Women in
African Parliaments

Women in African Parliaments

EDITED BY
Gretchen Bauer
Hannah E. Britton

LYNNE
RIENNER
PUBLISHERS

BOULDER
LONDON

Published in the United States of America in 2006 by
Lynne Rienner Publishers, Inc.
1800 30th Street, Boulder, Colorado 80301
www.rienner.com

and in the United Kingdom by
Lynne Rienner Publishers, Inc.
3 Henrietta Street, Covent Garden, London WC2E 8LU

Library of Congress Cataloging-in-Publication Data
Women in African parliaments / edited by Gretchen Bauer and Hannah E. Britton.
    p.   cm.
  Includes bibliographical references and index.
  ISBN 1-58826-427-0 (hardcover : alk. paper)
  1. Women in politics—Africa.   2. Women legislators—Africa.   3. Africa—Politics and
government.   I. Bauer, Gretchen, 1959–   II. Britton, Hannah Evelyn
HQ1391.A35W66 2005
320'.082'096—dc22

                                                       2005018517

British Cataloguing in Publication Data
A Cataloguing in Publication record for this book
is available from the British Library.

Printed and bound in the United States of America

The paper used in this publication meets the requirements
of the American National Standard for Permanence of
Paper for Printed Library Materials Z39.48-1992.

5   4   3   2   1

Contents

v

Acknowledgments

This book is the result of our experience at the African Studies Association's Annual Meeting in Boston in 2003. Interest in a panel that we co-organized at the meeting led us to recognize the need for an authentically comparative approach to understanding the role of women in African legislatures. Subsequently, we worked to secure a group of international scholars to contribute to this project. We would like to thank all those contributors for their hard work in crafting such in-depth analyses and for their patience in working through the drafts of their chapters.

We would also like to thank the African women parliamentarians who took time to work with each of us so that we could better understand the challenges they face. A special note of gratitude is due to the legislators who agreed to have their interviews published in the appendix so that they could explain in their own words their accomplishments and the obstacles that remain.

We would like to thank Lynne Rienner and her staff for their enthusiastic support of this project from its inception. Lisa Tulchin and Shena Redmond were invaluable in this process, and we appreciate their thoughtful reading of this work and careful editing of the final manuscript. We are also grateful for the comments and contributions of two anonymous reviewers. Finally, we would like to acknowledge our respective institutions, the University of Delaware and the University of Kansas, for their financial and professional support of the project.

On a personal note, this project has been a rewarding and valuable experience for both of us. Collaborative work can bring out either the best or the worst in people, and we are happy to report that the former is true in our case. After spending countless hours on e-mail, on the phone, and in person working through our manuscript, we feel we have a text that reflects the depth and breadth of the field and that we hope will contribute to a better understanding of political representation. We are also grateful for the support and understanding of our families and friends as we completed this project.

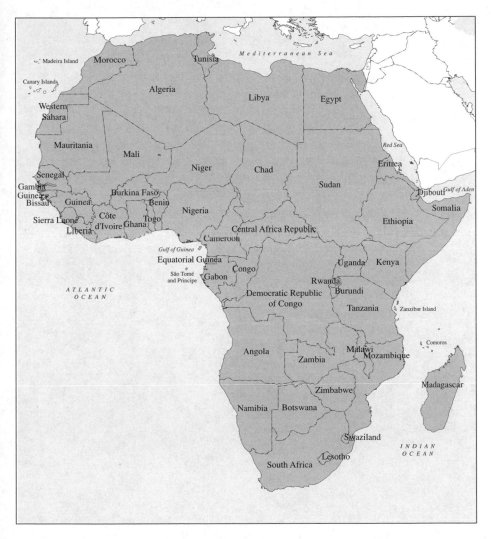

Africa

1

Women in African Parliaments: A Continental Shift?

Gretchen Bauer and Hannah E. Britton

In October 2003, less than a decade after the merciless genocide that claimed the lives of nearly one million people in a matter of months, the tiny East African country of Rwanda elected thirty-nine women to its eighty-member Chamber of Deputies. Overnight Rwanda replaced Sweden as the country with the highest percentage of women in its national legislature.[1] For decades a group of Scandinavian and Northern European countries had led the world in women's representation in parliament, with percentages ranging from 35 to 45 percent by the early 2000s. Such high percentages represented a slow and steady increase over time and resulted from a combination of factors, including the secularization of society, the development of an extended welfare state, women's increasing educational attainment and labor force participation, pressure from women's organizations on receptive social democratic political parties, and the selective use of particular electoral systems and party-based gender quotas (Dahlerup 2004). By contrast, in the course of just one election the percentage of women in Rwanda's national legislature had jumped to 48.8 percent.

Rwanda is not alone in sub-Saharan Africa. Over the last decade several African countries have moved from the very bottom to the very top of the list of countries in terms of women's representation in national legislatures. South Africa and Mozambique paved the way with elections in 1994 that saw significant numbers of women (25 percent) elected to their respective parliaments; in elections in 2004 both countries achieved a better than 32 percent representation of women in their national legislatures. In early 2005 three other African countries—Seychelles, Namibia, and Uganda—all had women in at least 24 percent of seats in their lower

1

or single houses of parliament. In other African countries women activists and women politicians were busy mobilizing civil society organizations and pressuring political parties to follow suit. This is a noteworthy development in a world in which regional averages for women's representation in parliaments range from 6 percent in the Arab states to only 18 percent in the Americas (approaching 40 percent only in the above-mentioned Nordic states).[2] This is also a remarkable achievement on a continent where women continue to lag behind even their developing world counterparts in any number of socioeconomic indicators, far surpassing them only in the HIV/AIDS infection rate.[3]

In this book we examine women's national political representation in six African countries. We explain how in five of those countries—Mozambique, Namibia, Rwanda, South Africa, and Uganda—significant advances in women's political representation have been realized despite pervasive gender inequality, patriarchal social relations, and historically male-dominated politics. In one other case investigated in this book—Senegal—women have not realized the same gains, and we explore why this is so. In addition, we provide a preliminary assessment of the impact and experiences of African women parliamentarians once in office. Mozambique, Namibia, Rwanda, South Africa, and Uganda have been chosen because they represent the five continental African countries among the top twenty-five worldwide in terms of women's representation in national legislatures. Senegal, with a lower, but growing, level of representation, provides an interesting counter-case from West Africa.[4] Together the six countries offer a sampling of African countries from the eastern, western, and southern regions as well as Anglophone, Francophone, and Lusophone traditions.

Though women members of parliament (MPs) outside Africa have attracted extensive scholarly notice (for example, Ross 2002; Tremblay 2005), African women parliamentarians, as a group, largely have not.[5] In recent years a few case studies have investigated women MPs in a single African country (Tamale 1999; Geisler 2000; Britton 2005; Bauer 2004).[6] In addition, three quantitative studies (Yoon 2001, 2004; Lindberg 2004) have examined the impact of a series of specific variables on women's parliamentary representation in Africa. Both approaches have their limitations. In this book we seek to move beyond single case studies and narrow quantitative approaches to provide a comparative study of African women MPs based on qualitative data gathered during lengthy field research in several African countries. In so doing, we hope to fill a wide gap in the comparative literature on women's political participation and representation around the world.

Why Elect More Women to Parliament?

Several arguments are made for increasing the level of women's political representation in elected office. Anne Phillips (1998, 228) identifies four groups of arguments: "There are those that dwell on the role model successful women politicians offer; those that appeal to principles of justice between the sexes; those that identify particular interests of women that would otherwise be overlooked; and those that point towards a revitalized democracy that bridges the gap between representation and participation." Phillips (1998, 228–238) privileges three of these four arguments, asserting that achieving gender parity in political representation is necessary because for men to monopolize representation is "patently and grotesquely unfair," because changing the composition of elected assemblies will help to increase and enhance democracy, and because without such change women's needs, interests, and concerns will not be adequately addressed. Although Phillips does not favor the "role model" argument, others have noted the powerful positive impact upon future elections of electing the first women into political office (Dahlerup 1988; Reynolds 1999; Lindberg 2004).

But can it be assumed that women's interests will be better represented simply by electing more of them to national legislatures? In general the literature on women's representation in legislatures draws a distinction between "descriptive" (or demographic) representation and "substantive" (or strategic) representation.[7] Anne Marie Goetz and Shireen Hassim (2003, 5) view this as the difference between a "feminine presence" and a "feminist activism" in politics. Richard Matland and Michelle Taylor (1997, 201) note that the degree of descriptive representation in a legislative body is important for three reasons:

> First, to the degree that groups are excluded because of some descriptive attributes (color, sex), the polity does not benefit from the talents of that portion of the population. To the degree that women are denied access, society loses the contributions of 50 percent of its most talented people. Second, to the degree that underrepresented groups have different perspectives on public issues, denying them access impoverishes the public debate. . . . Third, to the degree that these groups have different policy priorities, their lack of representation means the priorities of the elected assembly will not be representative of the public as a whole.

Goetz and Hassim (2003, 5) suggest that the distinction between descriptive and substantive representation may be overdrawn. In their view it may be more useful to consider descriptive representation as "a necessary first step to the institutional transformation that is required if substantive representation is to be achieved."

Underlying the notion of substantive representation, of course, is an assumption that there is a set of issues or interests that may be considered women's issues or interests and that once in office women will seek to act upon these. As Joni Lovenduski (1997, 718) notes for women parliamentarians, in order for them to make a difference, "it is necessary for women MPs to have distinct views on women's issues, to bring a women's perspective into political decision-making, or to bring a different style and set of role expectations to politics." A large literature, based primarily on the experience of women legislators in the developed countries, suggests that women politicians at the local and national levels are making a difference in terms of policy and implementation; indeed, they are representing women's interests (see Thomas 1991, Hyland Byrne 1997, Matland and Taylor 1997, Bochel and Briggs 2000, and Sainsbury 2004). In Britain, for example, Lovenduski and Pippa Norris (2003, 100) find that women in all the major parties "do bring a different set of values to issues affecting women's equality, in the workplace, home, and public sphere," and conclude that with time "the entry of more women into Westminster has the capacity to make more than simply a symbolic difference to the face of British representative democracy."

Now that they are 45 percent of MPs, women in Sweden have made two further advances with significant implications for elected women everywhere. First, according to Diane Sainsbury (2004, 65), they have "redefine[d] women's issues as demands for gender equality." In so doing, "they have transformed women's issues, which were earlier regarded as peculiar to women who were a special minority, into major party issues. In effect this change recast the conditions for substantive representation." Second, they succeeded in "gendering the demand for greater democracy. Framing the issue of women's representation in this way strategically converted political women from a minority within each of the parties into a majority of the citizenry—improving the potential for descriptive representation."

Finally, it has been argued that translating women's descriptive representation into an effective substantive representation requires that a critical mass of women—at least 30 percent—be elected into a given legislative body. The concept of critical mass as applied to women's representation in politics first appeared in the work of Drude Dahlerup (1988). Lovenduski and Azza Karam (2002, 2) note that Dahlerup's studies of women MPs in Sweden showed the impact of a critical mass:

"Women politicians worked to recruit other women, and developed new legislation and institutions to benefit women. As their numbers grew it became easier to be a woman politician and public perceptions of women politicians changed." At the same time, others have suggested that even a critical mass of women legislators may not be enough.[8] Citing the Kenyan, Ugandan, and South African cases, Hannah Britton (2005, 18) argues that many other factors may affect the ability for women to succeed in office, including patronage politics, patriarchal social norms, and social authoritarianism. Achieving a critical mass is not a panacea for undoing the imbalances of societal gender inequality. At the same time, as this book will demonstrate, there are clearly identifiable benefits of having a substantial number of women in elected office.

In June 2000 the Women's Environment and Development Organization (WEDO), based in New York City, launched the 50/50 campaign, an effort to raise to 50 percent the level of women's participation in politics and decisionmaking around the world. In launching the campaign WEDO organizers cited their reasons for joining the struggle for women's increased political representation: "We recognize that numbers are a necessary but not sufficient condition for women's full, equal, active and informed participation in economic, social and political decision-making. There is evidence, however, that when women enter decision-making bodies in significant numbers, such issues as child care, violence against women and unpaid labor are more likely to become priorities for policy-makers" (WEDO n.d.). More than a dozen countries have launched national 50/50 campaigns, including Namibia, South Africa, and Uganda. In those countries women activists are focused not only on the need for more women in politics but also on how to get them there.

How to Elect More Women to Parliament?

Assuming women and men should be equally represented at all levels of politics and decisionmaking, the question remains: How should that equal representation be accomplished? Existing research identifies a number of key factors that have helped to bring more women into national legislatures. These include the manipulation of electoral systems (the use of particular types of electoral systems and gender-based electoral quotas), the ideological orientation of the major political parties and the pressure exerted upon them by national women's movements, and social and cultural trends over time. Women candidates must also be available to stand for national political office.

Electoral Systems

Those countries that have historically had the highest representation of women in their national legislatures—Sweden, Norway, Finland, and Denmark (with 45.3, 38.2, 37.5, and 36.9 percent women, respectively, in early 2005)—all use a proportional representation (PR) electoral system and (with the exception of Finland) some form of voluntary, party-based quota, now or in the past (Ballington 2004, 125). The type of electoral system and use of electoral quotas are particularly significant because, "unlike other strategies to increase the level of women's legislative representation, such as changing political culture and the level of economic development . . . institutional structures are relatively easy to change" (Gray 2003, 55). As Matland (2002, 5) notes: "Changing the electoral system often represents a far more realistic goal to work towards than dramatically changing the culture's view of women."

Electoral systems are key because the choice of system "maximizes or minimizes the ability of political parties to manipulate the slate of candidates" (Meintjes and Simons 2002, 167). In general it is considered that PR systems are more favorable toward women than plurality-majority systems or semiproportional systems.[9] Julie Ballington (2004, 125) documents that in 2004 all but two of the fifteen countries with the highest rates of women's representation in the world used a PR electoral system (and the fifteen countries with the lowest rates used plurality-majority systems, averaging 1 percent of women in their legislatures). Staffan Lindberg (2004, 35), using a data set of 127 African elections held between 1989 and 2003, corroborates the general finding that "the more proportional the electoral system, the larger the share of the legislature that will be occupied by women." Several reasons are given for women's more favorable electoral outcomes under a PR than a plurality-majority electoral system. Most important, perhaps, is the fact that quotas are more easily implemented under a PR than a majoritarian system (Ballington 2004, 126). Another reason is that "contagion"—parties adopting the policies of other parties—is more likely to happen in PR systems than in majoritarian systems (Matland 2002, 7).

At the same time, not all PR electoral systems are the same, and certain factors help to further enhance women's representation (Matland 2002, 8–9). These include closed party lists, higher district magnitude, and high electoral thresholds. In a closed-list (as opposed to open-list)

PR electoral system, the party determines the rank ordering of candidates on the party list, and women's names cannot be removed from the list or moved downward by voters during an election, as experience has shown will happen with an open-list system. District magnitude refers to the number of seats per district. "As the number of seats per district increases, parties will go further down their lists (that is, win more seats) and more parties will have multi-member [presumably including more women] delegations." The most advantageous system for women is one in which the entire country is one electoral district. Finally, higher electoral thresholds are seen to favor women; low thresholds, according to Matland, encourage the creation of many "mini-parties, which often let in only one or two representatives. Overwhelmingly parties tend to have male leaders and party leaders inevitably take the first few slots on the list."

Gender-Based Quotas

Gender-based electoral quotas are meant to bring more women into politics and may take various forms. Although "some consider quotas to be a form of discrimination and a violation of the principle of fairness . . . others view them as compensation for structural barriers that prevent fair competition" (Dahlerup 2004, 17). Today, according to Dahlerup (2002, 1), quota systems aim at ensuring that women constitute at least a critical minority of 30 or 40 percent. They are typically applied as a temporary measure, until the barriers to women's entry into politics are removed. Quotas may be constitutional, as in Uganda and Rwanda; legislative, as in many parts of Latin America; or adopted by political parties, as in South Africa and Mozambique (Dahlerup 2004, 18). Uganda's 1995 constitution provides for "reserved seats" for women—one parliamentary seat in each of the country's districts is reserved for a woman. Provision is also made for other non-gender-specific reserved seats; women may run for these and other ordinary parliamentary seats in Uganda, and have done so successfully. In Latin America in the 1990s, eleven countries passed national laws requiring that at least 20 to 40 percent of candidates in national elections be women. Argentina has had the most success among these countries, utilizing a 30 percent quota in combination with a closed-list PR system to achieve a 31 percent representation of women in parliament (Gray 2003).

Political party–based quotas were used in the past by social democratic parties in some of the Scandinavian countries. In 1983 the Norwegian Labour Party decided that "at all elections and nominations both sexes must be represented by at least 40 percent." In 1994 Sweden's Social Democratic Party took the more dramatic step of introducing the principle of "every second on the list a woman" for its party lists (Dahlerup 2002, 4). Parties in Southern Africa have dubbed such rosters "zebra lists"—men and women alternate like the black and white stripes of a zebra. Many observers have attributed Scandinavia's high representation of women since the 1970s to the use of quotas. Dahlerup notes, however, that in Scandinavia quotas were never mandated by law and were adopted only at the level of the political party (and not all parties used them). Further, these party-based quotas were not introduced until women had already acquired around 25 percent of seats in parliament, a result of socioeconomic developments over time. Thus, Dahlerup (2004, 18) warns, "the Scandinavian experience cannot be considered a model for the 21st century because it took 80 years to get that far." Today, by contrast, "the women of the world are not willing to wait that long," so gender-based electoral quotas are being deployed with increasing frequency.

Political Parties and Women's Movements

Political parties are the gatekeepers to women's participation in politics because it is largely as candidates from particular parties that women stand for political office (Matland 2002). Ballington (2002, 77) identifies parties as "the final determinant of women's presence or absence in political institutions and consequently in the public domain." Moreover, in her late-1990s study of twelve advanced industrial countries, Miki Caul found that certain characteristics of political parties enhance the likelihood of women's increased political representation. Caul (1999, 94) argues that "high levels of institutionalization, a localized level of candidate nomination, and leftist and postmaterialist values all individually enable parties to increase the representation of women." Further, she contends that "high levels of women working at internal party offices and the presence of formal rules designed to increase the number of women MPs are both conducive to women's representation." Caul underscores the significance of women's party activism in increasing women's political representation. Such activism is crucial, she suggests, to the adoption of electoral and quota rules that will facilitate women's greater political participation.

Indeed, the importance of mobilized women's movements and the pressure they exert upon political parties has been noted repeatedly. In Scandinavia, according to Dahlerup (2002, 4), it was sustained pressure from women's groups within political parties and women's movements more generally that resulted in the adoption of quotas by several political parties. Steven Saxonberg (2000, 154–155) argues that in post-transition Eastern Europe a *lack* of strong women's movements has meant that the type of electoral system has had little impact on women's representation. Without the ability to pressure political parties to nominate more women to winnable seats, women's organizations stand little chance of increasing women's representation in parliaments. The support of women's movements has also been found to be crucial in ensuring that women legislators promote an agenda in which women's issues are prominent (Bystydzienski 1992; Carroll 1992). Moreover, as Sylvia Tamale (2000, 14) notes, a strong women's movement is particularly important in assuring that female legislators are aware of the strong need to "reconstruct political structures according to feminist principles."

Electing Women to Parliament in Africa

In those cases presented in this book in which women have gained substantial political representation over the last decade, the backdrop has been a political transition following a period of prolonged conflict. In Uganda in 1986, after a long guerrilla war, the National Resistance Movement (NRM) ousted the last in a series of dictators and assumed the reins of power. In 1990, after a twenty-five-year armed struggle led by the exiled South West Africa People's Organisation (Swapo), Namibia gained its independence from seventy-five years of de facto South African colonial rule. In Mozambique in 1992 externally brokered negotiations finally brought an end to seventeen years of brutal civil war, and in 1994 the first multiparty elections retained the Front for the Liberation of Mozambique (Frelimo) party in power. In South Africa in 1994 the venerable African National Congress (ANC) won the country's first-ever universal franchise elections, marking the formal end of decades of apartheid rule and a decades-long armed struggle. Also in 1994 the Rwandan Patriotic Front (RPF) proclaimed a new government after defeating the National Republican Movement for Democracy and Development (MRND) government whose supporters had fomented the genocide that had claimed the lives of nearly one million Rwandans. In Senegal a much less dramatic political transition has occurred, and not in the aftermath of a prolonged conflict—in 2000 Senegal's ruling Socialist Party, in power since independence in 1960, was voted out of office, and in 2001 a new constitution was adopted.

This set of transitions in six African countries is part of a larger set of transitions in Africa during the 1980s and 1990s from some form of authoritarian rule to a more democratic rule. This wave of transitions—part of the so-called third wave of democracy—has been referred to by some as Africa's second liberation, with the period of independence being Africa's first liberation. Indeed, in the 1960s, after nearly a century of European colonial rule, most African countries made the significant transition to political independence. In most cases, the transfer of power from the European colonial ruler to the newly independent African country was a relatively peaceful one. The exceptions tended to be the settler colonies, such as Algeria, where a devastating war was necessary to gain independence, or several countries in Southern Africa where independence was only attained in the 1970s, 1980s, or 1990s, after decades of diplomatic and armed struggle. For a few of these countries, Africa's second liberation was their first.

In the 1960s, the political system of the departing colonial power was typically adopted wholesale by the newly independent African country. In the former English (Anglophone) colonies the Westminster parliamentary model, with a prime minister and fused executive and legislative powers, was taken on, while the former French (Francophone) colonies embraced the French model of a president-centered system in which the executive and legislative branches were separate. A first round of universal franchise elections brought nationalist movements to power and filled the seats of national legislatures with eager members. In every independent African country women were given the vote, along with men, at independence, and in many countries women's participation in nationalist movements was rewarded with the establishment of national machineries for women and national women's organizations. But hopes for further advances were quickly dashed. By 1964 roughly two-thirds of independent African states had become one-party states. By 1970 about seventy coups or coup attempts had occurred in sub-Saharan Africa, and about one-half of then independent countries were under military rule. In the turn to single-party or military rule, constitutions were abandoned, political parties (except the ruling ones) proscribed, and civil society organizations banned. Most parliaments fell silent or became mere rubber-stamping bodies for the party in power. For women the only space for organizing was within an official wing of the ruling party or the national women's association, typically headed by the president's wife.[10] A few token women may have occupied the occasional seat in parliament or cabinet, but the most common role for party women was praise singing and dancing at official functions and ceremonies.

What then distinguishes the current spate of transitions, from which African women appear to have gained far more, from the transitions to independence in the 1960s? A number of factors are identified in the country cases that follow. First, as we noted before, the most significant advances have been made in postconflict states. Indeed, it appears that the disruptions to gender relations caused by prolonged conflict may actually offer opportunities for reconfiguring those relations in the postconflict period. Moreover, it appears that prolonged conflicts have produced a second factor, namely, a cadre of capable women willing and able to run for political office. Many of these women fought alongside their male counterparts during wars of liberation and/or had critical education and training opportunities overseas during years living in exile. Other women became activists at home struggling against an oppressive or dictatorial rule. Third, women and their organizations, emboldened by their experiences of struggle and learning at home and abroad, inserted themselves into the processes of crafting new constitutions and drafting new laws during the political transitions. New constitutions and new laws have, in turn, provided the legal foundations and political frameworks for the institutions and mechanisms to bring more women into political office. Critical to this process has been a fourth factor, namely, women's organizations and movements and the pressure that they have exerted on political parties to adopt the strategies and mechanisms that have led to women's increased representation in politics. Fifth, a global women's movement, to which many African women have been exposed in the course of conflict, has played a large role. African women have participated actively in and been strongly influenced by international forums such as the United Nations conferences on women.[11]

Postconflict States

In recent years it has been argued that violent conflict, which results in major disruptions to gender relations, can also provide "new opportunities to articulate debate about gender politics as well as for individual women to live in a different way." This is said to be all the more true when liberation movements have been part of that conflict (Pankhurst 2002, 127). Citing the examples of Uganda and some Southern African countries, Donna Pankhurst (2002, 123) suggests that violent conflict has offered significant opportunities for changes in gender relations in a number of African countries. Whether women took up arms from outside the country or took on male roles at home while men were "fighting, in prison, or dead," profound changes in gender relations ensued in the rural and urban areas as people called into question the need for rigid roles. Although the potential for backlash is great during the postconflict period, Pankhurst (2002, 124) argues that where liberation movements with some previously stated commitment to gender equality came into power, political space in which women could act opened. Indeed, Pankhurst suggests that access to this space, coupled with the "relatively new types of democracy introduced during the 1990s," allowed women to enter formal politics in increasing numbers and with increasing effectiveness. The case studies in this book largely confirm Pankhurst's observations about a connection between postconflict states and improvements in women's political representation.

Available Women Candidates

The conflict situations experienced in many of the countries discussed in this book seem to have resulted in an available cadre of women who have been involved in politics in one way or another for decades. Indeed, women in many of these countries have had experiences and opportunities not typical of the majority of African women. In Namibia and South Africa, for example, a significant portion of current women MPs spent many years in exile as members of Swapo and the ANC, respectively. In exile Namibian and South African women obtained training and education to which they never would have had access at home, with the result that many women MPs are highly skilled and educated. At the same time, many Namibian and South African women MPs joined their respective struggles as community organizers and antiapartheid activists fighting the wars at home. These women too have brought to national politics a unique and valuable set of skills gained during years of grassroots activity. Similarly, in Mozambique women participated as combatants and in other roles in the armed insurrection against the Portuguese that was required to attain independence. The Marxist-Leninist Frelimo movement incorporated women in various guises into the liberation struggle and included women's emancipation as one of its stated goals. This did not translate, in the postindependence period, into parliamentary gains for women. But, as Jennifer Disney argues in this volume, some of the impetus for women's legislative gains after the end of war in 1992 stems from this legacy.

In Rwanda women contributed to an emerging, thriving civil society in the 1980s and 1990s as they organized in response to deteriorating economic conditions and resulting growing social needs. As a result of the genocide in 1994, according to Timothy Longman, many of these same women's organizations were devastated when their leaders were killed or forced into exile. At the same time, importantly, the intense problems facing women in the postconflict period inspired many of these same women's organizations to assume important social roles. These groups' growing public influence then translated into concrete political power. Women moved directly from positions in civil society organizations to positions in government. In so doing, they also promoted the importance and legitimacy of women holding office.

Electoral Systems and Gender-based Quotas

One of the most significant opportunities to alter gender relations and to increase women's representation in legislatures has occurred during the post-transition period as new constitutions and laws have been written and new institutions created. Indeed, every country discussed in this book has adopted a new constitution since 1985, although the most prominent gains for women have been in the postconflict countries. South Africa provides the clearest example of women coming together with the express purpose of influencing the constitution and the post-transition political and legal framework. In 1991 women returning from exile and those from women's groups inside the country joined together to form the Women's National Coalition (WNC), a coalition of more than 100 women's groups, including representatives of all of the major political parties. The coalition then drew up the Women's Charter, one of the key goals of which was to advance women's equality in the constitution. In addition, the WNC lobbied for the creation of a Gender Advisory Committee to the (all-male) body negotiating the transition and new constitution. In part because of these efforts, Britton argues, the South African constitution has one of the broadest and most inclusive constitutional equality clauses in the world. Similarly, in Namibia in 1989 the six women members of the Constituent Assembly worked hard to shape a progressive constitution for that country, one that forbids discrimination on the basis of sex (and several other attributes), notes the special discrimination suffered by women in the past and the need to redress it with affirmative action, and states that customary law may remain in effect but only when it does not conflict with the constitution or other laws.

More important, perhaps, to the election of women to parliament is the choice of electoral system and use of gender-based quotas. Mozambique, Namibia, Rwanda, and South Africa all utilize a closed-list proportional representation electoral system for their parliamentary elections. Moreover, in each case the PR system is used in conjunction with some form of mandatory or voluntary gender-based quota. Uganda utilizes a majoritarian ("first-past-the-post") electoral system in combination with reserved seats for women. In South Africa, again under pressure from the WNC, the ANC instituted a 30 percent quota for women candidates on its party list in 1994 and for the 1999 and 2004 elections moved to a system by which every third position on the party's candidate list was occupied by a woman. Other parties also worked to increase female representation on their lists. In Mozambique since 1999 Frelimo policy requires that 30 percent of the party's candidates for the national legislature be women. Party policy also commits (though it does not require) the party to balance the distribution of women throughout the list, rather than grouping them all at the end. By contrast, the opposition party Renamo has no quota for women and no women's wing. In Namibia women activists have called on political parties to utilize zebra lists for national legislative elections. In the 1999 and 2004 elections close to 30 percent of names on the major party lists for the National Assembly were women. At the local level in Namibia such quotas are mandated by law.

Rwanda and Uganda use a slightly different system, but with a similar effect. In these two countries reserved seats for women in the national legislature have been introduced, in Uganda in 1989 and Rwanda in 2003. In Uganda one seat in the parliament is reserved for a woman in each of the country's fifty-six districts. In Rwanda 30 percent of seats in the Chamber of Deputies are reserved for women, allocated in such a manner that two women are sent from each of the provinces and two from the city of Kigali. In both cases, moreover, women have been elected to the national legislatures from more than just the reserved seats. In Uganda in 2001, 56 women won reserved seats for women in the districts; 13 won open constituency seats; and 6 won youth, labor, and disability reserved seats. In Rwanda in 2003, women were elected to 24 reserved seats and an additional 15 seats (out of 80). In neither case, then, have reserved seats represented a cap on women's election to national office. Furthermore, as Tripp and Longman point out, in both countries women have been elected to and selected for many other offices, such as judges and magistrates.

In Senegal, with 19 percent women in its National Assembly since 2001, a mixed electoral system is utilized for national legislative elections, with the proportion of PR versus plurality seats changing from one election to another. Lucy Creevey concludes that, by and large, the PR system does favor women more than the plurality system. Moreover, since 2002 several political parties in Senegal have agreed to a 30 percent quota for their candidate lists, although the Democratic Socialist Party, with the most women MPs in the National Assembly, does not use a gender-based quota.

Pressure from National Women's Organizations on Political Parties

As in other parts of the world, political parties and women's organizations play a tremendous part in electing women to national political office in Africa. Goetz and Hassim (2003, 10) note that despite a "feminist antipathy to parties" in many developing countries, there has typically been little choice but for women's movements to work with political parties, especially in Africa. In general two factors have challenged women's successful interaction with political parties in Africa. First, in those cases where nationalist or liberation movements became ruling parties, women's secondary status in the movements was replicated in the parties. Moreover, dominant parties also heavily curtailed civil society activity that could provide an alternative venue for women and their organizations. Second, because so many parties are so poorly institutionalized, lacking strong rules and procedures, challenging party practices can be difficult (Goetz and Hassim 2003, 10–11).

To a certain extent, political transitions in Africa in the 1980s and 1990s have improved the prospects for women's interaction with political parties. Indeed, the cases in this volume suggest that the role of parties remains paramount to women's election to national legislatures, particularly in those countries using PR electoral systems. For example, in Namibia, South Africa, and Mozambique, quotas have been adopted by political parties rather than mandated by national law. Indeed, political parties have been targeted by women activists and organizations keen to increase women's representation. In Rwanda and Uganda ruling parties or movements have institutionalized the reserved seats for women, though clearly pressured to do so by women's groups. It could be argued that all five of these parties are left-leaning, thereby verifying the assertion of many that such parties, as in Scandinavia, are more likely to help raise women's political participation. Finally, it has been hypothesized that the larger the share of the vote for the main political party, the more women in the legislature (Matland and Taylor 1997), and our cases appear to corroborate this assertion.

In addition, as elsewhere, pressure from women's organizations and movements on political parties and leaders has been critical to increasing women's representation. Aili Mari Tripp (2001a) early on identified the rise of independent women's organizations in Africa as one of the factors accounting for women's increased visibility as independent political actors across the continent in the 1990s. In her chapter on Uganda she notes that key leaders of the Ugandan women's movement visited Yoweri Museveni shortly after the NRM took power in 1986 to press for women's greater representation in government leadership, with immediate success. With the opening of political space in Uganda in the mid-1980s, Tripp continues, there was an extraordinary growth in the influence of women's movements, aided by increased educational opportunities for women that gave rise to stronger female leadership. Women's groups mobilized around a range of issues and pressed to improve leadership skills, encourage political involvement, advocate for political leadership, and more advances for women. In Rwanda, Longman notes, women's organizations stepped in to fill a social void in the postgenocide period. One group in particular, the umbrella organization Pro-Femmes, took the lead in lobbying the government on a series of women's issues, winning concessions from the executive and legislature. Longman argues that this extensive involvement of Rwandan women in civil society led directly to their increased presence in the national legislature.

In Namibia and South Africa women's organizations are clearly central to women's presence in politics today. We have noted the role of the WNC in establishing a favorable constitutional and electoral framework for women in South Africa. In Namibia women and their organizations have united around the goal of increasing women's national political representation. Indeed, after decades of party-political, racial, socioeconomic, and rural/urban divisions, women have mobilized around this issue. Moreover, there is significant interaction between women's organizations and the women who are being elected to office. As Disney observes for Mozambique, it is often the same women who are moving in and out of leadership roles in government and civil society.

In Senegal, where women MPs lag behind their Eastern and Southern African counterparts, increasing women's legislative representation is not high on the agenda of women's groups, according to Creevey. Rather, women are concerned about issues such as domestic violence, female circumcision, and equalizing economic opportunities. Moreover, so long as the National Assembly remains not much more than an "audience" for the decrees of the executive, it will not be much of a priority for Senegalese women, Creevey contends.

Influence of a Global Women's Movement

Though it is important to acknowledge the diversity of African feminisms and the ways in which they differ from other feminisms (Mikell

1997; Oyewumi 1997, 2003), it is also the case that women's organizations and movements in Africa have been profoundly influenced by a global women's movement. Decades in exile exposed some Namibian and South African activists to a diversity of feminist organizations, publications, thought, and activity. When they returned to Namibia and South Africa in 1989 and the early 1990s, the onetime exiles brought those influences with them. Britton notes the importance of political learning. She relates that women activists in political parties in South Africa, in contemplating the electoral framework for a new South Africa, were acutely aware of what had and had not worked for women in politics elsewhere on the continent. As Tripp and Gretchen Bauer indicate for Uganda and Namibia, meetings such as the United Nations conferences on women, particularly those in Nairobi (1985) and Beijing (1995), gave added impetus to national women's organizations as they sought to convince governments to adopt national gender policies and institutionalize national machineries for women. Many individual women MPs and activists spoke of the transformative impact that attending such conferences had on them, inspiring them to redouble their efforts at home. Donor agencies have also had a significant influence; as Tripp notes for Uganda, changing donor strategies that emphasize nongovernmental activities to a greater extent than in the past have also contributed to the extraordinary growth in women's political participation and representation. In Senegal, according to Creevey, it was the US-based National Democratic Institute that persuaded some political parties there to adopt gender quotas in 2002. In Southern Africa, regional organizations have also played an important role. The Southern African Development Community (SADC) Gender Unit spearheaded an (unsuccessful) campaign to have 30 percent of positions of power and decisionmaking held by women by 2005 and gained pledges of support from political leaders throughout the region. In 2002 the SADC Parliamentary Forum launched a regional women's parliamentary caucus, meant to provide support for the growing number of women parliamentarians in Southern Africa. In East Africa, regional influences have played a role as well. For Rwanda, Longman notes the clear influence of developments in neighboring Uganda (where many Rwandans spent decades in exile) on politics for women in Rwanda.

Impact and Experiences of Women in Parliament in Africa

Faced with a similar postcolonial framework—marked by issues of land rights, resource control, economic poverty, population growth, and internal conflict—autonomy, sovereignty, transparency, and democracy have become paramount for African MPs. Women MPs have the additional test of working against the impact of contemporary power patriarchies that are infused with the legacies of colonial economic, social, and religious patterns. Because colonialism served to undermine African women's status in society and restricted them to the domestic, private sphere (Amadiume 1997; Gordon 1996; Guy 1990), many women MPs have had to work not only to master the substance of their jobs as legislators but also to legitimize their presence in parliaments. African women MPs, perhaps even more than their counterparts in Europe and the West, have to work to define themselves as vital participants in the public space of elected office.

There is a deep commitment on the part of women leaders in Africa to improving the overall quality of life for women in their countries. It is from the backdrop of struggle that women are entering parliaments in Africa in significant numbers. Most African women MPs are finding parliaments to be new landscapes of struggle and are working to define new forms of agency and activism within their institutions with varied success. All are making visible changes in the political lives of their countries. Some women MPs' impact is felt within the institutional culture of parliament itself. Others' impact may be seen within their legislative goals and outcomes. And still others' impact is increasingly visible in new ways of organizing with women and organizations in civil society.

Impact on Institutional Culture

African women MPs have made varied but consistent changes to their parliamentary cultures. In cases where there has been a rapid influx of women into office, the physical presence of large numbers of women has had a visible impact on the institution of parliament. Rudimentary logistical accommodations often had to be made for women, such as building more lavatories for the large number of women elected in South Africa in 1994 who would otherwise have had to share the one facility in the parliament building. Women MPs across the continent have also begun to push for changes in the structure of parliamentary life to recognize that women have to balance domestic and professional responsibilities. They have demanded on-site child care facilities for MPs and staff, changed the hours of parliamentary work to end earlier, and changed the parliamentary calendar to match school holidays.

Most important, the presence of a large number of women MPs has changed cultural and societal perceptions about the nature of political leadership and governance. In Namibia, Mozambique, Uganda, South Africa, and Rwanda, as women entered the halls of parliaments, they too became faces and names associated with national office and legislation. Their presence and their success challenged the traditional perceptions of women as subordinates and men as leaders. And, as women's political participation becomes routine and legitimized, their absence from committees and delegations is rapidly becoming unacceptable. This normalization creates a positive environment for the active recruitment, advancement, and mentoring of younger women. What remains to be seen is how these newer generations of women MPs will differ from their mentors who first broke through the glass ceilings.

Throughout the continent, African women MPs have striven to create state institutions for the advancement of feminist change as part of long-term strategies for improving the quality of life for women in their nations. African women MPs recognize that their time in office is often short-lived and that state institutions are the key to ensuring that their goals and ideas become permanent features of government. Rather than demonizing the state as an entity of oppression, women are increasingly moving from *resisting* the state to *using* the state. Elisabeth Friedman (2000) estimates that over 90 percent of countries have some form of "state feminism," meaning that at least one national agency for women, such as a women's ministry, department, or commission, exists. The increasing reliance upon the state for feminist change in developed nations (Stetson and Mazur 1995) has had a clear impact on the turn toward the state by women in developing nations (Staudt 1998; Friedman 2000; Baldez 2001). This is also the emerging trend in Africa, even though it is widely recognized that the state has also been a source of African women's disempowerment (Parpart and Staudt 1989). Having now obtained positions of power in the institutions that previously oppressed them, African women MPs are turning that power on its head and are creating national state agencies to improve the status of women and to ensure that their basic needs are met.

The range of state institutions favored by African women MPs varies from legislative committees and parliamentary women's caucuses to government departments, women's ministries, national gender commissions, and women's budgets. For example, Namibia has a Ministry of Gender Equality and Child Welfare to oversee national gender policy and a Women and Law Committee to help draft new laws. South Africa has an Office on the Status of Women in the executive, a Commission for Gender Equality and a Women's Budget Initiative that involve both civil society and government agencies, and a Joint Monitor-

ing Committee on the Improvement of the Quality of Life and Status of
Women in parliament. In Rwanda the Forum of Women Parliamentarians has been instrumental in examining gendered aspects of new legislation, and in Uganda the Women Parliamentary Association has taken
an active role in legislative debates on gender issues. In almost all
cases, some level of institutionalization has been essential for the creation, implementation, and monitoring of government commitments to
gender issues.

Impact on Legislation

In addition to their work to create national machineries for women,
African women MPs have made remarkable progress in shaping the legislative agendas of their nations. Although parliaments vary in the number of women members, it is clear that women's activism within parliament has fostered an emphasis on addressing both the practical and
strategic needs of women in their societies. In fact, much of the legislative work of African women MPs serves to collapse the distinction between Maxine Molyneux's (1985) practical needs and strategic needs.[12]
For many African women, practical needs are in fact strategic needs.
Women's access to strategic needs is the only way to ensure the security
of their practical needs. As the cases in this book show, legislative agendas across Africa demonstrate this idea as lived practice. African women
MPs have an agenda that is demonstrably broader than the legislative
platforms of their counterparts in the North. Women MPs across the
continent have introduced gender into legislative debates and outcomes,
forcing national legislatures to recognize the differential impact of policies on women and men.

   For example, the legislative agendas of many African parliaments
are focused on land rights, and women MPs are challenging their male
counterparts to include the issue of gender within the discussion of land
rights and the context of customary law. Similarly, poverty alleviation is
central to the platform of parliaments across the continent, and women
MPs are beginning to push programs that recognize women's economic
roles and include them in the benefits of training and resource allocation. Women MPs are examining the gendered aspects of the HIV/AIDS
pandemic. They are attempting to find creative approaches that empower women to maintain or gain control over their sexual activity, they
are envisioning policies to accommodate the growing number of child-
headed households, and they are evaluating the most effective ways to
prevent the spread of the disease as well as outline the conditions for ad-

equate treatment and care. Finally, though violence against women has been utilized by colonial and more recent authoritarian regimes to maintain control over populations, discussion of the scope and nature of this violence has too often been absent in public dialogue. As women enter the halls of parliament across Africa, this violence is being named and strategies for its eradication are being devised.

The impact of women MPs on legislation is clearly evident in the cases in this volume. For Mozambique Disney uses the lens of the new family law to delineate the transformation of government attitudes toward the construction of "the family" and its subsequent meanings, to evaluate the changes in status and power of women within Mozambican culture, and to examine the new forms of interaction between women members of parliament and civil society organizations focused on women's rights. Disney asserts that in their revision of the family law, women MPs were able to work in concert with women in civil society to foster an exceptionally progressive version of the family law.

Writing about South Africa, Britton discusses multiple examples of how women MPs have influenced the initiation, drafting, or implementation of legislation. Women MPs have been involved in legislation dealing with abortion, pornography, employment equity, skills development, labor relations, basic income grants and maintenance, and domestic violence. Women legislators in South Africa have taken their role in the legislative process seriously and have had increasing effectiveness in terms of influencing the direction and scope of their parties' agendas.

In Namibia, Bauer finds that women MPs claim credit for a range of legislative initiatives and accomplishments. Indeed, the country's first women legislators, though few in number, maintain that they played a significant role in crafting the country's progressive constitution. One of those same women MPs was instrumental in the adoption of a mandatory gender quota for local-level elections. Namibian women MPs have worked to dismantle the apartheid-era legislation that discriminated against women and to foster legislation to assist in the economic and social development of women and girls. Women MPs have worked to engender legislation on affirmative action and labor relations, equality in marriage, land rights, gender violence, domestic violence, and child maintenance.

Yet, as the case of Uganda demonstrates, merely bringing women into national office does not necessarily translate into a consistent voice for women's rights. There is no question that women in the Ugandan parliament have had some fairly positive input into legislative debates.

But, as Tripp discusses in this volume, their record is uneven. Women legislators have worked to introduce or reform laws concerning gender violence and land rights, and they have been involved in debates concerning the regulation of bride price, marriage, and polygamy. But they have often been pressured by the ruling National Resistance Movement. For example, Tripp discusses the negotiations over the 1998 Land Act, in which women MPs and women's rights advocates were able to secure several provisions for the protection of women's land rights. However, a vital co-ownership clause was omitted against the wishes and lobbying activities of civil society organizations, and the NRM leaned heavily on women MPs to vote against the amendments. This example is essential for a fair assessment of the limitations of women legislators to challenge party leadership, especially when their political survival is dependent upon the approval of those leaders. Similar patterns can be found throughout this volume of women legislators finding themselves thwarted by the power of patronage, the traditions of parliamentary politics, and the demands of party leadership.

One of the biggest problems facing women legislators continues to be policy implementation. As Bauer concludes, the framework for women's equality has been enshrined in the new legislation and political institutions of postliberation Namibia, but the long-term challenge is the implementation of that framework. Here Bauer develops a key theme found throughout the book—that legislating policy is a necessary but not sufficient condition for ensuring the adequate implementation of policies to advance the status and position of women.

Just as important is the risk that women's legislative representation may be used by political leaders and parties to legitimize their agendas. This is seen most clearly in the Rwandan case. For example, Rwandan women legislators have been visible in the legislative arena. Through the work of the Forum of Women Parliamentarians, women legislators have contributed to debates on gender violence, inheritance rights, and gender discrimination. However, their actions are always governed by the agendas of their respective parties. As elsewhere in Africa, women legislators in Rwanda are constrained by the partisan nature of parliamentary politics because their political survival depends on their political parties. As the government in Rwanda has become even more authoritarian, the intolerance of dissent has led to a broader political intolerance and in some cases repression. Rwandan women legislators therefore find themselves facilitating policies that strengthen an authoritarian state and undermine individual civil liberties. Much as in the Ugandan case, Longman raises important questions about women in office doing more to legitimize and support the ruling party than to foster the gendered agenda many had intended.

Senegal extends this discussion by examining the ways women have been blocked from full participation in politics. Senegal is not an Islamic state governed by fundamentalists, but Senegalese politics are increasingly influenced by transnational Islamic attitudes. The convergence of religion and culture has served to reinforce notions that women ought not be part of formal politics, even though Senegalese women have more freedom and access to education and employment than women in many parts of the Middle East. As in Uganda and Rwanda, another obstacle blocking women in politics is the semiauthoritarian, highly centralized power of the executive that discourages full democratic participation regardless of gender. As Creevey notes in her conclusion, electing more women to parliament will not be a priority for women activists in Senegal until the National Assembly becomes a more autonomous body, not simply a rubber stamp for the executive.

Impact on Civil Society

Examining post-transition politics in Latin America and Eastern Europe, Georgina Waylen (1994) notes the chasm that often develops between women in office and women in civil society after a political transition. Because of the new institutional norms and values faced by women legislators who now have to answer to political party leaders and their constituents, women MPs and legislators often find themselves at cross-purposes with women's movements and organizations in civil society. As time passes, the usual tension between women in office and their female constituents frequently presents itself. Gender activists and women's organizations may find themselves walking a thin line between cooperation with the government and co-optation by the government. Women's organizations have often been some of the first groups to call for increased transparency, decreased corruption, and increased accountability in government.

Although their legislative and political agendas closely resemble those of their civil society counterparts, African women MPs are not immune to this division. As the cases in this volume indicate, a gap between women MPs and women activists can be found throughout Africa. Just as women MPs voice concerns about their political survival in office, so do women activists voice concerns that they have been abandoned by their MP counterparts who are interested only in self-preservation and self-promotion. There are often widely held attitudes that women MPs have been seduced by the power and once-in-a-lifetime financial security afforded by their positions.

Despite this schism, there is evidence that many African women MPs turn to and rely upon their civil society counterparts, and vice versa. Perhaps as a result of bonds formed among women during liberation struggles, many of the women described in this book maintained the hope that postliberation governments would be more open, transparent, and progressive than the oppressive regimes they replaced. These expectations are not unfounded. There are clear signs that women's groups should be more hopeful about the outcomes of parliaments that have high percentages of women members, based on the global experience of the legislative agendas and national machineries created by those parliaments.

Disney finds that autonomous women's organizations working specifically for the advancement of women were fairly circumscribed until the 1990s in Mozambique, and authentically progressive legislation protecting the rights of women, especially within the family, was limited at best. The transition from a Marxist-Leninist, one-party state to a neoliberal, multiparty state changed the nature of women's political mobilization, organizations, and participation. Prior to the 1990s women operated within party structures to support and foster the attainment of party goals and agendas. Once the transition to multiparty democracy created more political space, women were able to operate outside political parties in their own organizations and movements and focus on self-identified gendered goals. In this way the Mozambican case establishes a pattern seen within many of the countries in the text: Women's participation is only as viable as the political institutions and democratic processes within which they operate.

Unlike in Mozambique, where the previous one-party rule did not necessarily translate into women in office, Tripp presents the conditional assessment that Museveni's early one-party state fostered women's advancement because he could unilaterally adopt affirmative action measures such as the reserved seats that provided women with the political training and national exposure that would foster acceptance of them as political actors. Concurrently, women's organizations were working from the bottom up to strengthen women's power and status in Ugandan society by increasing their access to education and social benefits that would create the next batch of women politicians, leaders, and activists. These organizations began to address women's rights and heretofore hidden or unmentionable issues, such as gender violence, reproductive health, reproductive rights, and female genital cutting. Despite the potential for cooperation between women in office and women in civil society, Tripp notes the structural limitations placed on women in national office, who were in their positions in part because of Museveni's patronage. This limited women office holders from building sustained coalitions with the women's movement and from advancing a progressive legislative agenda on behalf of those groups. Tripp questions whether women in office may have done more to support Museveni and his regime than to support the gender issues that propelled many of them into office.

As in Mozambique, Britton finds that in South Africa women were initially focused on drafting legislation to improve women's position nationally. Women MPs also worked with gender consultants to design a set of institutions that would bring gender issues, and hopefully gender consciousness, into the mainstream throughout all branches of government. Despite the visible and notable progress toward gender equity in South Africa, there remain institutional obstacles for women in parliament as well as cultural norms that often hinder their full participation. This situation has contributed to a growing tension and lack of communication between women MPs and women in civil society. In Namibia women have historically had little success in developing an enduring national women's organization, but they do have a legacy of civil society organizations that fostered a range of social and economic development initiatives. As Bauer writes in this volume, during the transition process this legacy was critical to fostering an attitude of acceptance of women's rightful place in political life. It has also assisted in the enactment of progressive legislation, much of which will benefit women's long-term status and development. Bauer has also found evidence of a growing mobilization of women activists and organizations seeking to elect more women to political office. Although this effort predated the international 50/50 campaign, Namibia has since joined that global campaign for women's increased representation.

These findings are vital for understanding the potential for transnational feminist movements in Africa. Groups from throughout Africa have joined the movement to have 50 percent of elected offices held by women. The momentum for this campaign has spread rapidly across borders, and it is often a combined effort of gender activists and women politicians. Perhaps the most active support for the campaign has come in countries that already have a demonstrable level of women in office, such as Namibia and South Africa, indicating that success breeds success. Organizations in those countries can point to the impact of women in office as well as the international goodwill that often follows such success. But there is also the issue of timing. As high percentages of women in office become the norm and not the exception, nations that seek to follow suit will have precedents to follow.

Longman finds that women's groups were fundamental in the development of Rwandan civil society in the 1980s and 1990s and worked especially to assist grassroots economic development. These groups and women leaders expanded the focus on social services and development to push for democratic reform and political representation. The Rwandan story has the additional and tragic legacy of the 1994 genocide and its aftermath that also contributed to the now record levels of women's participation. After the genocide the entire institutional and social fabric had to be rewoven, and women's organizations were often in the best position to do this based on their earlier developmental activities (despite the fact that many of their leaders had been killed or exiled). Longman asserts that a key factor prompting women to run for office was the commitment on the part of the postgenocidal leaders in Rwanda to include women in political life. These leaders benefited from the timing of the transition because Rwanda could learn from Mozambique, Uganda, Namibia, and South Africa. Rwanda in many ways represents a process of collective social learning and cross-national feminism.

Creevey examines the role of women's organizations in Senegalese politics and finds that women's organizations in Senegal face the dual constraint of being elite-driven, thus lacking widespread support, and being influenced by the complexities of a growing anti-Western ideology. Women's groups must therefore craft their calls for political leadership and power in ways that do not appear influenced by Western feminism and that do not directly threaten the status quo. Political leaders have supported, at least marginally, organizations and leaders that successfully manage to negotiate this political quicksand. Despite these constraints, Creevey presents evidence that the number of women in legislative office continues to grow, albeit slowly, as does the number of women ministers and leaders in government. The path may be more delicate for Senegalese women, but Creevey finds that there is room for growth.

Lessons Learned and Challenges Ahead

The cases in this text contain the voices of African women who explain in their own words how they have achieved or continue to fight for electoral success, how they have learned to work with lifelong adversaries, and how they have begun to transform their parliaments in order to create space for women's issues to come to the fore. In many of the cases presented here, women and their organizations have seized the opportunities provided by their participation in decades-long conflicts and the transitions that accompanied the resolution of those conflicts. These cases demonstrate that, unlike many similar situations around the world, collaboration across class, ethnic, religious, or party lines is possible and may be successful given the right conditions. During times of national political transformation, for example, women may be able to secure significant gains by developing a broad, flexible coalition that allows for group differences. Such coalitions seem to function best when there is a shared identity of subordination and/or a shared belief in the necessity of group mobilization.

National women's movements in the cases presented in this volume have benefited from a growing collaboration with women's groups globally, for example, at international fora such as the United Nations conferences on women. African women activists and legislators have learned from the experiences of national movements for women's representation in the Americas, Asia, and Europe. They are members of international organizations and regularly exchange ideas with their sisters around the world. This text outlines women's domestic strategies but also highlights their links to international women's movements and organizations for gender equity.

The successes of African women MPs have been notable in many of these cases, especially those falling within the top twenty-five countries internationally. These leaders have been able to transform parliaments as well as shift legislative priorities to reflect the needs and interests of women in their nations. At the same time, many women MPs find that despite their increased numerical representation, they continue to face disproportionate challenges that deter their effective or equitable participation. These include, at least initially, lack of appropriate skills and training, even language barriers, continued lack of respect and collaboration from some male members of parliament, lack of constituencies beyond those provided by their political parties, and lack of independent funding and patronage sources.

The cases in this book reaffirm the growing comparative findings that electoral strategies, especially gender quotas, are often the most immediate and successful tools for increasing the number of women in national office. However, the African cases also reveal that relying on such quotas can be a double-edged sword. Depending on how the quo-

tas are constructed, women elected to reserved seats or who are in-
debted to party patronage systems often find their voices thwarted by
party loyalty. As we see in a few of our cases, one impact of strategies
such as quotas may be to support undemocratic movements, regimes,
or processes rather than to promote progressive or gender-sensitive legislation and institutions.

Another potential negative consequence of more women in parliament is the often unanticipated loss of women leaders from civil society organizations. As women across Africa have been pulled into the
halls of parliament, they often leave women's organizations and gender
advocacy groups without a second tier of leaders in place. Thus, while
getting women into office is a vital part of a national strategy for
women's empowerment, it is also important to maintain the strength of
civil society groups. Ensuring smooth and consistent cooperation between women in civil society and women in office is also a long-term
challenge. Given the professional and political constraints, women in
office are often unable or unwilling to maintain strong links to civil society groups. Once women in these groups recognize the limitations of
working with women MPs, their collaboration often falters. This is perhaps one of the most poignant lessons of this book, since it was often
such collaboration that brought women into office in the first place.

The cases in this book also remind us of the absolute necessity of
sustaining democratic transitions, indeed of consolidating democracy,
in order to assure women's continued electoral successes. We have
noted the way in which the global diffusion of multiparty politics has
paved the way for women's greater political participation and representation. By the same token, maintaining and deepening the institutions of political democracy will be essential to preserving women's
political gains. Otherwise, as happened in Zimbabwe, those gains will
be undone.[13] The Rwandan chapter in this volume warns of the dangers
of incomplete transitions and potential democratic reversals to
women's national-level political gains.

The cases in this volume are only a sample of the many stories of
women across the African continent who have struggled and continue to
strive for electoral reform, political representation, legislative change, and
institutional transformation. Although these cases are representative of
the successes and challenges of women in African parliaments, there are
countless other stories that could and hopefully will be told about how issues of gender are infusing contemporary African politics. It is our intention that this book be part of the continentwide movement for increased
women's representation, which in turn is part of the global movement for

political office. We hope our book will contribute to this process by out-lining multiple strategies of success pursued by African women as well as highlighting some of the institutional and cultural obstacles that continue to challenge women's representation and hamper their legislative impact. The lessons African women in parliament can teach each other, as well as the world, are invaluable for a truly comparative understanding of how social movements influence electoral politics, how gender may be in-cluded in the mainstream of legislative debates and outcomes, and how groups may find unity and strength within a shared identity.

Notes

1. National legislatures may be unicameral or bicameral. The cross-national comparisons of women in national legislatures, such as those main-tained by the Inter-Parliamentary Union (IPU), typically cite women's repre-sentation in the single or lower house of the national legislature.

2. www.ipu.org/wmn-e/world.htm.

3. In 2001 women in sub-Saharan Africa (SSA) were 15 million of the 18 million women living with HIV/AIDS in the developing world. SSA women experience a fertility rate of 5.4 children per woman in 2000–2005, compared to 2.5 and 3.3 children for women in Latin America and the Caribbean and South Asia, respectively. The adult literacy rate for women in SSA also lagged behind that of East Asian and Latin American women in 2001 (54 percent ver-sus 81 and 88 percent, respectively), though it was better than the rate for South Asian women (45 percent). www.hdr.org.

4. As of April 30, 2005, Senegal was forty-eighth worldwide, with 19.2 percent women in its National Assembly, still relatively far ahead of the bulk of African countries. The regional average for Africa was 15 percent in a sin-gle or lower house and 14.2 percent in a senate or upper house. www.ipu.org/wmn-e/classif.htm.

5. A vast literature spanning decades of research covers women in politics, including women legislators, primarily from developed countries. Some of that literature is cited in this book.

6. Two other recent studies (Geisler 2004; Morna 2004) focus on women in politics in Southern Africa, including but not limited to women legislators. Ballington (2004) focuses on quotas as mechanisms for electing more women to African parliaments.

7. Matland and Taylor (1997) and Goetz and Hassim (2003, 28) refer to Pitkin's (1967) distinction between "standing for" a particular group "as their literal biological copies in public" and "acting for or in the interests of a par-ticular group" as the difference between descriptive and substantive represen-tation. Hyland Byrne (1997) refers to a difference between quantitative and qualitative representation.

8. The application of the critical-mass concept to women's legislative representation has come under increasing criticism in recent years. See Childs and Krook (2005).

9. List PR systems are the most common of the PR systems. In a list PR system voters vote for a party rather than a candidate; parties receive seats in proportion to their overall share of the vote. Winning candidates are taken from the lists in order of their respective position. In closed-list systems electors cannot influence which party candidates are elected. The first-past-the-post system is one of four types of plurality-majority systems. Elections are held in single-member districts, and the candidate with the most votes (though not necessarily an absolute majority) wins. Semi-PR electoral systems, of which there are two types, fall between the plurality-majority and PR systems (Matland 2002, 2–3). Single-member district majoritarian systems (such as the first-past-the-post system, the world's most commonly used electoral system) "have consistently proven the worst possible system for women" (Matland 2002, 9).

10. See Ibrahim (2004) for an analysis of the impact of first ladies in politics in Africa, even today.

11. Two recent studies of women's increased electoral representation in Africa draw many of the same conclusions that we do. Ballington (2004) identifies the use of specific electoral systems and quotas, the strength and cohesion of national women's movements, pressure exerted by international women's movements and organizations, and the strategic use of windows of political opportunity as the factors giving rise to women's increased political representation in Africa in the 1990s and 2000s. Morna (2004) ties women's increased representation in a few Southern African countries to a PR electoral system and party-based gender quotas or reserved seats for women. She also finds that countries with the highest proportion of women in politics have recently emerged from struggle or conflict situations, or have ruling parties with social democratic inclinations, or both.

12. Molyneux defined women's practical needs to include the most pressing basic needs for safe shelter, adequate nutrition, health care, and clean water for themselves and their families and the necessity of secure employment to ensure their continued access to these basic needs. Beyond these basic necessities for survival, Molyneux delineated women's strategic needs that would drastically improve their status in society, such as legal protections, educational access, employment and land rights, and an end to gender violence.

13. Ranchod-Nilsson (1998, 274) attributes the 1999 repeal of the Legal Age of Majority Act in Zimbabwe to an increasing consolidation of power by a single-party state, resulting in a transformation of the state's "gender ideology," and a dramatic change in the "cast of state insiders and outsiders."

2

Mozambique: Empowering Women Through Family Law

Jennifer Leigh Disney

With nearly 35 percent of its National Assembly seats held by women, Mozambique had one of the highest percentages of women in parliament in mid-2005, ranking second in Africa and ninth in the world.[1] This is an amazing achievement for one of the poorest countries in Africa. Yet Mozambique has a Gender-Related Development Index of 0.339, according to the *2004 UNDP Human Development Report*.[2] It appears, then, that there is a gap between the quantitative representation of women in parliament in Mozambique and the qualitative capacity of women to effect change on behalf of women's political, economic, and sociocultural rights and interests.

Women's political representation numerically does not necessarily translate into women-centered policy initiatives substantively. In other words, the representation of women in national legislatures is a necessary but not a sufficient condition for women's empowerment. The successful achievement of 34.8 percent women members of parliament (MPs) in Mozambique must be analyzed both in terms of how this representation was achieved and to what extent it has resulted in the implementation of a policy agenda focused on improving the quality of women's rights, status, and lives in Mozambique, thereby raising the question of what constitutes a feminist policy agenda in Mozambique and for Mozambican women.

In this chapter I will discuss the political representation of women in Mozambique and attempt to assess the impact of such representation. Tremendous achievements have been made in terms of political representation and basic constitutional equality for women. However, years of legal inaction and pervasive cultural patriarchies continue to prevent significant challenges to women's oppression in the spheres of home and family, particularly in the areas of domestic labor, reproductive rights, and domestic violence. Women's subordinate status in the sphere of the family, both culturally and materially, was not adequately addressed by the Front for the Liberation of Mozambique (Frelimo) revolution, but it is finally being addressed legally in the postrevolutionary, multiparty Assembly of the Republic, due, to a large extent, to the lobbying efforts and advocacy of women.

After a brief history of women's experiences in Mozambique and a discussion of their path to political office, I will use the New Family Law as a case study to analyze the impact of women in parliament. The New Family Law, in draft form for over twenty years before getting through the Mozambican parliament in December 2003, epitomizes both the historical and cultural impediments to change as well as the legal and material achievements of Mozambican women lobbying in parliament and organizing in civil society. Through a combination of government initiatives, efforts of women MPs, and, most importantly, pressures and demands placed on both by women's organizations in civil society, an extremely progressive Family Law was passed after years of research and struggle. In this chapter I highlight that process, with a particular focus on the relationship between women MPs and women leaders in civil society. Finally, I conclude with an assessment of the possibilities and limitations women face for future organizing in the Mozambican National Assembly by addressing the issues raised by women MPs about the (as yet unattained) creation of a bipartisan parliamentary women's caucus.[3]

A Brief History of Women in Mozambique

One interesting feature of Mozambique that sets it apart from many of its neighbors is the Marxist-Leninist ideology of its successful national liberation movement, which became the ruling political party at independence and still governs today in the post-transition period. Mozambican independence from Portugal was won through the success of several anticolonial guerrilla movements that joined under the leadership of Eduardo Mondlane and Frelimo to fight for an independent Mozambique. In 1974, after a ten-year war of liberation (and a military coup d'état in Lisbon), Frelimo seized state power and became the government of an independent Mozambique. In 1977 Frelimo officially adopted Marxism-Leninism as its ideology. In 1992, after a sixteen-year war against the Mozambique National Resistance (Renamo), a foreign-created and -funded counterinsurgency force established in 1976 by Rhodesian intelligence and subsequently funded by South Africa's apartheid regime,[4] Frelimo embraced multiparty democracy. A United Nations peacekeeping operation in Mozambique was created to monitor the implementation of the 1992 Rome Peace Accord, demobilize Renamo and Frelimo soldiers, transform Renamo from a military force into a political party, and create a stable environment for the country's first multiparty elections in 1994.

Mozambique's transition from a Marxist-Leninist, one-party state to a neoliberal-democratic-capitalist, multiparty state in the 1990s has had a significant impact on women's organization and participation in politics. Women in Mozambique have transformed themselves from being mobilized by Frelimo for the purpose of achieving the nationalist and socialist goals of the party to organizing themselves for feminist political change within an active and growing women's movement. During the revolutionary rule of Frelimo in the pretransition period there was only one women's organization in Mozambique: the Organization of Mozambican Women (OMM). The OMM was created during the national liberation struggle in Tanzania in 1973. Former OMM secretary-general and current Frelimo MP Salome Moiana explained: "The OMM did not arise as an autonomous initiative of women. It was, rather, an expression of FRELIMO's will to liberate women" (Women's International Resource Exchange [WIRE] 1980, 31). The OMM accepted the analysis that the goal for which Frelimo was fighting was the "liberation of all the people from the exploitation which is also the cause of the oppression of women" (WIRE 1980, 31).

The OMM grew out of the first Frelimo women's organization, the Women's Detachment, a military unit created in 1968 as an experiment to see how women could contribute to the armed struggle. In many ways the presence of armed women in and of itself served as a critical form of political education to "dispel myths about the innate incapacity of women" (WIRE 1980, 31). At the very least, it sparked a discourse about the differences and similarities between men and women. Manuel Tome, former Frelimo secretary-general and current Frelimo MP, described the debate that took place "trying to give women their adequate place in the armed struggle," culminating in the creation of the Women's Detachment in 1968: "There were very interesting discussions: women cannot do fighting versus women can do the same work. Of course, women and men are not biologically identical, but we are essentially the same. The Women's Detachment was a turning point for women in Frelimo: not only were they taking care of children and old people, but they were also freedom fighters."[5]

Women's involvement in the Mozambican revolution as freedom fighters helped challenge traditional notions of women's inferiority.[6] Indeed, some have claimed that it was women's military involvement in the war that gave them greater credibility in the early 1990s when they started demanding peace.[7]

One of the most important legacies of Frelimo's Marxist-Leninist doctrine was the incorporation of women into the national liberation struggle and the inclusion of women's emancipation as one of the party's stated goals. However, this same legacy contains several key limitations: (1) the assumption that the exploitation of all Mozambicans and the exploitation of Mozambican women was the *same* exploitation, and that a fight to end the exploitation of (paid, male) workers in the public sphere of the market would also automatically eliminate women's oppression, and thus necessarily liberate women; (2) the focus on state-led, large-scale economic development projects despite the fact that the most popular form of agricultural production was family farming and was performed predominantly by women; and (3) the productivist, economistic way that women's emancipation was conceptualized, thus increasing women's work burden by bringing them into the paid labor force while ignoring their oppression in the sphere of the home and family, and not simultaneously encouraging men to engage in reproductive labor.[8] Thus, while the Marxist-Leninist (male) leaders of Frelimo deserve credit for integrating women into the revolutionary struggle, they also deserve criticism for circumscribing and limiting women's roles once they got there.

However, several important laws were passed in Mozambique after independence to grant women rights in the economic sphere. The Law of Sixty Days, passed in 1976, permits pregnant women workers sixty days' paid leave. Article 228 of the Rural Labor Code grants all women workers the right to miss two days of work per month without losing any salary. And in 1981–1982, the Labor Act was passed to protect women from job and wage discrimination. Yet all of this legislation applies to women in the formal sector labor force, although there are very few. More than 95 percent of women in Mozambique work in subsistence agriculture. Women "are the main people directly responsible for food production, and through their domestic work ensure the reproduction of the labor force. Due to their excessive workloads and low educational levels, women continue to occupy the worst paid jobs and to have difficulty in obtaining formal employment" (*The Situation of Women in Mozambique* 1994, 29).

Mozambique's 1975 constitution contained several strong statements against oppression and exploitation and for women's empowerment. The constitution declared "the elimination of colonial and traditional oppression and exploitation structures and their related mentality." It also stated that women's emancipation is "one of the essential tasks of the state" and established that "women and men have equal rights and duties in the economic sphere." This principle is restated later when the constitution declares that "women and men have the same rights and are subject to the same duties" and that this notion should guide "all state legislative and executive action" that "protects the marriage, the family, motherhood and childhood."

Despite the constitutional mention of the family, fatherhood is conspicuously absent from the list of things the state must protect, suggesting that the discourse of Frelimo was at best gendered and at worst patriarchal. The sphere of home, family, and marriage continued to be understood as the sphere of women and children, thus perpetuating the sexual division of labor that allows men to abdicate their responsibility to engage in the reproductive labor of the household, including family farming, food provision, cooking, cleaning, and child care. The history of male labor migrancy in Mozambique has often been cited as a major contributing factor to this sexual division of labor. In fact, migrant labor has both contributed to and challenged the sexual division of labor in Mozambique in interesting ways. Men's migration to urban areas left women in the rural areas tending to the fields and engaging in all of the labor of the family economy. It also created the conditions for women to become heads of household, pursue income-generating survival strategies, and assert decisionmaking power in the family. Still, while women were encouraged, and often through necessity forced, to engage in the "productive" labor of the money economy, men were not equally encouraged to assist in the unpaid labor of the family economy.

Though equality between men and women was established in the 1975 constitution, it was not codified in the civil or customary law. This contradiction was most evident with respect to the Nationality Law and the Family Law. The Nationality Law (enacted on the same day as the constitution of 1975) deprived Mozambican women of their citizenship when they married foreign men, though not Mozambican men when they married foreign women (Berg and Gundersen 1992, 252). This law remained in effect until 1987, despite its unconstitutionality. At the second national congress of the OMM in 1976, President Samora Machel argued that Mozambican women were weaker than Mozambican men and thus would be influenced by foreign men in a way that Mozambican men would not be by foreign women. Even the OMM claimed that enemy infiltration was easier with women due to women's "unbalanced development" compared to men:

> Mozambican woman's present situation manifests her unbalanced development in relation to man in cultural, socio-political and economic terms. It derives from her discriminatory education in traditional society which was aggravated by racial, social and sexual discrimination that Portuguese colonization imposed. It is in this context that we should understand why illiteracy, obscurantism, tribalism, regionalism, and racism, as well as inferiority complexes are more ingrained in women. . . . Woman is frequently the transmitting agent for wrong ideas because of her feeling of inferiority and insecurity. That is how enemy infiltration is made easier. The enemy will freely propagate lies thus trying to degenerate the Mozambican Revolution. (*Documentos da 2 Conferencia da Organização da Mulher Mocambicana Realizada em Maputo, 10 a 17 de Novembro de 1976*, 1977, 1, 11)

This passage attempts to explain the rationale behind the unequal, gendered nature of the Nationality Law: women's "unbalanced development," "inferiority complexes," and "discriminatory education." Discrimination against women notwithstanding, this discourse clearly "blames the victim." The Nationality Law has often been cited as evidence for the charge that Frelimo's support for women's emancipation was more in the realm of rhetoric than reality.

Legislation concerning the family provides an important lens through which to examine women's empowerment. Throughout the years of independence, Mozambique attempted to create a unitary, hybrid legal system, a combination of formal law and customary law. Much of the formal law in Mozambique was carried over from the period of Portuguese colonial rule. As a result, many of the laws in effect in the postindependence era, such as the Family Law, Civil Code, and Penal Code, remained the laws of the colonial era. For example, under the Portuguese Civil Code, the man was defined as the head of the family. This means that women have been subject to the "marital power" of their husbands, required their husbands' consent before taking paid jobs, and have not been owners of household property. Thus, the Civil Code has openly violated the clause in the Mozambican constitution that has asserted the equality of the sexes since 1975. Carla Braga describes the discriminatory treatment women have received by Portuguese law, and subsequently, by Frelimo inaction, for the past twenty-eight years: "In the Portuguese Penal Code, crimes such as adultery were defined and punished in different ways, more harshly on women. Legal reforms are in process, but twenty years after independence, these laws are still enforced and still on the books! Why did Frelimo or the OMM *not* take this as their charge? You can always blame colonialism, even after independence."[9]

Many women in Mozambique have worked for years to reform the Civil Code. One of the first attempts at legal reform in the revolutionary period was directed at the Family Law. In 1980, a Draft Family Law was prepared by the Ministry of Justice and the Faculty of Law at Eduardo Mondlane University as part of a Family Law Project. It was designed to replace the Portuguese Family Law and to reform discriminatory customary law without directly addressing the diverse marriage systems that exist throughout Mozambique.[10] From 1982 to 1990 parts of the Draft Family Law were put into use as a result of a Supreme Court of Appeals directive, but not until 2003 was the draft law, after several years of consultation, research, and reflection throughout the country, actually debated in parliament. In 1999 Terezinha da Silva, then director of the Faculty of Social Sciences at Eduardo Mondlane University, spoke of the organized efforts of the late 1990s among academic feminists to lobby parliament about the Family Law: "Two months ago, there was a proposal or request of the Ministry of Justice to discuss the Family Law. Men had attitudes at the issues raised. Some of us decided let's organize a group of women, feminists, to organize, to influence the parliament. On which issues can we get success? If you start with abortion, you'll go down. So, we started with property rights, inheritance, maintenance. Mostly academic feminists . . . We were so horrified with the attitudes of lawyers, educated men in Maputo, middle-upper class."[11]

For the most part, achievements for women in the legal sphere in Mozambique have been limited by legal inaction and cultural norms. Only recently have significant legal changes been made on behalf of women's equality in the family. Two factors in particular are worth noting on this path toward success: the role of women parliamentarians in the Assembly of the Republic and the role of women's organizations in civil society. Although the OMM was the only organization for women in the revolutionary period, today there are more than fifty women's rights and gender-based nongovernmental organizations (NGOs) in the country that have had a tremendous impact on the nature of women's organizing, the quality of women's lives, and the achievement of gender-based initiatives in postrevolutionary Mozambique. In the rest of this chapter I will explain the interactive role of women parliamentarians and women activists in Mozambique by exploring women's political organizing efforts both in and out of office.

Path to Political Office

Mozambique has done very well in increasing the political representation of women for a few key and internationally recognized reasons, most specifically, the adoption by Frelimo of a quota for women candidates and the use of a proportional representation party-list electoral system. At its sixth congress in 1992, the Frelimo party decided to introduce quotas to ensure greater representation for women at all levels and in all bodies of the party (Abreu 2004, 6). Frelimo party policy requires that 30 percent of the party's candidates for the National Assembly be women. In addition, Frelimo's policy also commits (though it does not require) the party to balance the distribution of men and women throughout the party list.

Soon after independence, the representation of women in Mozambique ranged from 12 percent at the national level to 28 percent at the local level (see Table 2.1). During the first multiparty parliament from 1994 to 1999, Frelimo boasted a very high representation of women at the national level (see Table 2.2). For Frelimo the 30 percent quota for women is no ceiling; indeed, 43 percent of Frelimo MPs in 1999 were women. This number represents a doubling since 1992.

The visibility of women in leadership positions in Mozambique has improved dramatically over the past fifteen years. In 1990 the representation of women in management positions within government ministries ranged from 0 percent in the Ministries of Defense, Interior, and Justice

Table 2.1   Women's Representation in Assemblies, 1977 (percent)

	National Assembly	Provincial Assembly	District Assembly	City Assembly	Local Assembly
Women	12.39	14.70	23.81	20.87	28.30
Men	87.61	85.30	76.19	79.13	71.70

Source: OMM 1980.

Table 2.2   Women's Representation in Frelimo, 1999 (percent)

	Members of Frelimo Party	Members of Central Committee	Deputies of Assembly of Republic
Women	42	28	43
Men	58	72	57

Source: Frelimo Central Committee 1999.

to 25 percent in the Ministry of Agriculture and 33 percent in the Ministry of Culture (Casimiro 1990). In 1993 women occupied 10 percent of the 105 leadership positions in the civil service (*Situation of Women in Mozambique* 1994, 13). By 2004 Mozambique proudly boasted a woman prime minister (Luisa Diogo), a woman minister of higher education and technology (Lidia Brito), and two women spokespersons in the National Assembly for Frelimo (Veronica Macamo, First Deputy Speaker of the Assembly of the Republic) and the Renamo-Electoral Union (Renamo-UE) (Zelma Vasconcelos). After the 2004 elections women took on an even greater role in administrative positions, with seven appointed as ministers and four as deputy ministers (see Table 2.3).

Having women in leadership positions is an essential component of any project of women's empowerment, not to mention dispelling myths of women's incapacity and achieving a truly democratic society. However, the extent to which women will lobby for women-centered initiatives or further a feminist policy agenda once they get into leadership positions is as uncertain in Mozambique as it is anywhere in Africa or the world.

Obede Baloi of European Parliamentarians for Africa (AWEPA) argues that Frelimo's decision to set quotas for women's representation has had a very important impact on women, not only in parliament but also in society: "Women are not only to be in the kitchen, they can be in the parliament! Frelimo did more. Virgilia Matabele, a woman MP, was the Deputy Chair of the Frelimo group in parliament. Having a woman communicating decisions of the ruling party has an impact."[12] Sabina Santos, former director of the OMM National Training Center in Machava, reflects upon Frelimo's openness to OMM demands for the greater political representation of women in the 1990s: "It was a necessity to put women in government as ministers and vice ministers. So, we had a direct discussion—give us names of women working in factories, graduates. The president asked if he could get a list of names. Then, we had one minister and four vice ministers. It was a very good

Table 2.3   Women's Representation as Ministers and Vice Ministers, 1999 and 2005

	1999	2005
Number of Women Ministers	3/24 (12.5%)	7/26 (26.9%)
Number of Women Vice Ministers	5/18 (27.8%)	4/15 (26.7%)

Source: Joseph Hanlon, Mozambican Government, February 2005.

thing for us. We never had women in those areas before."[13] Sérgio
Vieira, founding member of Frelimo, also applauded the party's accomplishments in bringing more women into parliament, though he
suggested that many more women need to be governors of provinces
and district administrators.[14]

The gains in women's political representation in Mozambique are
often cited as evidence of the party's commitment to the emancipation
of women. For Gertrudes Victorino, that commitment is obvious: "Of
course they [Frelimo] had an analysis of women's oppression. They
gave us space. Otherwise, we could not be in the parliament, for example. Women are inside Frelimo, in the government at every level: city
council, provincial, national. Ministers and vice ministers, directors of
firms and factories . . . Women are studying at the university."[15] Edda
Collier, United Nations gender specialist in Mozambique, credits the
Marxist perspective of Frelimo with helping women gain greater political representation than in many liberal democracies: "The Marxist perspective was clearly reflected in the constitution of 1975—equality for
everyone—'sex' included. . . . The 1990 constitution also has no discrimination based on sex."[16] Collier feels it was this framework that enabled the OMM to lobby for a quota for women within all Frelimo organs and decisionmaking bodies.

The relationship between Frelimo and the OMM is an important
factor in understanding women's path to political office in Mozambique. The OMM was an instrument through which Frelimo was able
to mobilize women in the revolutionary one-party state; in the postrevolutionary multiparty state, the OMM is doing more, with the help of
autonomous organizations in civil society, to lobby Frelimo. But one
thing seems clear: The women who rise within Frelimo and the OMM
are the same women. Signe Arnfred, a Danish sociologist who worked
with the OMM, argues that the organizational identity of the OMM was
determined by Frelimo: "All the time I was there, from 1980 to 1984,
they didn't do anything that was not confirmed by the party. They never
took initiatives; there was never disagreement. The party sent initiatives down to the OMM. On the whole, in the OMM the line was very
much in my view given from the top down. The OMM was taking too
much direction for my liking."[17] Arnfred's perception of the nature of
the relationship between the OMM and Frelimo was confirmed by Ana
Rita Sithole, Frelimo MP and OMM member. She noted: "Sometimes
we feel Frelimo uses us for mobilization for elections and that we are
not a part of the big decisions. There is a tense relationship. However,
most of the OMM leaders have Frelimo responsibilities. If not, they
will not rise—they will not become an OMM leader."[18]

Apparently, not only is party support important for becoming an OMM leader, but membership in the OMM is an important prerequisite for women who wish to become party candidates for public office. Perhaps one of the most important roles of the OMM today is submitting names of women to the party for elected positions. Generossa Cossa was elected to the Maputo city council working in the areas of gender, youth, social assistance, and civic education: "I was elected as an OMM member. I am still an active member of OMM. It is a really strong organization. If you go to a meeting, you'll feel that! People fight to get seats, to get elected."[19] The OMM seems to be the path toward electoral success for women not just on the local but also on the national level. Cossa noted that the secretary of the OMM of Maputo City had a list of six hundred women who want to be members of the National Assembly: "The OMM is one of the ways to get into parliament."[20]

Despite a brief period of autonomy, the shift from a revolutionary one-party state to a postrevolutionary multiparty state propelled a major transition for the OMM, from being the organization of all Mozambican women to being the women's organization of the Frelimo party. Renamo does not have a party quota for women, nor does it have a women's organization. Thus, women's path to political office in Mozambique tends to be a partisan issue: Frelimo seems more committed than Renamo to the representation of women in parliament.[21] Indeed, despite the desire and efforts of several Frelimo and Renamo women MPs to create a women's caucus in the National Assembly, partisan divisions have made it difficult for women from both parties to come together as women in parliament to effect political change. This begs the question: What impact have women MPs had in the Mozambican National Assembly once they have gotten there?

The Impact of Women MPs in Mozambique

Women's increased political representation does not necessarily translate into women-centered or feminist policy initiatives. As the Mozambican National Assembly just completed its second term under the multiparty constitution in 2004, it may be too early to tell. However, concerns have been raised by women activists in civil society, and expectations are high. Elisa Muianga and Celeste Bango, formerly of Women, Law, and Development Organization (MULEIDE), share their cynicism, speaking of the difference between the quantitative and qualitative aspects of women's representation after the first multiparty parliament in Mozambique from 1994 to 1999: "In Africa, Mozambique has the second-highest percentage of women in parliament. The question is to know if they are fighting for women inside. Are they representing women? Probably not Frelimo, but women in parliament are discussing it in meetings with other organizations. We cannot be happy with the number of women in parliament but with the *quality* of women in parliament. This is the first parliament. It is a quick evaluation, but we are not satisfied. But, they are learning now. They have no practice. We must give them time, then criticize them" [emphasis added].[22]

Ivete Mboa of the Association of Housewives (ADOCA), a women's NGO in Matola, also shared her skepticism regarding the difference between the quantity and the quality of women serving in parliament. According to Mboa, although many women have ideas, some "choose the party and not the people."[23] In discussing the composition of political power in parliament, Carla Braga concurs that numbers are not enough: "How many times did this woman make an intervention in parliament? How many times was she heard?"[24] Despite the fact that there has been an increase in the number of women elected to parliament and appointed to ministerial positions, many women continue to assert that "you don't necessarily get empowerment from participation."[25]

The passage of the New Family Law in the National Assembly in December 2003 acts as a critical case study to begin to assess the impact of women MPs in Mozambique and the extent to which women's political participation in parliament has resulted in women's empowerment. The history of the Family Law is a long one, involving actions on the part of executive governmental commissions, legislative assemblies, and NGOs in civil society. The successful passage of a flawed though extremely progressive Family Law in the Mozambican National Assembly was the result of a concerted cooperative effort among and between women MPs and women in civil society. However, when asked directly about the role each group played in the contemporary period, most women MPs and women activists gave women in civil society more credit for putting pressure on parliament to make it happen. According to Maria Angelina Dique Enoque, Renamo-UE MP, "I think that very honestly the pressure was from women in civil society. I do not want to say that women MPs were not interested in the law, because we were. [But] the Family Law was one of the moments society used women MPs to help in this project."[26] In other words, despite the necessary efforts of governmental commissions and the national legislature, it was women's organizations in civil society pushing from the outside and pressuring such governmental agencies on the inside that did the most to achieve the passage of the Family Law in the National Assembly in December 2003.

In 1998, after twenty years of a law in draft form, the Ministry of Justice, under the direction of the president, ordered the Commission for Legal Reform to study, research, and draft a new version of the Family Law in consultation with civil society. Such women's organizations as Forum Mulher (Women's Forum), MULEIDE, Women and Law in Southern Africa (WLSA), and the Association of Women Lawyers not only played a crucial part in drafting the law but also assisted in the process of conducting research throughout the country to determine the attitudes of women and men in various communities about the family and the Family Law. The draft itself was taken back out into the countryside to assess attitudes toward several key provisions; community discussions were held in every province. From 1998 to 2001 there was a real attempt to identify the attitudes of Mozambican citizens in urban and rural areas both before and after the new version of the law was drafted.

However, once a new draft was sent to the National Assembly in 2001, it stalled and failed to be debated in parliament. According to Celeste Nobela and Emanuela Mondlane of Forum Mulher, from 2001 to 2003, parliamentarians made numerous excuses for why the law was not being addressed. It was simply pushed off the legislative agenda because it was not a priority—or perhaps because a fundamental restructuring of the Mozambican family was too controversial. After two years of delay more than 1,000 women marched to the National Assembly building in November 2003 and demanded that the president of the Assembly of the Republic, Eduardo Joaquim Dinis Erasto Mulembwev, come out and address them. Women leaders in civil society had written a statement that they read to Mulembwev, demanding that the Family Law be discussed during the current session of parliament. Amazingly, after twenty years of legal inaction and two years of stalling within parliament, the bill was passed in December 2003, just one month after the march. Pressure from organized coalitions outside government is often required to help even well-intentioned, if not stalling or outright resistant, MPs to take action for change. In fact, some would argue it is the only such influence that ever succeeds.

The New Family Law

What Does the Law Accomplish for Women?

The New Family Law, deemed everything from progressive to feminist, makes great strides in challenging the history of traditional family structures in Mozambique. Overturning years of patriarchal privilege in the family, property rights, and divorce law, the new law recognizes shared leadership and property in the family and two types of divorce: that based on mutual consent and that sought by one spouse through litigation. The law works hard to recognize religious law and customary law alongside civil law, perhaps its most difficult challenge. In April 2004 President Joaquim Chissano returned the law to parliament, claiming that the sections dealing with the mutual recognition of religious, civil, and customary marriages were unconstitutional. The National Assembly's Legal Affairs and Social Affairs Commissions reworked the law in light of Chissano's objections. On August 24, 2004, during an Extraordinary Session of the Assembly of the Republic, the amended bill was passed unanimously and with acclamation.[27]

Historically, customary law in Mozambique recognizes monogamous and polygamous marriages, hinders women from obtaining contractual capacity, and favors the father or his male relatives in custody situations. Only the man has been allowed to initiate a divorce because in patrilineal systems women go to live with the family of the husband after the payment of *lobolo* (bride price) and because in Muslim societies women are often not considered legal adults. Lobolo is paid by the family of the groom to the family of the bride in patrilineal systems, representing a shift in "ownership" and responsibility for the bride, as she will leave her family and go to live with her husband's family. Originally, lobolo signified only an alliance between two families. Money was first introduced into this custom during colonization (WIRE 1980, 30). Lobolo has been found to discourage divorce in patrilocal societies because the control of the woman is given to the husband and his family through an economic bond, meaning that the woman would be expelled without her children following a divorce, and the lobolo would be paid back. It also indicates that the woman's autonomy even after the husband dies is circumscribed (Women and Law in Southern Africa 1997). In matrilineal systems women have more power in terms of property and divorce because after marriage the husband goes to live with his wife's family, so he would be the one expelled from the home upon divorce. The New Family Law attempts to provide protection to women and children within these varied situations without challenging the traditional or religious belief systems of polygamy, patrilineality, or Islam.

One of the most important achievements of the law is its challenge of the assumption of a male head of household. Under the New Family Law a woman or a man can be the chief of the family. Moreover, the law recognizes both customary marriages and de facto unions. A de facto union is defined in the law as a woman and a man cohabitating for at least three years but not marrying legally. De facto unions are the most prominent form of relationship in urban areas. Under the new law, women in de facto unions and traditional or religious marriages would be able to seek alimony, maintenance, or custody in the case of divorce or separation, even though the couple may never have legally married.[28] Only about 10 percent of marriages in Mozambique are official, civil marriages through the state. Ninety percent are customary, traditional, or religious. Maria José Artur, national coordinator of WLSA, explains the thinking behind the New Family Law's treatment of alternative forms of marriage: "The Family Law set out to give recognition and legal status to traditional and religious marriage. The idea is that it doesn't make sense to say to people, 'Get married in a civil marriage after your traditional or religious marriage.' According to the old law, traditional and religious marriages did not count. Our proposal was that if you are eighteen years old, monogamous, with two witnesses, that would count and should be recognized. The idea is to respect other forms of marriage and not only civil marriage."[29]

Most important, the recognition of noncivil marriages affords the law the opportunity to protect the children of these unions. The New Family Law eliminates the distinction between "legitimate" and "illegitimate" children and affords equal rights to both. In addition, the law raises the minimum age of marriage for boys from sixteen to eighteen and for girls from fourteen to eighteen, although it allows exceptions for girls at sixteen "under special circumstances" and with parental consent.[30] The law also makes it easier for couples to adopt children and acknowledges the concept of "foster family" for the first time in Mozambican history. The practice of taking in foster children has become very common in Mozambique because of the number of children orphaned or abandoned during the war years, or whose biological parents are dying of HIV/AIDS.

Throughout the 1990s the draft law was circulated around the country and became the subject of heated debates because of its challenge to the patriarchal family structure. According to the Mozambican Information Agency, many organizations contributed substantially to the development of the New Draft Law, including MULEIDE, Forum Mulher, the National Union of Cooperative Farmers, the Association of Women Lawyers, and the Association of Mozambican Women Journalists. It was reported that during the debate the first deputy speaker of Parliament, Veronica Macamo, asked if it was time to challenge "the exercise of marital power" by the husband in the name of equality.[31] In addition, Sérgio Vieira, founding member of Frelimo, "questioned the legal recognition of 'de facto unions,'" suggesting that this would just encourage men not to get married. The practice of lobolo is often regarded as mercenary, but Vieira declared that it was a form of "'pre-nuptial' contract, which should be included in the law."[32] Ultimately, the law goes very far in improving the status of women in the family in three key areas: (1) The husband is no longer automatically head of household, and no longer automatically represents the family—either partner may do so; (2) the right of a husband or wife to work may not be restricted by the other partner, and the wife no longer needs to ask her husband's permission to go into business or contract debts; (3) the children of traditional, customary, religious, and civil marriages will have the same protections under the law.

Limitations of the Law

Mozambique is a culturally diverse society. Not only are there regional differences from the south to the center to the north of the country, and religious differences from traditional African religions to Islam to Christianity, but there are also patrilineal and matrilineal marriage systems in the country as well as traditions of polygamy in both the Muslim and African patrilineal communities. As a result, a real effort was made to draft a family law that would respect the cultural diversity of the country while also protecting the rights of women and children. This goal was not easy to achieve and in fact proved to be quite controversial in several key areas, especially with regard to polygamy. In this section I discuss some of the debates that arose around polygamy and assess how the compromises that were made during the parliamentary passage of the law in December 2003 further women's rights and women's empowerment. I also hope to shed light on the impact of women MPs and women leaders in civil society in their attempts to extend their own forms of feminist empowerment throughout Mozambique.

Polygamy

The debates surrounding polygamy, both on the floor of the Assembly of the Republic and in community meetings in civil society,[33] proved to be the most controversial, with no consensus emerging among the women or men involved in the debates. For the leaders and members of women's organizations in civil society, one thing was clear: Their goal in the New Family Law was to protect the women and children of polygamous marriages without defending polygamy. This proved to be extremely difficult, though necessary. As Zelma Vasconcelos, MP and spokesperson for the Renamo-UE in the National Assembly, argued: "There is a provision in the law that states that if a man dies, wife number two, number three, and number four should have legal recourse. The law should not be saying that. That in effect condones polygamy!"[34] When asked whether such a provision was designed not to protect polygamy but rather to protect the women and children who, though perhaps unfortunately, currently live within polygamous marriages, Vasconcelos responded: "We are trying to create a society. We should be writing laws for the way we want society to be. We should be writing laws for the future, not for the present."[35]

In response to the points made by Vasconcelos, several women leaders in civil society articulated the difference between defending polygamy as a system and defending the women and children who currently live within polygamous relationships. According to Terezinha da Silva, president of the Board of Forum Mulher: "There is polygamy in Mozambique. The law is not protecting polygamy. The women and children need to be protected. . . . We interviewed the children, men and women, girls and boys, children of polygamous marriages. We interviewed Islamic and non-Islamic [families]. . . . Everybody is saying, 'No! We suffered from a polygamous marriage. Only children of the first wife got benefits, privileges.' This led to a bad economic situation for many. . . . And with AIDS, it is just not possible to have polygamy."[36]

Isabel Casimiro, longtime feminist activist, scholar, and researcher of women's organizing in Mozambique and former Frelimo MP, asserted that not everyone was against polygamy in the debates in parliament and society at large: "I think if I know this version [of the law] it tried to take all things into consideration."[37] Casimiro agrees with Vasconcelos that the law is written for the future, but she also says it needs to take into account present realities: "When we say women and men are equal, we know it is not true. But we write it for the future. But the future must also take into account the past. Polygamy is a reality."[38]

It is interesting to note that men on the floor of the National Assembly tended to make arguments in favor of polygamy, while men in the communities often spoke about the economic difficulties of polygamy and the responsibility of caring for several wives and all their children. These different perspectives among men seem to highlight the class system that polygamy in fact is: Those elite men who can afford to have several families want to protect the tradition, while those who cannot are beginning to recognize that it may oppress not only women.

It has been very difficult for women in Mozambique to reach consensus about the relationship among polygamy, feminism, and religious freedom, both in terms of the theories of feminism and the provisions of the Family Law. In Islamic communities in Mozambique, the arguments for and against polygamy are less economic than religious and generational. Selma Augusta, a woman who joined Forum Mulher to represent Muslim women during the public discussions around the Family Law, stated that the Koran allows men to have up to four wives and that it is not her place to question that. It is a matter of faith.[39] However, she argued adamantly that the Koran also clearly states the conditions under which a man should take up to four wives: Those conditions include equality, dignity, and respect.[40] Augusta also asserted that the Koran states that only if a man can treat his wives equally in terms of material and nonmaterial resources (for example, economic resources and emotional love) should he take on more than one wife. Selma's son, Aly Elias Lalá, said that he does not believe equal emotional love would be possible, which is why he does not plan to take more than one wife.[41] Generational differences also emerged in the Muslim community meetings that took place around the Family Law. Aly had conversations with several young Muslim women who do challenge the Koran: "I understand their argument. And if it were me, I would probably feel the same way. I do not want to be one of four, or three, or even two. But for me, it is not my place to question the Koran. Allah is all knowing. . . . There are things that can be seen and known that we would not think of. It is a matter of faith."[42]

Protecting the women and children of polygamous marriages without either defending or condemning polygamy within the provisions of the Family Law proved to be the most difficult aspect of negotiation. Several other areas of the law were also controversial and ended in compromises being made by women leaders in civil society and parliament in order to ensure the passage of the law. One such compromise was the clause allowing girls to marry at sixteen, two years younger than boys. Because of the strong lobby of traditional communities in the country, the commitment to an equal age for girls and boys to marry was compromised despite the seemingly unanimous commitment to encouraging both to stay in school longer. Obviously, these kinds of goals require cultural change, not simply legal change.

After thirty years of promises, twenty-five years with a draft law in place, and eight years of research, revisions, discussions, and debates, how do feminists in Mozambique assess the recent passage and final version of the New Family Law? Perhaps Maria José Artur of WLSA said it best: "This was the best law that we managed to pass according to the conditions we have in Mozambique. The main rights of women and children are respected. Of course, we wanted to go farther. For example, legalizing gay and lesbian marriage, or providing more for women's rights like recognizing the possibility of rape in marriage. This is currently not in the penal code. But the Law has the basic rights to educate future generations."[43]

Future Directions

One of the most interesting developments in post-transition Mozambique is the continuing interaction between women MPs in the National Assembly and women activists in civil society. The growth of autonomous women's NGOs in civil society has dramatically increased in the postrevolutionary period, from 1 in 1992 to 25 in 1997 to over 50 in 2004. Ana Maria Montero, former co-coordinator of the NGO Development Project of Eduardo Mondlane University, believes that the primary reason there are so many women's organizations in Mozambique today is that for so many years women could participate politically, economically, and socially only in the OMM: "Women had to be a member of the OMM to have the opportunity to participate or give their experience. When the country gave the opportunity to all people to organize in associations, . . . women found a place to exchange ideas and discuss their situation in Mozambique. Associations give excluded women the opportunity to show the people that they have the capacity to do anything in different sectors."[44]

Today there are strong connections between women MPs and women leaders in civil society. Often the same women move in and out of leadership roles in government and civil society. In addition, autonomous NGOs in civil society often have strong ties with the Frelimo party and Frelimo women leaders because of the process of democratization and the recent development of a multiparty system in the post-transition period.

The future of women's organizing in Mozambique will be to further codify connections between women MPs of all parties and women activists in civil society through the establishment of greater links, networks, and structures through which women can come together and work for change. Renamo-UE MP Maria Angelina Dique Enoque spoke about the historical development of democracy and the shifting identities of the OMM in Mozambique from an organization for all women to an organization for Frelimo women, expressing her hope for a future bipartisan national women's organization: "With the multiparty system, there are new women's organizations for each political party. I keep saying the OMM is the women's organization of Frelimo. In the future, one day, women from Frelimo, Renamo will all be a part of a national women's organization. I don't know if I'll be alive, but . . ."[45]

One of the most important bipartisan initiatives that has been on the agenda of women MPs in Mozambique since the first multiparty parliament in 1994 to help achieve the goal of more coordinated women's organizing on a national level is the creation of a parliamentary women's caucus. According to Isabel Casimiro, MP in the first multiparty parliament from 1994 to 1999: "We tried to create a women's caucus. We had all the conditions. AWEPA was supporting us. It was not a question of not having the money. There was the money. But we couldn't do it."[46] Why have women MPs been unable to create a parliamentary women's caucus despite the material incentives to do so?

Perhaps the most interesting discourse to emerge from my recent interviews with women parliamentarians and leaders in civil society is the limited extent to which having a high percentage of women in the Assembly of the Republic of Mozambique makes a difference. This discourse is inextricably linked to one of the most consistent issues raised by women MPs when asked about women's organizing and feminism in Mozambique: the lack of a parliamentary women's caucus. Although women MPs could not agree as to whether or not their high percentage in parliament makes a difference, one thing they all agreed upon was that their ability to make a difference was dramatically constrained by two factors: party politics and the absence of a women's caucus.

Zelma Vasconcelos, Renamo-UE MP and spokesperson for the Renamo opposition, stated emphatically that having a high percentage of women MPs in the Mozambican parliament does not make a difference: "Our society is a society of men. Women in the government only say, 'Yes.' No! No! It doesn't make a difference! It is only numbers. . . . If you ask women in parliament, 'What projects do you do for women?' No. . . . It's true for all parties. Women are spokespersons for their parties."[47]

Several other women leaders agreed with Vasconcelos's assessment of the inability of women to express themselves as women within the structure of political parties in Mozambique: "Unfortunately, she's right" was a phrase repeated by several prominent parliamentarians and self-identified feminists in civil society.

However, some took issue with Vasconcelos's argument that having women in parliament makes no difference. Rafa Machava, executive director of MULEIDE, summarized the impact this way: "They are from the government, but they are still women! It gives us more status as women, more power to demand women's rights, more power to demand women's emancipation."[48] One leader of a prominent NGO in civil society understood Vasconcelos's argument in completely partisan terms: "She is from the opposite party speaking about not having a voice. Maybe that's the way it is with her party, but not with our women! I know I am not supposed to identify myself with my party, but I think for her side, it may be more difficult because their men are suspicious. They are very controlled by their men."[49]

Not all Renamo-UE MPs were as pessimistic as Vasconcelos about the possibility of establishing a women's caucus. One, Maria Angelina Dique Enoque, said: "One of the aspects that is very sad about the Mozambican parliament is that a women's caucus doesn't exist."[50] Enoque explained that several women have been trying to create a women's caucus within the Assembly of the Republic that would act as "a link to women on the outside and would work to put pressure to get laws passed. . . . I am one of the women, and I am getting frustrated. My mandate is finishing now, and we didn't manage to achieve this goal for women in civil society."[51] Enoque spoke quite passionately about the need, desire, and possibility of creating a women's caucus that would bring women MPs together across party lines:

> One of my Frelimo colleagues was in an accident and lost her life. . . . I wanted to achieve this goal as a memorial to her.[52] The point of the women's caucus meeting would be to be without the name of the party, but rather to join together to solve women's problems. Women are all equal when it comes to violence—we don't have a party name written on our back. And we have young parliamentarians from the provinces who have kids. There is no child care set up for parliament. Women MPs in a women's caucus could work on this. . . . It is true that women MPs are getting closer to each other. In the main building, when a woman is speaking, the other women often clap their hands. There is not a very bad relationship between women from both parties, but they are still covered up by parties. As a woman, I believe women can work across party.[53]

Ana Rita Sithole, Frelimo MP, expressed a similar frustration. As a member of several international and regional parliamentary organizations that have spaces for women's caucusing, Sithole expressed regret that Mozambique stands out for its absence of a women's caucus: "We need to create this women's caucus. In all these international forums, there is always a meeting of women. This means, Mozambican women have to go to these meetings with ideas of what is happening to women in Mozambique. . . . I feel for the next term, we have to create this group. There is no other way. Otherwise, we cannot participate with other women in other meetings."[54]

Although Sithole shares Vasconcelos's concern that women MPs are too controlled by their parliamentary groups, she disagrees with the other's assertion that party divisions are too strong in Mozambique to make a women's caucus a reality. Sithole is more optimistic and more committed to trying to create a bipartisan women's caucus. Frelimo MP Filipa Baltazar da Costa raised issues about how the women's caucus would be structured. Would it be formal or informal? To what extent would it be politically and economically integrated into, and therefore accountable to, parliamentary structures, and to what extent would it operate outside such structures? And, of course, there is the question of leadership. Former MP Isabel Casimiro summarized this issue: "Our problem is a power problem. We couldn't organize. We couldn't decide who was going to be the head of it."[55]

The challenge for women MPs in a multiparty Mozambique, it seems, will be to increase women's focus on their gender identity and not just their party identity. For a country just completing its second multiparty parliament, it doesn't seem unreasonable for party identity to remain the primary organizing principle. However, the success of future women's organizing in Mozambique will depend upon women MPs strengthening their gender identities, thinking through the structural issue of organization, and further coordinating their links and networks with the many autonomous women's NGOs in civil society in order to continue to work together, as successfully as they did to pass the New Family Law, toward the creation and implementation of a woman-centered, feminist policy agenda.

Conclusion

Mozambique's transition from a one-party Marxist-Leninist state to a multiparty liberal-democratic-capitalist state has ushered in new organizing opportunities for women. Frelimo has always been committed to women's participation in the party structure and in the OMM, but the extent to which women have had the autonomy to question the party and/or develop a feminist agenda has been questionable, to say the least. The fact that Mozambique has achieved such a high percentage of women in parliament can be attributed to the legacy of Marxism-

Leninism, the Frelimo party commitment to a 30 percent quota for women candidates, and the use of a proportional representation party-list electoral system. The question of what women have been able to do in the Assembly of the Republic since they have been there is the relevant issue that I have tried to address in this chapter.

After years of inaction, a progressive New Family Law has been passed, establishing women's legal equality and expanding their empowerment in the family. The role of women MPs and autonomous NGOs, such as Forum Mulher, MULEIDE, and WLSA, outside the realm of Frelimo and the OMM has been crucial to such legal achievements. The interaction between women MPs and women's organizations in civil society has dramatically increased, shaping the discourse around these issues by setting the terms of the debate and putting women and women's empowerment at the center. Moreover, women's organizations in civil society have influenced women MPs through their research, lobbying efforts, and pressuring of parliament to achieve legal changes for women from a feminist perspective. Maria José Artur of WLSA summarized the influential effects of women's NGOs: "The government had a very important role. Women's organizations also had two important roles. They pressed the government. Forum Mulher asked for an audience to speak with important people in government. And, in terms of media and public opinion, they wrote things in the newspapers to influence people. There was a big contribution of women's organizations all over the country: Forum Mulher, WLSA, MULEIDE. They talked to women about their expectations of what should be in the law."[56]

The women MPs and NGOs of today will have the responsibility of continuing to address the issues of importance to Mozambican women, such as economic development, women's legal equality, and education, and of highlighting the issues that historically have been difficult to get on the agenda, such as violence against women and reproductive rights. Moreover, women MPs will have the challenge of working across party lines to cultivate women's gender identities within parliamentary structures and work toward more bipartisan women-centered policy initiatives.

Obviously, legal change is not all that is needed. Carla Braga, involved with a group of women from Eduardo Mondlane University doing activist work on the New Family Law in 1999, expressed some concern about how much good the new law would actually do, even after being passed: "I'm giving it so much importance. How many women will this actually affect? Most women live by customary law versus written law. . . . There is little knowledge of the law, even among literate people. Statistics say 80 percent are illiterate, and 20 percent are literate, knowing how to read and write."[57] Obviously, legal change can only go so far. Cultural and educational change must accompany any legal program for expanding women's rights in Mozambique. However, the codification of legal equality between women and men, particularly in the family, achieved through the recent passage of the New Family Law because of the tireless efforts of women MPs and women activists in civil society, represents a fundamental feminist step toward the achievement of women's empowerment.

Notes

Special thanks go to Hannah Britton and Gretchen Bauer, both for inviting me to participate in the African Studies Association panel from which this edited volume emerges and for their detailed edits and suggestions to several drafts of this chapter. Moreover, I would like to thank Lenny Markovitz, Frances Fox Piven, and Hester Eisenstein for their comments on earlier iterations of this research and their continued mentorship and support.

1. Inter-Parliamentary Union, *Women in National Parliaments,* as of April 30, 2005, women's representation in a single or lower house of parliament. http://www.ipu.org/wmn-e/classif.htm. Mozambique has a unicameral national legislature. The Assembly of the Republic is also known as the National Assembly, and the two terms are used interchangeably in this chapter.

2. The Gender-Related Development Index is a composite index measuring average achievement in the three basic dimensions captured in the human development index—a long and healthy life, knowledge, and a decent standard of living—adjusted to account for inequalities between men and women. http://hdr.undp.org/reports/global/2003/indicator/indic_196_1_1.html.

3. Research for this chapter was conducted during two trips to Mozambique. The first took place in July–August 1999, when I conducted fifty in-depth, open-ended interviews with women and men who had been active leaders in the revolutionary struggle, both within the Frelimo party and within the national-level women's organization, the OMM. I also interviewed Frelimo parliamentarians and leaders and members of autonomous women's organizations and other NGOs that have emerged during the 1990s. In 1999 I traveled to each of the three regions of the country—Nampula in the north, Beira in the center, and Maputo in the south—interviewing women from both patrilineal and matrilineal societies. In 2004 I updated my research, focusing primarily on women parliamentarians and activists in Maputo. Interviews were conducted in English and Portuguese and were assisted by a translator when necessary. Both the original language and the translations were recorded to ensure accuracy. Unless otherwise stated, all interviews took place in Maputo.

4. Tens of thousands died and hundreds of thousands were displaced in the war with Renamo. Addressing the magnitude of human loss, destruction, and

tragedy due to the war is outside the limitations of this chapter. Numerous other sources attempt to address the impact of the wars. See, for example, Magaia 1988; Minter 1994; Vines 1990.

5. Interview by the author on July 29, 1999.

6. Ali Mazrui emphasizes the importance of Frelimo's use of women combatants through his definition of a new type of resistance that he feels was implemented in Southern Africa, inspired by the Marxist tradition: androgynous warriorhood. Androgynous warriorhood is defined as "a principle which seeks to end the masculine monopoly of the skills of war" (Mazrui 1976, 189). Citing Frelimo's use of women as early as the late 1960s, Mazrui asserts that the leftist regimes in Africa, particularly in former Portuguese colonies, seriously attempted to incorporate women militarily into their struggle (1976, 191).

7. Interview by the author on July 30, 1999.

8. Several scholars have discussed the gendered nature of Frelimo's philosophies, decisionmaking structures, and rural development plans (Urdang 1985, 1989; Bowen 2000; Disney 2002, 2004). The revolutionary analysis adopted by the Frelimo party was framed by Marxist-Leninist understandings of the causes and thus the solutions of women's oppression. As a result, the theories and practices of the OMM, created by Frelimo, were also framed by Marxist-Leninist analyses of "the woman question" that focus primarily on a "productivist" model of integrating women into the revolutionary cause via "productive labor" without an analysis of (1) the gendered division of labor and women's primary participation in "reproductive labor"; (2) the intersections between women's practical gender needs and strategic gender interests in the interconnected spheres of production and reproduction; and (3) women's input into the overall revolutionary vision for society. Basically, although the discourse of "women's emancipation" was seen as critical to the articulation of the revolution, the achievement of the "socialist revolution"—and the mobilization of women in defense and production that was required to accomplish it—was seen as synonymous with the liberation of women. There was no alternative or autonomous discussion of what women's liberation might entail.

9. Interview by the author on July 15, 1999.

10. Mozambique is unique in that the country contains quite a diverse set of marriage and kinship systems. The northern region is predominantly matrilineal, while the southern region is patrilineal. In addition, the country is one-third Christian, one-third Muslim, and one-third traditional African religions, with traditions of polygamy in both the Muslim and African patrilineal systems. Muslim communities can be found predominantly in the north, center, and coastal regions of the country.

11. Interview by the author on July 23, 1999.

12. Interview by the author on July 23, 1999.

13. Interview by the author in Machava, July 20, 1999.

14. Interview by the author on July 15, 1999.

15. Interview by the author on July 14, 1999.

16. Interview by the author on July 30, 1999.

17. Interview by the author on November 17, 1999.

18. Interview by the author on July 15, 1999.

19. Interview by the author on July 13, 1999.

20. Ibid.

21. In the second parliamentary session from 1999 to 2004, Frelimo had fifty-four women MPs, and Renamo had twenty-three.

22. Interview by the author on July 21, 1999.

23. Interview by the author in Matola, July 7, 1999.

24. Interview by the author on July 15, 1999.

25. Interview by the author on July 30, 1999.

26. Interview by the author on July 6, 2004.

27. The New Family Law took effect 180 days after its publication in the official gazette, the *Boletim da Republica,* to allow time for changes in other legislation affected by the law, such as the Inheritance Law, and to train registrars, and religious and traditional dignitaries, in what the law requires of them. *Assembly Passes Revised Family Law*, Maputo, August 24, 2004. Mozambican Information Agency–AIM.

28. *Assembly Debates Radical Change in the Family Law,* Maputo, April 29, 2003. Mozambican Information Agency–AIM.

29. Interview by the author on July 5, 2004.

30. *Assembly Debates Radical Change in the Family Law*.

31. Ibid.

32. Ibid.

33. These accounts come from several parliamentarians, women's organization leaders, and community members whom I interviewed who had been present at debates in the National Assembly and throughout the country.

34. Interview by the author on June 29, 2004.

35. Ibid.

36. Interview by the author in Matola, June 30, 2004.

37. Interview by the author on July 8, 2004.

38. Ibid.

39. Interview by the author on July 7, 2004.

40. I include this discussion not to take a position on the Koran but rather to try to adequately represent the diversity of views expressed in debates about the Family Law by Mozambican women, and hence to reveal the complicated situations within which Mozambican feminists and women's movement activists found themselves when trying to act as advocates for "women's rights" in the country.

41. Interview by the author on July 7, 2004.

42. Ibid.

43. Interview by the author on July 5, 2004.

44. Interview by the author on July 8, 1999.

45. Interview by the author on July 6, 2004.

46. Interview by the author on July 8, 2004.

47. Interview by the author on July 29, 2004.

48. Interview by the author on July 1, 2004.

49. These partisan references are from an interview by the author in 2004 with a woman in civil society who claimed that Frelimo women have more of

a voice than Renamo women. On the one hand, this seems true prima facie, as Frelimo has adopted a party quota for women whereas Renamo still has not. On the other hand, despite this obvious difference in each party's commitment to women's equality, I think it is safe to say that women's ability to assert a gendered or feminist identity is often still curtailed in Mozambique, even in Frelimo.

50. Interview by the author on July 6, 2004.
51. Ibid.
52. Reference to Yudite Anegelina Mocâo.
53. Interview by the author on July 6, 2004.
54. Interview by the author on July 4, 2003.
55. Interview by the author on July 8, 2004.
56. Interview by the author on July 5, 2004.
57. Interview by the author on July 15, 1999.

3

South Africa: Mainstreaming Gender in a New Democracy

Hannah E. Britton

Women in South Africa cut their political teeth during decades of anti-apartheid struggle. They were a powerful but often invisible force in the liberation movement that fought against government-imposed segregation and discrimination. Apartheid was a reification of colonial hierarchies of ethnicity and gender, and women worked collectively to oppose the white-minority government, often building coalitions across racial or ideological divisions. This political experience was essential for the strategies women used during the transition to democracy in South Africa. Once it was clear that apartheid was ending and the transition to a multiethnic democracy was assured, there was space on the national political agenda to address issues such as gender discrimination. Women used their political skills during this brief window of opportunity to influence the constitution-writing process and to pressure their individual political parties to advance women candidates for national office. After the first free democratic election in South Africa in 1994, women occupied approximately 26 percent of the seats in the National Assembly.[1] This was the first step in a continuing process of integrating gender issues into the legislative process and of securing equitable gender representation in office.

Based on five research trips to South Africa, including the most recent trip in May–July 2003,[2] I assert in this chapter that South African women are now actively engaging the structures of political and institutional power. Women parliamentarians have chosen to work within the system to champion additional legislative reforms and to transform the status and role of women in society. However, despite significant legislative and institutional accomplishments, women parliamentarians are faced with obstacles that challenge if not undermine their efficacy in office. The institution of parliament, with its traditions and norms, remained essentially static following the election, despite the fact that the faces and parties within it had changed completely. Many women have fared well in their roles as members of parliament (MPs) and delegates; however, most often these women come from affluent backgrounds, have extensive professional or educational experience, or come from an ethnic group that was privileged during apartheid. This means that the parliament of South Africa is rapidly becoming filled with women from professional, educational, and political backgrounds that may be associated with typical traditional Western legislative bodies. Granted, the gender and ethnic composition of the South African parliament is monumentally more progressive and representative than most; however, the rapidity with which the women in parliament have become "professionalized" is remarkable. Interviews with women lead me to predict that this emerging trend will become a norm for South Africa; the interviews also indicate that women in parliament will continue to pursue insider strategies, such as state feminism, to achieve pragmatic gains for women nationally. In many ways this emphasis on pragmatic insider strategies lessens the revolutionary potential and radicalism of a social movement. Yet such strategies have promoted institutionalized reforms that have had immediate practical social benefits for meeting women's basic needs. Despite the limitations of reform strategies and state feminism, many women's groups in civil society have opted to continue the pragmatic approach of political representation, and these groups are leading the 50/50 campaign to mandate that a full 50 percent of seats in parliament are held by women.

A Brief History of Women in South Africa

The history of women in South Africa can not be separated from the history of colonization, white-minority rule, and apartheid politics that dictated every aspect of people's lives and created vast inequality along racial and gender lines. Apartheid, which formally institutionalized the decades-long practice of racial separation, was legislated into national law in 1948. The pattern of exploitation and enslavement of the indigenous population had started as early as the 1400s, when explorers started to use South Africa as a refueling station on their way from Europe to Asia. Both the people and the resources were seen only as a means of extending the needs of European explorers, missionaries, settlers, and eventually colonists.

As Beth Goldblatt and Sheila Meintjes (1998) argue, both colonialism and apartheid were founded upon and extended existing racial and gender hierarchies. These systems worked in tandem to solidify white male power and diminish what power women did have in society. Jeff Guy (1990) delineates the power, albeit circumscribed, that women had in the precolonial, precapitalist society in Southern Africa. Women were valued not only for their productive labor but also for the reproductive potential they represented. Guy argues, "This control and appropriation of the productive and reproductive capacity of women was central to the structure of southern Africa's precapitalist societies. It was *the* social feature upon which society was based" (1990, 40). Guy similarly reports that although many women suffered varying degrees of exploitation during this period, they maintained some level of power because their labor and fertility were "the bedrock upon which these societies were built" (1990, 47).

Gender difference was clearly a pattern in precolonial South Africa, but the intrinsic value of women was undermined by colonial and apartheid norms that stripped women of their social status and became appendages of the political system. The patterns of racial and gender exploitation can still be seen today in democratic South Africa. Although South Africa is 52 percent female, there are vast inequalities between white and black South African women. For example, the maternal mortality rate is 58 per 100,000 live births for black women and only 3 per 100,000 for white women. Other vital indicators of health and social development also bear the imprint of apartheid inequality. The death rate at birth is 54 per 1,000 for black South African babies and only 7 per 1,000 for white babies (Baden et al. 1999, 18). Black South African men live on average 60 years and women 67 years. Colored men live only 59 years on average, women 65 years. Indian men live 64 years on average, women 70. White men live 69 years on average, women 76 years (Budlender 1998, 32). Educational statistics similarly reveal the vast inequality of apartheid rule. Whereas all white men and women have received some level of formal education, 16 percent of African men and 23 percent of African women have never received any formal education (Budlender 1998, 27).

Violence was a central element of the foundation upon which apartheid rested, and gender violence was central in the apartheid state's control of the population. Rape was used regularly as a tool to maintain social control, to destabilize the black population, and to extend threats against rebellion and protest. Gender violence continues to haunt the new democratic government as a continuing reminder of the patterns of exploitation and power that shaped the apartheid era. South

Africa continues to top the international list in the number of reported incidents of violence against women. South Africa consistently has the highest per capita rate of reported rapes internationally, and these levels are increasing. The South African police force estimates that only 3 percent of all rapes are actually reported (Govender et al. 1994).

Women in South Africa did not passively or silently accept the racial or gender discrimination enforced by apartheid. Throughout the history of the liberation movement, women were involved in all aspects of the antiapartheid struggle, even though the vocal and visible male leadership often overshadowed women's contribution. What is striking about the South African case, however, is that women from all ethnic, religious, and political backgrounds often found themselves in unified opposition to the apartheid system. Although the male leadership tried to use legal challenges to the racial discrimination that eventually became apartheid, women were involved in mass action beginning in the early 1900s. Women unified around their gender identity to oppose the Pass Laws, which strictly governed African women's movement from one area to another (Wells 1993; Kadalie 1995). They often pursued mass action because they were infused with a need to maintain their domestic roles and traditional gender identities, the primary location of their strength and power.

Rather than overtly challenging both the racism of the apartheid government and the sexism within the patriarchal society, women instead developed a strategy of conservative militancy. This approach preserved their subordinate gender status but utilized nontraditional methods of resistance against apartheid, including mass action, labor union activity, and political mobilization. Oftentimes their actions were quite militant and aggressive, and most often they were clearly outside the traditional activity and norms of a subordinate, passive female role. But their activities did not directly challenge gender hierarchies as much as they opposed racial oppression. As Jacklyn Cock indicates, "'Motherhood' was a mobilizing role" (1991, 182). It was an identity through which to challenge apartheid's violence and discrimination. Women of all ethnic groups were involved in this form of conservative militancy, as especially witnessed in the multiracial protests of the Pass Laws in the early 1900s and again in the 1950s, led by the multiracial Federation of South African Women.

Accordingly, women in the resistance became known as the "backbone" of the struggle or the "silent strength" of the movement (Liebenberg 1995; Russell 1989; Walker 1982). They developed key skills that would serve many of them well after the transition to democracy. Collaboration, networking, and mass action were invaluable tools that women mastered during the resistance. Although women acquired essential skills during the struggle and were a vital foundation for the resistance movement, the physical face of leadership was almost exclusively male. Women were the backbone, but the men were the voice of the opposition.

One of the main political parties fighting for liberation was the African National Congress (ANC). The ANC was founded in 1912 on a philosophy of multiracialism that advocated that South Africa should belong to all its peoples, not just the white minority. The ANC and the women's branch of the party, the ANC Women's League, were banned by the apartheid state in 1960. Just as the struggle within South Africa was dependent upon the structures developed by women, women in exile were simultaneously developing their own set of skills, training, and ideas. Again, women were not at the visible forefront of the movement in exile; however, much like their domestic counterparts, they were actively providing the foundation for the exile wing of the struggle. They were receiving military training in Africa and the Soviet Union, pursuing advanced academic degrees in Europe and in Africa, and networking with women at international conferences. From this background South African women in exile learned of the problems faced by women in Angola, Mozambique, and Zimbabwe after liberation. Women in these countries told stories of how their male counterparts had thanked the women for their participation and service and then dismissed them back to traditional female roles. Women's participation in those struggles did not guarantee them a place in formal politics after the transition. In fact, almost the opposite was true. Many leading South African women in exile learned that their only chance of ensuring that they would have a voice in national politics was to unify before the first election, not after.

Because of their training, research, and networking abroad during the antiapartheid struggle, South African women's rights advocates and gender consultants were familiar with numerous international women's agencies and feminist institutional strategies. From this knowledge base, they became singularly focused on ensuring women's place within formal political life after the transition to democracy. The women leaders in exile primarily focused on propelling institutional and legislative changes to foster improvement in the quality of women's lives. The new government was clearly going to benefit the entire nation and work to end the discrimination of apartheid. Women wanted to be certain that it also worked to advance gender equality.

The Path to Political Office

The steps to national political office taken by women in South Africa have now been well documented (Goetz 1998; Ballington 1999a; Britton 2002a). Women returning from exile combined their plan for a national women's organization with the structures and organizations of the women's groups that remained in the country during the struggle. The focus of this national women's organization was to develop a national plan of action and to influence the constitutional negotiations. This national women's organization, called the Women's National Coalition (WNC), was launched in 1991 and unified over one hundred women's groups, including representatives of all the major political parties (WNC 1994; Tripp 2000a). This organization developed the Women's Charter, which was a detailed platform of action for the movement as a whole.

One of the key goals of the Women's Charter was to advance women's equality in the constitution. The WNC was able to maintain its unity within the fractured and politicized South African context because of women's exclusion from the process of negotiation. There were no women in the leadership positions of their respective political parties, and none were present at the negotiating table for the new constitution. Through extensive behind-the-scenes networking, women from opposing political parties worked together to pressure the male leaders to allow women's voices in the negotiations and to guarantee women's political equality in the constitution (Steyn 1998; Britton 2002a). Women used the strength of the WNC unity to press for a growing attention to women's needs and issues. They forced their individual parties to turn rhetorical promises for women's equality into practical reality. Their actions created the Gender Advisory Committee (GAC) for the Convention for a Democratic South Africa (CODESA), the body negotiating the transition from white-minority rule to multiracial democracy. Women then became concerned that gender issues would be relegated to the GAC alone rather than being a significant element of the negotiations. Therefore, women advocated the addition of one member to each party in the negotiating council under the condition that the member was a woman from the party. This proposal has been seen as the first major victory for women in South Africa (Britton 2002a; Ballington 1999c).

In part because of these efforts, the South African constitution has one of the broadest and most inclusive equality clauses internationally. A brief statement of rights indicates that "the state may not unfairly discriminate directly or indirectly against anyone on one or more grounds, including race, gender, sex, pregnancy, marital status, ethnic or social origin, colour, sexual orientation, age, disability, religion, conscience, belief, culture, language and birth" (Chapter 2, The Constitution of the Republic of South Africa, Act 108 of 1996). Although additional rights and protections are delineated in the thirty-two sections that follow, this brief statement is clearly a response to South Africa's legacy of discrimination, which made the rights of the majority invisible. Further, South Africa "became the first [nation] in the world expressly to prohibit discrimination on the basis of sexual orientation" (Croucher 2002, 315). Although many argue that it may take decades for South African society to "catch up to" the constitutional protection, gender activists and practitioners celebrated the fundamental enshrinement of gender equality in the constitution. Its inclusion creates a solid legal foundation for future legislation and court action to extend women's rights in practice. The women I interviewed linked the success of women gaining entrance to the negotiating table to their successful cross-party coalition building within the WNC.

Securing a seat at the negotiating table was only the first step in the strategy of women leaders. Their next step was to create a system that would assist women's representation in political office. In addition to drafting the constitution, the negotiations focused specifically on creating a new political and electoral system, and women at the table were equally concerned that such a system be conducive to electing women into office. Drawing upon their international networks, the constitutional consultants—especially those with an interest in gender equality—researched political systems internationally to determine which electoral system would be most beneficial in fostering ethnic unity in South Africa, in minimizing the ideological cleavages that historically had led to violence, and in facilitating the election of members of socially subordinate groups to office. South Africa adopted the multimember district electoral system with party-list proportional representation (PR). This is the same system that, not coincidentally, is found to be most likely to enhance women's representation internationally (Castles 1981; Duverger 1955; Lakeman 1970; Lovenduski and Norris 1993; Matland 1993; Rule 1987). This system is most beneficial for women because parties are more likely to create a list of candidates that reflects the actual population in both ideological and demographic makeup. They do this in order to attract broad-based support from the electorate. In single-member district systems, parties are less likely to risk their only seat on a woman candidate.

Gender considerations were in no way the only, or arguably the most important, reason for adopting the multimember district system with party-list PR system. The predominant force propelling this system was the fact that it would guarantee a political voice for minority parties, thereby lessening the chance for political fragmentation and violence in postapartheid South Africa (Reynolds 1995). PR gives a voice to small and powerful minority parties, bringing them into the context of a unified elected body rather than marginalizing them without a voice in government. This system fosters party-list heterogeneity in ethnicity and ideology as well as gender.

Once this system was in place, women had the standing they needed to press for additional, concrete measures to secure national office. Again, using the growing strength of the WNC, women were able to pressure the male leadership within their respective parties to advance women in their party lists. Most parties were able to increase women's place on party lists through some sort of affirmative action measure, including the active recruitment of women candidates into the party. However, the most visible and effective action was taken by the ANC, which instituted a 30 percent quota for women candidates. This quota was in many ways a goal for which ANC women had been fighting for years. Long before the end of apartheid was in sight, ANC women had pushed party leaders to enshrine women's equality in the party's message of human rights and equal rights. By the time the negotiations for the 1994 election were a reality, ANC women could refer back to several years of party promises for gender equality.

Because of their international networks and the advice from gender activists globally, women leaders in all of the parties were familiar with the importance of using quotas to overcome gender imbalances. The effectiveness of quotas has been extensively documented (Caul 2001; Rule and Zimmerman 1994; Jones 1996, 1998; Steininger 2000; Phillips 1991) and is much faster than other methods of attempting to bring about societal change (Norris 1996; Jones 1998). Because of this coalition and its strategies, women in South Africa gained over 26 percent of the seats in the National Assembly in the first democratic election in 1994. This significant number was due in large part to the quota put in place by the ANC leadership (Ballington 1999b; Britton 2002a.) For both the 1999 and the 2004 National Assembly elections, the ANC moved to a system of having every third position on the list occupied by a woman, ensuring the election of women regardless of the party's popularity. This is also one step closer to the zebra-list system, in which a woman holds every other seat on the party list.

The ANC was the only party to implement a gender quota in 1994 and in 1999, yet most parties worked to encourage female representation in some form (see Tables 3.1 and 3.2). Of the parties reporting their national lists, five increased the percentage of women on their national lists. The African Christian Democratic Party increased the percentage from 13 to 29, the African National Congress from 32 to 39, the Freedom Front from 12 to 16, the Inkatha Freedom Party from 10 to 22, and the Pan-Africanist Congress (PAC) from 12 to 22. Although the two prominent majority-white parties, the New National Party and the Democratic Party (DP, now Democratic Alliance), did not create national lists for the 1999 elections, the DP increased the actual percentage of women MPs from 14 to 16. The actual percentage of women MPs from the New National Party decreased slightly from 1994 to 1999, perhaps reflecting its loss of overall seats more than any intentional decision to have fewer women in office. The composition of the New National Party's regional lists reveals that in fact there was an increase of women, from 11.4 percent in 1994 to 18.4 percent in 1999. These numbers conditionally support Richard Matland and Donley Studlar's (1996) theory of party contagion, which postulates that women's representation levels increase more rapidly within multimember PR systems because parties within such systems respond more quickly to the pressure of a rival party's nomination of women. One caveat is that the proliferation of minor parties in the 1999 elections—parties that took a smaller number

Table 3.1   1994 Elections

Party	Women National List (%)	Women Regional Lists (%)	Number of MPs	Number of Women MPs	Women as Proportion of MPs (%)
African Christian Democratic Party	12.9	9.6	2	0	0
African National Congress	32.2	32.6	252	90	35.7
Democratic Party	31	19	7	1	14
Freedom Front	12	7.8	9	0	0
Inkatha Freedom Party	10.4	15.9	43	10	23.3
National Party	N/A	11.4	82	9	11
Pan-Africanist Congress	11.8	12	5	1	20
Total			400	111	27

Source: Ballington 1999b.

Table 3.2   1999 Elections

Party	Women National List (%)	Women Regional Lists (%)	Number of MPs	Number of Women MPs	Women as Proportion of MPs (%)
African Christian Democratic Party	29.0	24.0	6	2	33.3
African National Congress	39.0	34.0	266	96	36.0
Afrikaner Eenheids Beweging	14.5	18.5	1	0	0
Azanian People's Organization	18.0	15.6	1	0	0
Democratic Party	N/A	21.0	38	7	15.8
Federal Alliance	13.0	13.6	2	0	0
Freedom Front	16.0	17.7	3	0	0
Inkatha Freedom Party	22.0	28.6	34	7	20.6
Minority Front[a]	14.0	1.6	1	1	1
New National Party	N/A	18.4	28	3	10.7
Pan-Africanist Congress	22.0	19.0	3	1	33.3
United Christian Democratic Party	26.0	24.7	3	0	0
United Democratic Movement	23.0	19.0	14	2	14.3
Total			400	119	29.8

Source: Ballington 1999c.
Note: a. The Minority Front chose after the election to put Sally Rajbelly into its only winning seat in parliament.

of seats and filled them with men—contributed to an overall decline in the number of women in opposition parties if taken as a whole. However, the impact of contagion may be seen in several parties, especially those that held their ground or increased their seats in parliament.

The 2004 elections also showed an interesting trend. Although almost every party increased the number of women on its preelection party list, women in opposition parties were typically placed in "unwinnable" positions. The ANC continued to increase the number of women on its list, bringing it to 35.4 percent of the seats. Since the ANC swept the elections with almost 70 percent of the vote, the number of women in parliament increased to 32.8 percent in the National Assembly. In 1999 there were 119 women in the National Assembly; this increased to 131 in 2004, with 107 of those women coming from the ANC. Additionally, President Thabo Mbeki of the ANC has won praise for his appointments of women to cabinet positions, which, according to Amanda Gouws, is "approaching the 50 percent mark with 41.2 percent ministers and deputy-ministers and premiers at almost 45 percent."[3]

According to Table 3.3, of those parties reporting figures, the number of women on preelection party lists increased from 1999 to 2004. However, the gains by the ANC meant losses for the opposition parties. Since women are often at the bottom of preelection party lists for the opposition parties, those parties' number of women in office is often not as high as the female candidates' overall percentage on the party list. The Democratic Alliance has 10 women out of 50 seats, the Inkatha Freedom Party has 6 women in its 28 seats, the United Democratic Movement has 3 women out of 9, the Independent Democrats have 2 out of 7, the New National Party has 1 out of 7, the African Christian Democratic Party has 1 woman out of 6, the United Christian Democratic party has 1 woman out of 3, and the Minority Front has 1 out of 2. The Freedom Front, the Azanian People's Organization (AZAPO), and the PAC have no women in office.[4] So, while party contagion continues to impact preelection party lists and is therefore useful for opposition parties in justifying gender representation, the impact of contagion is not as apparent in the actual numbers of seats held by women after the election.

Table 3.3   Women on Party Lists for 1999 and 2004 Elections

Party	Women on Lists, 1999 (%)	Women on Lists, 2004 (%)
African Christian Democratic Party	N/S	31.8
African National Congress	35	35.4
Azanian People's Organisation	N/S	37.0
Democratic Party/Democratic Alliance	20	31.59
Independent Democrats	N/A	30.33
Inkatha Freedom Party	22	31.82
National Party/New National Party	12–15	25.21
Pan-Africanist Congress	N/S	33.64
United Democratic Front/UD Movement	N/S	24.94
Freedom Front Plus	16	23.39

Source: Women's Net through Genderlinks: http://www.genderlinks.org.za/article.php?a_id=290.
Note: N/S = not specified; N/A = not applicable.

Impact of Women in Office

Once in office, women in South Africa began to implement their vision of feminism that utilized the state as a means of securing long-term benefits for women. Drawing from the lessons learned during exile from women in other nations (Seidman 1999, 295–296), the South African women's agenda became focused on mainstreaming gender issues throughout all levels and branches of government. Having observed the problems associated with grouping women's issues into a· single women's ministry or department within the executive branch or a gender committee within the legislative branch, South African women focused their attention on creating a national machinery for gender equality that encompassed all levels and spheres of government. This plan came through the combined vision of women MPs, gender consultants, and grassroots activists.

First, the original speaker and deputy speaker in the democratically elected parliament spearheaded the campaign to make parliament more "women-friendly" and thus also more "parent-friendly." Then Speaker Frene Ginwala and Deputy Speaker Baleka Mbete worked together to make key cultural changes to the environment of parliament that honor and accommodate the domestic obligations of members of parliament. During the first five years of democracy, the parliamentary calendar was reorganized to match the school calendar. Thus, when students are on holiday, members of parliament are either in recess or have constituency time. Debates ended much earlier in the evening, recognizing the need of many members to be at home to take care of familial responsibilities. A day-care center was provided for the young children of members and staff. These are a few examples of how key leaders in parliament are working to widen the space for women and parents so that they may balance their professional and personal responsibilities.

Second, women in parliament have secured significant legislative advancements for women. Although the primary leadership has come from the women of the ANC, most legislation has involved women from multiple parties. Examples of legislation with a gender focus include the 1996 Choice on the Termination of Pregnancy Act, which extends abortion rights to all women on demand. The 1996 Films and Publications Act is invested with protections against the degradation of women and children. The 1996 Commission for Gender Equality Act created the national oversight commission focused on gender equality and the status of women, discussed below. The 1998 Domestic Violence Act increased the legal and institutional protection for victims of domestic abuse. Women parliamentarians have also had vital input into the Maintenance Act, the Employment Equity Act, the Skills Development Act, and the Labour Relations Act.[5]

Third, the leaders of the women's movement and the women in parliament implemented a framework of structures to mainstream gender consciousness throughout the South African government. This decision was based on the advice of gender consultants and international experts, as I noted earlier. Rather than implementing a women's ministry or a department of women's affairs, South Africa adopted the National Machinery for Advancing Gender Equality (NGM) in South Africa (see Figure 3.1). Parliamentarians learned that the model of a single women's ministry led to the marginalization and ghettoization of gender issues into one institution. Consequently, the plan in South Africa was to create institutions within parliament, the government, and civil society that fostered women's issues and gendered consciousness.

There are three main areas within the NGM: parliament, executive, and civil society. Once women were located in parliament in critical numbers, they needed committees and groups within the legislative branch to facilitate their work. Although these committees and groups have gone through several iterations, there has always been a focus on providing a vehicle for cross-party collaboration on women's issues.

One such parliamentary organization that started soon after the first democratic elections in 1994 was the Parliamentary Women's Group (PWG). The PWG had the laudable yet unattainable goal of bringing the women's movement into the halls of parliament. Gender activists and women MPs wanted to preserve the cross-party collaboration that helped propel women into office. The PWG was also tasked with addressing issues facing women MPs in order to overcome any gender-specific obstacles to their full participation as national legislators.[6] Due to the constricting nature of parliamentary politics, the ability of the PWG to focus on political issues and to build coalitions was thwarted. Women MPs were first and foremost members of their own political parties. Their very existence in parliament was due to the parties that put them on the party lists, brought them into office, and kept them as sitting members. If women consistently worked against their party ideologies, their seats would be jeopardized. Cross-party collaboration of women was possible in civil society, but such unity was severely constrained within parliament. Despite its auspicious beginnings in the 1994 parliament, the organization has for all intents and purposes ceased to exist. Yet women had found another avenue to facilitate gender-sensitive legislation within parliament. During my research trip in May–July 2003, when I asked

Figure 3.1 National Machinery for Advancing Gender Equality in South Africa

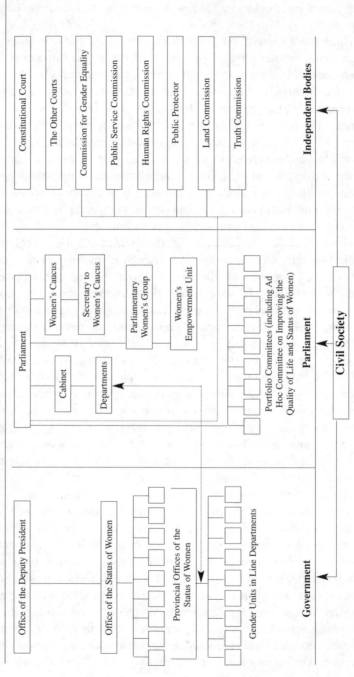

A model developed by Cathy Albertyn, Centre for Applied Legal Studies, and adapted by Santha Naiker, Human Sciences Research Council of South Africa. As cited in Baden et al. 1999.

about cross-party collaboration, women MPs instead discussed the activities of the Joint Monitoring Committee on the Improvement of the Quality of Life and Status of Women (JMC).

Although it functions now as a multiparty body, the JMC is the result of ANC leadership. Specifically, Speaker Frene Ginwala's office initiated the JMC in 1996 to monitor the government's implementation of the United Nations Convention on the Elimination of Discrimination Against Women (CEDAW). There was a clear recognition by 1996–1997 that the PWG would be captured by the divisive nature of party politics and that a new vehicle for legislation had to be created. The JMC was, therefore, given the specific mandate of monitoring legislation for gender sensitivity. Originally the JMC was an ad hoc committee that was given very few resources and was accorded a low status among opposition parties. However, one of the first missions of ANC leader Pregs Govender was to move it to the status of a permanent committee. Govender brought to the committee her reputation as a national gender and labor leader and her already notable success as a leader in legislative affairs. The JMC rapidly became a focal point for gender issues and, some would say, an unrelenting challenge to the vestiges of male power within parliament, parties, and society. Govender and the committee set a broad yet clear legislative agenda and had significant input into legislation affecting labor laws, sexual harassment, poverty, domestic violence, parental rights, maintenance, and most dramatically HIV/AIDS. By Govender's own estimation, 80 percent of the legislative priorities she and the committee set were enacted.[7]

Govender left office in 2002 to return to civil society and leave the confining environment of parliamentary politics.[8] The JMC has new leadership that promises to carry forward its past success, but there is no question that losing a power broker like Govender on the committee and in parliament is a significant blow to the long-term success of women in office. It is also a provocative statement that a leader in the ANC itself found that parliamentary politics often ties the hands of women. With the shift from the informal Parliamentary Women's Group to the institutionalized Joint Monitoring Committee, women leaders in parliament and in the ANC recognized the limitation of cross-party collaboration. The JMC became an avenue through which women from multiple parties could monitor legislation and make significant contributions to legislation while it was in the process of being drafted. Yet it clearly reflected ANC goals. For such a widely recognized and celebrated woman leader as Govender to recognize that the challenges by her committee have been met with inaction from her own party calls into question whether the JMC can maintain its position as a site of cross-party collaboration.

The second main area of the NGM focuses on the executive branch of government. Within that branch, the Office on the Status of Women (OSW) strategically falls under the Office of the Deputy President. The OSW is an oversight and visionary body that works to monitor government spending and implementation in regard to gender issues. The OSW also coordinates the activities of the provincial OSW branches as well as working with the cabinet in parliament to monitor and assist the Gender Units in each of the government departments. These units were envisioned as a way of diffusing gender consciousness throughout the entire government. The placement of the Gender Units in the line departments recognizes that the most direct contact of citizens with the government is through service delivery. Ten years into the new democracy in South Africa, these Gender Units are still fairly uneven in their power, funding, and effectiveness. The OSW has undertaken a process to evaluate the ideal placement for Gender Units within departments and to advise each department on the function of these units.

The OSW has a gargantuan task, given its lack of human resources and staff, and therefore it has come under scrutiny for its effectiveness— for example, it has no powers of enforcement. Regardless of these challenges, the OSW is growing in importance as a coordinator for the NGM. The OSW is working to convene meetings of representatives of the NGM at least six times a year, drawing together MPs; representatives of NGOs, community-based organizations (CBOs), Gender Units, and provinces; and activists. These meetings focus on increasing communication and developing a national direction for women's issues.

The third area of the NGM is civil society. The visionary charge by the women who created the NGM was to ensure that there were institutions in civil society that would work to draw closer connections between civil society and government. Two main bodies have been created and have successfully started to fill that gap: the Women's Budget Initiative (WBI) and the Commission for Gender Equality (CGE).

Drawing upon a similar institution in Australia, the Women's Budget Initiative monitors government spending with a uniquely gendered lens.[9] Recognizing that money equals results, the WBI formally recognizes that legislation and implementation are only as good as the money behind them. It is not a separate budget for women's issues but a process of budget analysis. The WBI currently does not have a function for measuring the impact of spending and is limited only to tracking the spending itself. It was started by the Institute for Democracy in

South Africa, the JMC in parliament, and the Department of Finance in the executive branch. It is hoped that through its links to groups and NGOs in civil society the WBI's findings and assessments will be more legitimate and less partisan than if it were simply a part of parliament.[10]

A second civil society component is the Commission for Gender Equality, enacted in 1996. The CGE is charged with monitoring institutions in both government and civil society to ensure that they comply with the constitutional mandate of gender equality. With both national and provincial branches, the CGE is attempting to retain a national voice for gender issues as well as reflect the regional variation in the needs of women and men. The CGE is a highly visible body involved in monitoring national progress toward CEDAW, evaluating government policy and parliamentary legislation, fostering a land restitution project targeting rural women, and initiating national education campaigns on gender equity and women's rights.[11] Most recently the CGE has also been one of the key agents in the 50/50 campaign pushing for increased representation of women in office.[12] Much like the OSW and the JMC, the CGE had to spend much of its initial time and energy on fighting for equitable status and funding. At its inception it received less government support and financial resources than many other national commissions, such as the Youth Commission and the Truth and Reconciliation Commission.[13] These financial deficits translated into deficits in staffing and human resources. It was only after intense public pressure that the CGE received equitable funding and could focus fully on its original agenda.

Through all three of these areas—parliament, executive, and civil society—the National Gender Machinery was envisioned to foster widespread action and awareness of gender issues. The women parliamentarians and gender activists who created this vision wanted to avoid marginalization of women's issues into one branch of government, as had been the case in so many other postliberation contexts (Mabandla 1994). This goal has become a reality in South Africa because gender issues are found throughout the areas of policymaking, in government offices, and even in civil society. However, this diffusion has also meant that the gender movement may be spread through too many places and issues at once, thus diluting its effectiveness and overextending its supporters.

As I met with members of the NGM in 2003, I spent time evaluating what each branch felt it was intended to do. Clearly the members in parliament recognized that their main role was legislation; similarly, the members in the executive branch identified their main goal as implementation. However, members of the JMC, the OSW, and the CGE all felt that they were responsible for monitoring governmental compliance with the goal of gender equality. The actual business of implementation, the key to making sure the machinery has a product and not just a process, is left to the Gender Units in the government departments. To date, these units are the most uneven and underdeveloped part of the machinery. Clearly a key goal of the second ten years of democracy must be to focus on implementation.

One key area blocking the full realization of gender equity has been the remaining vestiges of a resistant civil service, retained from the apartheid civil service, and the sometimes invisible gendered obstacles that have blocked women's full participation in office. The masculinity of the state and its institutions was not replaced through democratic elections. In fact, many of the same masculinist norms and values were quickly replicated within the new 1994 government. These masculinist norms continue to present challenges for women in office.

Challenges Facing Women in Office

Despite significant legislative accomplishments, women elected to office in South Africa have faced several forms of institutional sexism that have hindered their full participation. First, women in parliament have had to face a "gendered workload." In addition to their assigned committee work and chosen legislative agendas, they are often called into debates that deal with gender issues such as abortion, surrogacy, health, and welfare. In this way women MPs are carrying more than the normal committee load and often juggle additional responsibilities. Second, women have faced resistance from their male counterparts that has taken several forms, from overt sexual harassment to marginalization in the party. Third, women often face exclusion from informal political spaces where important deals are struck and personal bonds are formed. For example, the all-male rugby team was not intended to be a place of political networking, but cross-party conversations and friendships are fostered in such spaces. These bonds may be used later to secure collaboration on formal political goals. Fourth, the most significant obstacle faced by women in the South African parliament is the double workday. Women in parliament are expected to run the country and still maintain their households rather than diminishing their domestic obligations as their professional expectations increase. Although most male members of parliament have the support of a wife, mother, or daughter at home, women MPs often are the wife, mother, or daughter in their own family system. Women MPs often expressed to me their frustration with the pressure placed on them by the members of their families. Indeed, family members often are more concerned with women MPs' diminished attention to the family than with their accomplishments and challenges in office (Britton 2002b).

In part because of these gendered obstacles, women in the South African parliament have faced a rotating door as many self-select themselves out of office. Over one-half of the women that I interviewed in 1996–1997 told me they were planning to leave parliament before or during the next election cycle in 1999. Over one-half of the women I interviewed in the 1994 cohort have in fact left office, returning to a life as grassroots activists or pursuing other professions. The women most likely to leave had a specific profile: They were most often black women from previously disadvantaged socioeconomic backgrounds. Most had little formal education or political training, although they possessed a wealth of local knowledge and community experience that would have been invaluable to the policy process. This applied knowledge, however, did not readily translate into the norms and expectations of the day-to-day operations of an MP or delegate. Initiating, drafting, and debating legislation are processes that require a different set of professional skills than those held by many of the women in the 1994 cohort. The irony, of course, is that most of the legislation in the 1994–1999 parliament focused on areas that ought to be informed by local knowledge and community experience, yet these voices were the most silent.

Despite the number of women I interviewed who have left parliament, the overall number of women in office actually increased with the 1999 election to 29.8 percent. This second generation of MPs was markedly different from the first in several ways. Most specifically, the women of the 1999 cohort are marked by a general trend of professionalism in their political, educational, and occupational experience. Women who remained in parliament were those already familiar with the policy process, those with substantive education in a related field, those who could rapidly assimilate into the procedures and norms of Westminster-style politics, or those from professional backgrounds and careers. Similarly, those who are now being recruited into parliament are often from professional or educational backgrounds that translate more naturally to the cerebral life of a national legislator than the hands-on life of a grassroots activist.

Given the challenges faced by women in the national parliament, one may ask why the numbers have actually increased. The answer is twofold. First, because of the highly celebrated gender quota for the

ANC party lists, other parties have been pressured to increase the numbers of women on their own party lists. In line with Matland and Studlar's (1996) theory of party contagion in PR systems, parties are more likely to increase the number of women on their party lists to attract a broader segment of the vote and to defuse criticisms that their party has no women of merit. Unlike single-member district systems, voters in a PR system are voting for a party platform rather than individual candidates. It is easy for voters to see from the party lists which parties are supporting women candidates and which are merely paying lip service to gender equality. Although no other major South African parties have implemented an official quota for women's representation, almost all have attempted to increase the number of women on their party lists. They have utilized other methods of affirmative action, recruiting women in business or education, or grooming women from provincial and local governments to run for national office.

In one sense the increase of women with political backgrounds is part of the natural progress of social development within a newly freed society. There is a much broader pool of women experienced in policymaking and implementation at the lower levels of government. Prior to 1994 women from all backgrounds were discouraged from participating in formal political life, and the majority of South Africans—the black population—were actually barred from participating. Since 1994 women and men from all backgrounds have taken seats at all levels of elected office. The broader pool of potential candidates has assisted party leaders in promoting from within the realm of elected office.

Several key trends are now evident within the 1999 cohort of women in office. Each trend indicates how the institution of parliament is rapidly becoming professionalized. Because of this professionalization, the women now being recruited or self-selecting into office are better prepared for the demands of the job than the 1994 cohort. In that way, women in parliament are now prepared to survive their jobs as MPs. A remaining question is whether they will be allowed to thrive in their jobs.

First, as I stated before, a majority of the women MPs whom I interviewed in 2003 indicated that they had held prior political office at a local or provincial level. These women were much better prepared for the time commitment and professional responsibilities of elected office. Unlike the 1994 cohort, the women in 1999 had made the transition from being activists at a lower level of elected office in 1994—years before they reached national office in 1999. Many women MPs in 1994 had moved from the liberation struggle into the halls of parliament.

Thus, they experienced a greater culture shock than that experienced by women coming from a background of provincial and local office, who often remained within their social networks and home districts. Since the demise of apartheid, even women from previously disadvantaged groups are now able to advance through traditional political ranks, cutting their political teeth at a lower level of government. These women have learned the tools and goals of legislation before reaching national office. What is noticeably different is the lack of revolutionary fervor shown by the 1999 cohort. This revolutionary drive has been replaced with a push toward legislative prowess.

Second, the majority of the women whom I interviewed in 2003 came from advanced educational or occupational backgrounds. Unlike the 1994 cohort, which represented an impressive breadth of backgrounds (Britton 2001), the women who remained in office and joined in 1999 are primarily women who have completed Grade 12 or advanced degrees. Several women hold Ph.D.s or are physicians or lawyers. Similarly, every woman I interviewed was proficient in written and spoken English. Although parliament is able to support each of the eleven official languages, there is a growing preference for English, and most committee work and debates occur in English. The women I interviewed similarly were from nontraditional career fields for women, such as business, journalism, academics, research, or the law. Many fewer women came from traditional career backgrounds as nurses, teachers, domestic employees, or farmers.

Third, the way women in the 1999 cohort approached their jobs was markedly different from the approach of the 1994 cohort. The favorite aspect of the job for women in the 1999 cohort was the debates. Strikingly, this was the most problematic aspect of the job for women in 1994, as most felt threatened and humiliated by the fast-paced jeering in the chambers. The goals and issues raised by the second generation were also different. Many women elected in 1994 spent as much time on community work and grassroots projects as they did on legislation. When I asked the 1999 cohort what their main goals and issues were, almost all responded that they were focused on drafting specific legislation. Only a small number mentioned any other projects or initiatives for which they were responsible. The few women with community-based work experience were women in the ANC, Inkatha Freedom Party, and Democratic Alliance who had direct connections to specific projects. To some degree, this change is indicative also of the professionalization of parliament in terms of role clarification. The primary focus of parliamentarians is legislation. The primary focus of employees and appointees within government departments is implementation. The women in 1994 who were most focused on community development projects and hands-on development have moved back into the nongovernmental sector. Women who focus on legislation have replaced them. What is similar about the two generations is that they are all interested in broad topics, ranging from HIV/AIDS to housing, education, health care, unemployment, child abuse, violence against women, and the environment. Yet, the way the cohorts approach these issues is different: The first generation had more women interested in implementation, and the second is almost exclusively composed of legislators.

Finally, I found a vast difference in the needs and obstacles faced by the two generations. Women of the 1994 cohort were faced with significant gendered obstacles that blocked their participation in office. The women in the 1999 cohort had two clear needs: better access to information, and more funds for constituency-based projects. Their problems were not with the demands of the job or the attitudes of their male counterparts. In fact, only one woman spoke on the record about male resistance. Instead, the key call from women in the 1999 generation was better access to the resources they need to excel in their positions. These resources were, first, well-trained researchers who can assist in the creation of policy and, second, financial support for the projects of their constituents.[14] Women MPs recognize that they need resources to support their constituents' ideas and projects. As with legislators the world over, supplying requested funds is how they can establish themselves politically with their constituents. In fact, information resources and funding support are two key ingredients for all elected officials. Here again we see the trend toward a professionalized parliament.

Future Directions: Developing Pragmatic Feminism

What are the long-term implications of this study for women in South African politics, and what general lessons may be useful for other contexts? First, the South African case demonstrates that cross-party collaboration is most successful when the goals are focused and issue-based. Women were able to gain significant representation in the first election because of strategic alliances among women leaders focused on the specific goal of electoral success. This level of female representation has afforded South Africa international praise and recognition, and the nature of the proportional representation system has pressured other parties to increase the numbers of women on their lists as well.

The gains made in 1994 were extended in 1999 and promise to continue in the future.

Second, women in South Africa have chosen to implement their own feminism by creating and using state institutions for feminist change. Rather than relying solely upon continued grassroots activism and social movement methodology, South Africa was in a privileged position to use the state to gain progressive legislative and societal change. This is an ironic twist of fate since the apartheid regime had used the state for ethnic and gender repression. What the South African case indicates is that state feminism may work faster in postliberation contexts. Whereas state feminism in nonrevolutionary contexts must be folded into "normal" politics, this may not be the case in newly emerging states. Strategic mobilization allowed women in postapartheid South Africa to envision and implement an intricate and powerful system of institutions that ought to ensure lasting change. Had they not acted quickly or had the entire framework of government not been up for grabs, their level of influence and progress might have been minimal.

Third, South Africa has opted for the decentralized model of state feminism, with very uneven results. The diffusion of institutions has also meant a diffusion of financial resources and human capacity, which has limited the short-term viability of most of the state organs. However, South Africa is just ten years into democracy, and these institutions are still quite new. The leaders in these bodies are gaining a better sense of their role and their relationship with other institutions in the NGM. The long-term impact of the NGM remains in question, but several key lessons have been learned. Contrary to the cases described by most of the literature in the field, the South African case indicates that legislative bodies can also be highly effective tools of state feminism. The JMC has been one of the most visible and consistently effective tools for actualizing gender issues. With the recent departure of the power broker Pregs Govender, questions remain about whether it is the institution or the person that made such change possible. Yet all the women in my study indicated a commitment to the committee and to continued attempts at strategic cross-party collaboration.

What was most striking during my 2003 research was that despite the limitations of state feminism and the professionalization of women parliamentarians, there is still strong support within civil society for increasing the number of women in parliament and bolstering support for the institutions of formal politics. There is no doubt that there is a solid portion of women's groups and gender activists that feels that women in parliament have "sold out" or have become too distant from the grassroots. Yet the primary impetus for increasing the representation of women in office has come from organizations within civil society—not from the women in parliament. The 50/50 campaign is a joint initiative of several NGOs: Institute for Democracy in South Africa, the Gender Analysis Project, Gender Links, and Women's Net. These NGOs have linked with the Commission for Gender Equality and the international 50/50 campaign to mobilize support within parliament and within civil society to mandate a 50 percent quota for women. Several women within parliament quickly joined the call for "50/50 by 2004," but the initial push came from outside parliament. This indicates a continued belief in the effectiveness and importance of having women in parliament.

How likely is the 50/50 campaign to succeed? There is no question now that 50/50 by 2004 was unsuccessful, as the ANC retained its commitment to a 30 percent quota and its practice of listing women candidates in every third slot on the party list. However, the groundwork may be set for the next election. Members of the 50/50 campaign that I interviewed outlined two different strategies. One is pursuing the legislative quota enforced by the government, as has been the pattern in a few Latin American countries. According to my interviews, the possibility of the ANC implementing such a quota seems highly unlikely, given the continued preponderance of male leadership throughout the party. Additionally, there is a great deal of quiet antagonism to the ANC's voluntary quota of 30 percent on its list. A jump from 30 percent to 50 percent at this stage would be dramatic.

An ANC mandate may not be likely, but it is in fact possible given the current position of the party. During the floor crossing in 2003, when several MPs from opposition parties defected to the ANC, the ANC gained a two-thirds majority in parliament. This two-thirds majority guarantees that the party can, in effect, change the constitution unilaterally. The ANC could therefore mandate a 50/50 legislative quota, fulfilling its rhetorical commitment to women's equality. But the ANC leaders have indicated that they will not utilize their current right of unilateral constitutional revision for any issue, so this strategy is not likely.

The second option is to mobilize wider support within civil society for "women voting for women." In this way, women's voting power will influence parties' agendas and the representation of women. This is a much longer-term strategy that was obviously not achieved before the 2004 elections. But the campaign itself has again raised the issue of women's representation in the South African parliament. More importantly, the 50/50 campaign indicates that at least one portion of the women's movement in South Africa is focused on pragmatic approaches to improving the quality of life and status of women. There may be significant obstacles faced by the women in parliament, but the legislative and institutional changes they have accomplished in just the first ten years are remarkable. Clearly, increasing the number of women in parliament is only one piece of a comprehensive societal change, yet it has been and continues to be a viable option for South Africa.

Notes

1. The South African Parliament is bicameral. The National Assembly is the lower house, and the National Council of Provinces (NCOP), which was originally known as the Senate, is the upper house. The National Assembly's four hundred seats are chosen every five years through direct election. Election statistics in this chapter refer to the National Assembly unless otherwise noted. The NCOP is composed of nine provincial delegations of ten people each. In each delegation, four delegates come from the provincial legislature, including the premier or someone appointed by the premier to lead the delegation, and six permanent delegates are chosen by the parties following the general elections and based on a party list. Political parties are represented in the delegation based on their proportion in the province. The goal in the reconstitution of the NCOP from the Senate was to institutionalize a direct, regular, and equal representation of each province and to ensure a clear voice for provincial politics, issues, and needs. Interviews were conducted with both MPs and delegates.

2. The paper draws upon five research trips and three qualitative research methods: semistructured intensive interviews, participant observation, and archival research. Over the course of the five research periods, I have interviewed sixty women members of parliament—in both the National Assembly and the National Council of Provinces—and conducted an additional 140 interviews with women in civil society organizations, NGOs, CBOs, government departments, the Commission for Gender Equality, and the Office on the Status of Women. This paper focuses primarily on the interviews with women MPs and delegates from both the 1994 cohort and the 1999 cohort as well as members of civil society organizations working on the 50/50 campaign, although the additional interviews provide background information for the discussions of the coalition strategies. Pursuant to the regulations of the Institutional Review Boards of Syracuse University and Mississippi State University, all interviews were conducted in English and all nonelected participants were given pseudonyms to protect their confidentiality.

3. Amanda Gouws, "After Casting Our Vote: A Look at Who's in Power and Accountable," *Womensnet*, May 18, 2004. http://womensnet.org.za/Elections2004/index.shtml.

4. Ibid.

5. The primary agent of change for gendered legislation has come through the Joint Committee on Improving the Quality of Life and Status of Women, discussed later.

6. One of the first bodies created to support the work of women MPs was the Women's Empowerment Unit. This unit was focused on capacity building and skills training for new women MPs. There was widespread, international recognition that most of the new women MPs came straight from the struggle and had not had the opportunities of formal education or traditional political experience that most national legislators have before coming into national office. The unit worked to develop an understanding of the legislative process and the professional norms and expectations of national office. Yet these standards and norms were often defined by international consultants and advisers and thus reflected international definitions of professionalism. The funding of the unit was from international sources, and it is now less visible, reflecting the fact that many current women MPs have had prior political experience in office or the fact that international funding sources are often temporary.

7. Pregs Govender, "Gender Budgeting Was Removed, Not Committee's Funding," *Mail and Guardian,* August 17, 2001, 1–2. http://archive.mg.co.za/.

8. Many members of the JMC indicated to me in May–July 2003 that Govender left parliament soon after the release of the HIV/AIDS report from the JMC. This report was a significant challenge to the government's, and thus the ANC's, inaction on HIV/AIDS. Official accounts differ; see, for example, "Two Top Women Quit Parliament," *Mail and Guardian,* May 31, 2002. http://archive.mg.co.za/.

9. Several women MPs mentioned this fact-finding mission to Australia, where they encountered the Women's Budget.

10. Colleen Lowe Morna, "Gender Budget on the Rocks?" *Mail and Guardian*, August 4, 2000, 1–2. http://archive.mg.co.za/.

11. See the Commission for Gender Equality's home page: http://www.cge.org.za/.

12. Eddie Jayiya, "Commission Calls for More Women in Government," *Star*, October 21, 1999, 1–2. http://www.iol.co.za.

13. Ferial Haffajee, "Women's Day: Big Hopes, Little Funding," *Mail and Guardian*, August 8, 1997, 1–2. http://archive.mg.co.za/.

14. The call for financial resources came almost exclusively from women in opposition parties, who have much less access to government funds than ANC MPs.

4

Namibia: Losing Ground Without Mandatory Quotas

Gretchen Bauer

When Namibia's fourth National Assembly took office in early 2005, 25 percent of voting members were women. This is slightly down from late 2004, when 29 percent of voting members of the third National Assembly were women. Nonetheless, this is a considerable accomplishment for an African country that only attained independence in 1990. Moreover, 5 out of 27 ministers were women and 4 out of 20 deputy ministers were women, as were the deputy prime minister, the deputy speaker of the National Assembly, and the deputy chairperson of the National Council.[1] At the local level, women were even better represented. Forty-three percent of local councilors elected in 2004 were women, as were the mayors and deputy mayors of many towns and villages in the country. But even these numbers were not good enough for a highly mobilized contingent of Namibian women activists. Since 1999 Namibian women (and men) have joined forces in a campaign to demand that women occupy at least 50 percent of positions of power and decisionmaking in the country.

The high percentage of women members of parliament (MPs) in the National Assembly in 2005 represents a steady increase in the years since independence in 1990 (leveling off since 1999). In Namibia's first National Assembly, 6 of the 72 voting MPs (8.3 percent) were women.[2] The second National Assembly in 1995 had 9 women MPs (12.5 percent, with 2 added in 1996 for a term total of 15.3 percent), and the third National Assembly in 2000 had 18 (25 percent, with 3 added midterm for a term total of 29.2 percent). Local-authorities elections in 1992, 1998, and 2004 brought large numbers of women into local councils— 31.5 percent, 41.3 percent, and 43.4 percent, respectively. In the 1992 regional council elections, by contrast, only 3 of 95 regional councilors elected (3.2 percent) were women, in 1998 only 4 of 102 regional councilors elected (3.9 percent) were women, and in 2004 only 12 of 107 regional councilors elected (11.2 percent) were women. Interestingly, more than half (7) of those women regional councilors were sent to the National Council, whose 26 members are selected from the country's 13 regional councils (Frank 2004b).[3]

In this chapter I examine Namibian women's electoral successes at the national level since independence. First, I present a brief history of women in Namibia. This section shows that the majority of Namibian women continue to experience the effects of the twin legacies of colonialism and apartheid. Moreover, until very recently, women and their organizations in Namibia have been divided along party-political, racial, ethnic, geographic, and other lines. Second, I investigate the factors responsible for Namibian women's national-level electoral successes. These include a combination of electoral-system manipulation, a nascent women's movement with links to global women's movements, and the role played by women in Namibia's decades-long liberation struggle. Third, I elaborate the impact and experiences of women MPs in Namibia. Indeed, since independence a bevy of progressive new laws has been passed, including those that deal with marriage, rape, domestic violence, child maintenance, and land tenure. Moreover, a number of important institutions have been established in government. At the same time, elected women as well as ordinary Namibian women continue to face a host of challenges in their efforts to improve gender relations and the lot of Namibian women in an independent Namibia. Finally, I conclude by considering future directions for women MPs in Namibia.

Brief History of Women in Namibia

Despite independence in 1990 and the increasing number of women in parliament in Namibia today, the twin legacies of colonialism and apartheid continue to have a profound impact on the lives of most ordinary Namibian women. One hundred years of colonial rule, in particular 75 years of South African white-minority rule, created enduring racial and ethnic categories within the small Namibian population. Moreover, a migrant labor system founded by the Germans in the late 1800s, combined with apartheid policies imported from South Africa, ensured that racial and ethnic categories largely coincided with clear class distinctions. Thus, race and ethnicity formed the basis for significant social, political, and economic discrimination against the majority of Namibians. For the majority of women in Namibia—who are black and live in the rural areas—gender oppression has been intertwined with significant race and class oppression. Moreover, rural black women in Namibia suffered disproportionately from the effects of the decades-long war for national independence that largely played itself out in the country's rural north.

In the years since independence a new black elite has emerged that shares some common interests and aspirations with the white middle class, thus blurring racial distinctions among the privileged few in Namibia (Hubbard and Solomon 1995, 165). For the majority of women in Namibia, however, subsisting on agriculture in the rural areas, the triple oppression of race, class, and gender remains a potent force.

The University of Namibia's 2000 *National Gender Study,* like the 1991 and 2001 censuses,[4] found that women continued to be the majority among Namibia's population of nearly two million, outnumbering men at a ratio of 100 women to 95 men (Iipinge et al. 2000, 264). The study also found that women are poorer than men and they are less likely to own, or have access to, land (Iipinge et al. 2000, 265). Nearly 40 percent of households in Namibia are female-headed. Such households are less likely to own durable goods or have access to electricity, water and sanitation facilities, and health care than male-headed households. In general, female-headed households offer a worse standard of living for members than male-headed households (Iipinge et al. 2000, 22).

An earlier study from the University of Namibia found that while women in Namibia are economically active, their participation in and contribution to the Namibian economy tend to be undervalued (Iipinge and LeBeau 1997, 14–16). Most women in Namibia remain concentrated in subsistence agriculture in the rural areas or in domestic service in the urban areas. With less access to land and credit than is available to men and largely confined to a narrow range of low-income and low-status jobs, women are prevented from participating more fully in Namibia's economic development. With women more likely than men to live in the rural areas (in part because of patterns of male migration), they are also more prone to food insecurity and less likely to have access to much-needed social services. Women also suffer from lack of adequate child care and child maintenance arrangements. Though women are currently taking advantage of adult literacy programs in large numbers, girls remain discriminated against in the formal education system (Iipinge and LeBeau 1997, 15). Girls are more likely than boys to drop out of school at the secondary level, primarily because of pregnancy and family work demands and because school curricula, at all levels, remain gender biased. At the same time, from 1994 to 1998, more females were enrolled in school than males—at all levels (Department of Women Affairs [DWA] 1999, 24–25).

Despite improvements to their legal and social status since independence, women in Namibia experience unacceptable levels of violence made worse by poverty, unemployment and high rates of alcoholism among men, cultural norms, and women's perceived low status (LeBeau and Spence 2004, 42). Violence against women (and children) includes physical, psychological, sexual, and financial abuse and comes primarily from those closest to them (Iipinge and LeBeau 1997, 16). According to the 2000 *National Gender Study,* "the most endemic form of violence against women . . . is wife abuse or abuse of women by intimate male partners" (Iipinge et al. 2000, 160). Among other things, this violence "makes women and children feel insecure. This, in turn, prevents women from moving about freely, having access to basic resources, and from taking active part in public activities, all in fear of violence" (DWA 1999, 45). Rape is on the increase, and although more men than women are infected with AIDS in Namibia, since 1998 women have accounted for 53 percent of all new reported HIV cases (DWA 1999, 35).

Given the disadvantages with which so many Namibian women contend, one might anticipate a highly mobilized women's movement in the country. And yet it is only in very recent years that such a movement has emerged. Rather, Namibian women and their organizations have been seriously divided along a number of lines—racial and ethnic, party-political, urban/rural, among others—for decades. Until recently most of the organization of women in the country was through churches at the local level or through women's wings of political parties, both of which reinforced the strong divisions among women. In an interview in 2002, Congress of Democrats (COD) MP Nora Schimming-Chase lamented the power of party political divisions over women: "All of the participation of women has always been within political parties. We let ourselves be put in the corner of women's leagues, Swapo, Swanu, all of them." Indeed, in the late 1970s a South West Africa People's Organisation (Swapo) Women's Council (SWC) was established by the exiled liberation movement, to be followed by a Democratic Turnhalle Alliance (DTA) Women's League in 1980 and similar bodies in the smaller parties.[5] Not only have the women's wings contributed to a lack of unity among women, but they have also lacked autonomy from their parties (Becker 1995, 294, 302).

In the mid-1980s two efforts to bring women together across the historical dividing lines were made, only to be thwarted by the liberation movement, Swapo, and other political parties. COD MP Nora Schimming-Chase recounts the attempt by women who had been in exile but returned to the country in the mid-1980s to organize the Namibian Women's Association (NAWA):

> When we came back we started NAWA, and that was the first time that women came together across political lines. It was also the first time that black and white women could share experiences because women were surprised to find that when we sat down white women were equally oppressed, white women were equally marginalized. . . . But we became such a threat to the political parties that the major parties like Swapo and Swanu and the DTA went as far as to instruct their women what they were supposed to do, and it [NAWA] was sidelined.[6]

Also in the mid-1980s, urban township women organized themselves outside the confines of the liberation movement with the goal of addressing some of their practical gender interests—unemployment, alcoholism, and juvenile delinquency, among others—and their strategic gender interests—gender relations and the oppression of women generally (Becker 1995, 205). This organization, Namibian Women's Voice (NWV), has been described as the "first major women's group to operate independently of party-political, church, or other superimposed structures" and has been hailed for providing "a forum where gender issues were not subordinated to other priorities" (Hubbard and Solomon 1995, 170). But despite (or perhaps because of) the NWV's success in organizing women in several regions of Namibia, it was quickly disbanded under pressure from the externally based liberation movement that could not countenance what was perceived as a separate feminist stance that diverted attention from the more important goal of national liberation. In early 2002 COD MP Rosa Namises blamed continuing divisions among women on Swapo's early refusal to sanction the development and growth of the NWV: "The reason that we feel divided and we are divided and there is such a lack of a move towards a national women's movement comes from the fact that already in 1985 Swapo came back and stopped our Namibian Women's Voice. And from that time women have felt broken and it has taken time to rebuild ourselves."[7]

Attempts to organize women into one national organization in the early years after independence also failed, despite a general feeling among women activists that a strong women's network was necessary "to support women and to provide them with a political base to advocate for social and political change" (former NWV general secretary Nashilongo Elago, cited in Becker 2000, 192). According to most observers, this was, again, because of party-political and other divisions among women and a failure to find one or two issues around which women could organize themselves. According to Heike Becker (2000, 29–30), "personal jealousies and political power struggles between leading female politicians, representing their respective political parties' women's departments, prevented a successful outcome."

The situation appears to be changing, however. In Namibia today, one detects the emergence, after many years, of the elusive unified women's movement. Interestingly, this movement has come together largely around a single issue, namely, electing more women to political office. In many ways, this road to a more cohesive women's movement in Namibia parallels the situation in Botswana, where a women's rights movement developed as a result of an intensive mobilization around a single initiative, namely, the challenge to the nation's Citizenship Law, which determined children's citizenship on the basis of the father's nationality only (Van Allen 2001). Namibia's emerging women's movement is one of the factors that has put more women on the path to political office in Namibia; it is discussed further later in this chapter.

The Path to Political Office in Namibia

Several factors have come together in Namibia to bring a large percentage of women into the National Assembly. These include use of a closed-list proportional representation (PR) electoral system, together with agitation for gender-based quotas, pressure from an emerging women's movement on fairly receptive political parties, and the availability of a cadre of women candidates, many of whom gained training in politics and/or were influenced by a global women's movement through their participation in the country's twenty-year liberation struggle. Moreover, as with most cases in Africa where large numbers of women have been elected to political office, the backdrop has been a political transition—in Namibia's case from an authoritarian colonial rule to a more democratic independent rule. Many of these factors are consistent with years of research and scholarship on the factors that help to propel women into politics.

The first factor, a closed-list PR electoral system combined with mandatory quotas at the local level and voluntary quotas on the part of some political parties at the national level (with a serious campaign under way to make those higher and mandatory), represents the collective learning of decades of experimentation with alternative electoral systems and different types of quotas (see Dahlerup 2002; Matland 2002; and Gray 2003, among others). Namibia's experience to date largely mirrors experiences elsewhere. For regional council elections, where women have fared poorly, a winner-take-all electoral system is utilized. By contrast, local authority and National Assembly elections use a closed-list PR electoral system. Indeed, the significance of the type of electoral system to the number of women elected is broadly recognized in Namibia today. Originally, the type of system used in local-authorities elections was to be changed from a party-list PR system to a ward system. In 2002, however, the Local Authorities Act was amended so that all future local elections will be conducted by a party-list PR system. In motivating the amendment, the deputy minister of Regional, Local Government and Housing argued that the PR system would ensure a greater representation of women (Thiel 2003, 3).[8] While there is no evidence that the original choice of a closed-list PR electoral system for National Assembly elections was motivated by a desire to increase women's political representation, it is now recognized as key to bringing more women into national office (Bauer 2004).

At the local level the PR electoral system is used in conjunction with a mandatory quota that requires that nearly one-third to one-half of candidates on party lists be women, depending on the size of the local authority (Hubbard 2001, 11). Interestingly, one woman MP (now the deputy prime minister), then minister of Local Government and Housing, Libertine Amathila, is credited with adding the quota to the Local Authorities Act when it was drawn up in 1992 (discussed later). At the national level, no such mandatory quota exists. Since just before the 1999 election, however, considerable pressure has been exerted upon political parties to have 50 percent of their candidates for the National Assembly be women. Parties are also being urged to ensure that their party lists are "zebra lists," which means that men and women are listed alternately, like the black and white stripes of a zebra. While no party has yet agreed to even a voluntary quota, the parties did heed the call for more women candidates in the 1999 National Assembly election. Twenty-eight percent of the ruling Swapo party's candidates, 33 percent of the COD's candidates, and 21 percent of the DTA's candidates were women. Though none of the lists were zebra lists, women were fairly well distributed throughout each party list.[9]

Clearly, in closed-list PR electoral systems, political parties play a critical role in the task of bringing more women into political office because they compile the party lists for each election. In interviews in early 2002 Eunice Iipinge of the Swapo Women's Council and Maria Lourence of the DTA Women's League both expressed strong commitment to demanding more women on their respective party lists in the 2004 election and to ensuring that their lists be zebra lists.[10] As the SWC's Eunice Iipinge noted: "We really want to have half of it; that's why we are calling for the zebra list. To us that constitutes justice . . . it constitutes legitimacy. . . . Women are the majority in the country, so if women are not involved in decisionmaking, then the question of legitimacy comes up. . . . So we really want to see the zebra list introduced."

Swapo, DTA, and COD women MPs all voiced the same intention in 2002—to focus on increasing the number of women on their parties' 2004 lists.[11] In the event, like all party wings, the SWC was invited to submit names to Swapo's October 2004 electoral convention to select the party's list, and put forward 10. In addition each of 13 regions was invited to submit 2 names, one of which was to be a woman. Finally, President Sam Nujoma also had the prerogative of submitting 10 names, 6 of which were women. In the end, there was only 1 woman candidate among Swapo's top 10.[12] Interestingly, with 15 of 18 women MPs in the fourth National Assembly from the ruling Swapo party, Namibia demonstrates the potential impact of one dominant political party receptive to pressure for party-based quotas on women's electoral outcomes.

The second factor, a nascent women's movement, again speaks to decades of experience and research that show that an association with women's organizations is critical to the success of women officeholders, both in getting them elected and in helping to assure that they promote women's interests once in office (see, for example, Bystydzienski 1992 and Carroll 1992). As I noted before, for the first time in Namibia a somewhat unified women's movement has emerged in the country. The movement has its origins in a March 1999 workshop held by Sister Namibia, a long-standing feminist organization based in Windhoek,[13] for nongovernmental organizations (NGOs), political parties, and elected women at all levels of government to discuss ways of increasing women's representation in politics. At the workshop Sister Namibia was mandated to lead the NGOs, women's wings of political parties, and other groups in their preparations for the December 1999 National Assembly elections. Among other things, workshop participants decided to draft a manifesto that would outline their demands in a number of key areas. In September 1999 the *Namibian Women's Man-*

ifesto was launched, translated into six languages, and distributed throughout the country.[14] One of the manifesto's seven aims was a 50 percent quota for women on party lists, lists that were also zebra lists (Sister Namibia 1999, 3). Within a year, the Namibian Women's Manifesto Network (NWMN) was born. In September 2000 the NWMN formally launched a 50/50 campaign. The 50/50 campaign, later linked to a global effort sponsored by the Women's Environment and Development Organization (WEDO) in New York City, called for the 50 percent representation of women in all areas of politics and decisionmaking by 2005.

To date, the campaign has generated widespread debate throughout Namibia. Between July 2001 and March 2002 the NWMN held 105 workshops around the country involving more than 3,500 people focused on the issue of women's participation in politics. Following the workshops, network members and supporters visited 70 schools, 88 churches, 9 traditional leaders, 17 regional councilors, and 32 local councilors. They also held meetings with NGOs and the leaders of the major political parties. Finally, they organized marches, distributed thousands of pamphlets, and collected thousands of signatures in support of a proposed 50/50 Bill (Khaxas 2002). In its fourth phase by 2004, the campaign, with the support of more than 40 NGOs and 30 women's groups across the country, worked hard to convince women to be candidates and voters in the 2004 local authority elections and to persuade political parties to draw up zebra-style lists (Frank 2004a, 2004c). This kind of countrywide mobilization and unity around a women's issue is unprecedented in Namibia. In many ways it verifies Gwendolyn Mikell's (2003, 104) observation that "the pragmatics of women's political representation in the 1990s are shaping the emerging African women's movement."

The campaign has also garnered widespread support from diverse corners. In the past, the contact between women MPs and women's organizations was fairly limited. Very few women MPs, with a few notable exceptions such as former COD MP Rosa Namises and Swapo National Council deputy chairperson Margareth Mensah, were activists in women's organizations before joining parliament.[15] The closest most other women MPs came to a women's organization was the women's wing of their political party or a church-based women's group. But women MPs are largely supportive of the call for an equal representation of women and men in politics and decisionmaking, with only 2 of 15 women MPs interviewed in 2002 hesitating to express unequivocal support for the campaign.[16] At the same time, many women MPs cited the Namibian government's 1997 commitment to 30 percent women at all levels of government by 2005 (as a signatory to the *Southern African Development Community [SADC] Gender Declaration*) and felt that this was a more realizable short-term goal. Moreover, Namibian women MPs participate actively in the newly created SADC Regional Women's Parliamentary Caucus, an objective of which was to "engage leaders of political parties in six countries scheduled to hold elections in 2004–05 and lobby for at least 30 percent women candidates on their election nomination lists for Parliament" (*Launch of the Southern African Development Community [SADC] Regional Women's Parliamentary Caucus: Voice of Women Parliamentarians in SADC* 2002, 3).[17] Rumbi Nhundu, gender program officer for the SADC Parliamentary Forum in Windhoek, observed in 2002 that the goal of 30 percent women by 2005 should be seen as a starting point, as "laying the foundations for the campaign for the 50 percent."[18]

A whole range of women's organizations is also behind the campaign, and it is especially in this regard that one may speculate on the emergence of a cohesive women's movement in the country for the first time—organized around a specific initiative. Sister Namibia provided the impetus for the organization of the NWMN and continues to supply essential support to the campaign. Other groups actively supporting the campaign include Women's Action for Development (WAD), a grassroots-based organization that works toward the economic and political empowerment of rural women, the Namibia Girl Child Organization, which targets schoolgirls with the goal of preparing them for future political participation and has chapters in dozens of schools around Namibia, and the Namibian Media Women's Association, which seeks to monitor the portrayal of women and highlight their concerns in the popular media. Many other Namibian NGOs have also pledged their support.

In a July 2002 meeting two organizations of elected women, the Parliamentary Women's Caucus (PWC) and the Namibia Elected Women's Forum (including elected women from the local, regional, and national levels), pledged that they would fight for a 50 percent representation of women at all levels of government. At a preelection workshop of the Regional Elected Women's Forum in Windhoek in late 2004, local, regional, and national women politicians called for continued unity in the effort to increase the number of elected women.[19] In addition, leaders of both the Association of Local Authorities of Namibia and the Association of Regional Councils stated their strong support for the campaign. Finally, many ordinary Namibians support the campaign. In a 2003 Institute for Public Policy Research survey, 81 percent of respondents stated that it was important "to have equal numbers of men and women as candidates" in elections in Namibia (Thiel 2003, 9). Thus, after a long history of division along a range of fault lines, Namibian women are mobilizing in an unprecedented way around the issue of electing more women to political office.

Not only is this nascent women's movement mobilizing to elect more women to parliament, it is also spearheading campaigns to influence specific pieces of legislation. On International Women's Day in 2004 women activists led civil society organizations in a march to parliament to deliver a petition on women's and children's rights. Indeed, fifteen civil society organizations had signed the petition, calling for changes to the Children's Status Bill and the Labour Bill then under consideration by the National Assembly. Accepting their petition, the secretary of the National Assembly "encouraged the women's rights campaigners to make use of all avenues available to them to make their voices heard" ("Civil Society's . . ." 2004, 2).

The emerging women's movement and women politicians in Namibia have also been influenced in not insignificant ways by a global women's movement. While the demand for the 50 percent representation of women in politics in Namibia predates the launching of the WEDO 50/50 campaign, the campaign is now linked to a global one.[20] Namibian women MPs belong to organizations such as the Pan African Women's Organizations, the Inter-Parliamentary Union, and other organizations that have exposed them to political practices around the world. In addition, Namibia is a signatory to a number of international protocols and conventions, including the Protocol to the African Charter on the Rights of Women in Africa, ratified by Namibia in 2004 (Hubbard 2004).[21]

Namibian women politicians and activists have also been profoundly influenced by their participation in international conferences, in particular the Fourth United Nations World Conference on Women held in Beijing in 1995.[22] The first minister of Women Affairs and Child Welfare, Netumbo Nandi-Ndaitwah, headed a fifty-six-member delegation to the Beijing conference, including many of the prominent women politicians and activists in Namibia today. National Council deputy chairperson Margareth Mensah, who attended the Beijing conference, observed: "Beijing really brought us together internationally, and we learned a lot, a lot. We shared a lot of experiences and the networking thing really helped, regionally, internationally, etc. Getting the information, molding the laws the way that we have, came from the information that we shared, that we received."

PWC chairperson Teopolina Mushelenga described how women's organizations throughout Africa, including in Namibia, are "drawing their strength" from the Beijing Platform of Action. DTA MP Patricia Siska reported in 2002 that she and other Namibian delegates came back from Beijing "energized," ready to take a fresh look at Namibian laws. From that point on, she asserts, "a lot of things have changed."[23] Indeed, in the post-Beijing period a National Gender Policy and a number of progressive new laws were adopted, and the Department of Women Affairs (DWA) was transformed into the Ministry of Women Affairs and Child Welfare.

Regional influences have also had an impact. For example, women from Sister Namibia compiling the *Namibian Women's Manifesto* were well aware of the launching in 1994 of a *Women's Manifesto* in Botswana by the Emang Basadi Women's Association (Machangana 1998). In addition, the more moderate goal of 30 percent women in politics and decisionmaking by 2005 was put forward and endorsed by the SADC, a regional body. Women MPs in Namibia and Southern Africa were very aware of this and set their sights, not always successfully, on 2004 and 2005, when nearly every country in the region held national legislative elections (Southern African Development Community Gender Unit 1999).

Only a very few women MPs in Namibia considered the influence of the global women's movement to be negative or of no consequence, and they tended to be from Namibia's first generation of women activists (and exiles). For example, former minister of Health and Social Services Libertine Amathila drew a clear distinction between the kinds of issues women in Namibia are struggling with and those that, in her view, preoccupy women activists internationally: "This movement of women we have here has come from our background of the struggle. We were actively involved in the war. I would be careful not to mention this, but if you look at the movement of the Europeans—since Europe has developed further than us here, European women tend to discuss issues like lesbianism and freedom to have sex that we haven't reached here. We haven't reached that yet . . . so I wouldn't say there is any influence on us." The COD's Nora Schimming-Chase charged that the international women's movement failed Namibian women by favoring, indeed only supporting, those women's groups associated with the liberation movement, now the ruling party: Swapo.[24]

The global women's movement may have influenced Namibians the most during the years of exile, from the late 1960s to the late 1980s, when tens of thousands of young Namibians left the country for the rest of Africa, Europe, and North America. In South Africa, when young students and exiles returned home in the early 1990s, armed with a new feminist vocabulary, they challenged "earlier assumptions about the role of women in democratic struggle and the nature of women's political aspirations" (Seidman 1999, 295). They also insisted that feminist concerns not be postponed until after the transition. In Namibia, as in South Africa, women former exiles have entered parliament in large numbers.

The third factor, the timing of Namibian independence and Namibian women's significant contribution to it—as armed combatants, "radical mothers," community activists inside Namibia, university and vocational students trained abroad, and the backbone of exile camps in neighboring Angola—demonstrates that the result of liberation and nationalist struggles, revolutions, or democratic transitions need not always be the demobilization of women and the deactivation of their demands.[25] Rather, as in South Africa, Uganda, and Mozambique, women in Namibia have built upon the experiences and training they received in the course of struggle, and the support they garnered as a result of it, and they have been able to push a forward-looking gender agenda that includes greater representation in political office. The timing of Namibia's independence—when gender issues were "at a high peak"—helped.[26]

Women's participation in Namibia's independence struggle was great. For nearly twenty-five years the liberation movement Swapo waged a war against the South African occupiers in Namibia, from exile bases first in Tanzania, then in Zambia, and, finally, in Angola. Northern Namibia, the most densely populated region of the country, was the war zone. By the mid-1970s about 20 percent of Namibian exiles were women, and, at their own insistence, all who were unmarried and childless received the same military training as the men exiles. Taking up arms was a crucial step for women. According to Becker (1995, 149–150), "the participation of women in armed fighting caused men to revise their perception of women and added much to women's self-confidence." Young Namibian women's self-confidence was also bolstered by the study and training opportunities that exile provided to many—opportunities that they never would have had at that time in Namibia. In fact, there were often more female than male students sent abroad, and many young women moved into engineering, law, medicine, and other fields previously seen as male domains (Becker 1995, 151–152). Because they were more often than not abroad on their own, women also developed a high degree of autonomy. Becker (1995, 153) concludes: "Many educated young Namibian women in exile were no longer prepared to be subordinate to male dominance but claimed equality and power-sharing with men on all levels, including politics."

Namibian women who remained behind were also often part of the resistance movement, playing a supportive role to Swapo combatants or those sought after by the police, in particular in the rural northern war zone (Soiri 1996, 58–59). As such, these women have been identified by Iina Soiri as "radical mothers," that is, mothers taking an active part in political struggle based on their responsibilities and capabilities as members of a community under threat. The women "acted as mothers, daughters and sisters utilising the potential opportunities given by their traditional role. They were not aware of or even interested in feminism or its analysis of their situation, but were still empowered as women."[27] Urban women also participated in the struggle for independence. Indeed, Anna Mungunda is typically cited as the first Namibian to die in the "modern" period of Namibia's anticolonial struggle. In December 1959 Mungunda led a group of Old Location residents in protesting their relocation to a new township in Windhoek, and was gunned down for doing so. By the time of the transition to independence, according to Becker (2000, 26), "women had become visible in Namibian politics" and they had become an important new target for political parties: "The major political parties contesting the elections included 'women's issues' in their campaigns to canvass the female electorate, which constituted more than half of the adult population."

In all, 10 of 21 women MPs in the third National Assembly and 1 of the 2 women members of the second National Council had gone into exile with Swapo, usually in their teenaged years, including 2 who later became members of the opposition COD party.[28] All of these women when interviewed confirmed the transformative impact of the exile experience on their lives—providing a range of skills, from a facility in English and public speaking to advanced degrees and confidence-building—leading in many cases to their involvement in formal politics. Most of the other women MPs in the third National Assembly had participated in the struggle for independence from inside the country— as township activists, community organizers, nurses in the border war zone. Only one woman, COD MP Dr. Elizabeth Amukugo, former University of Namibia department head and former Swapo exile, dissented from the view of the liberation struggle as having brought more women into political office. She observed: "If gender issues were taken more seriously at that stage, we would be having more than 25 percent [women in parliament]."[29]

Women's role in the liberation struggle also gained them the support of an important player in Namibian politics, President Sam Nujoma. Repeatedly, Namibian women MPs from all political parties cited the president's role in promoting women in politics and other sectors. This role has manifested itself in various ways, including Nujoma's (unsuccessful) efforts to single-handedly put 15 women at the top of the Swapo party list for the 1999 National Assembly election (and 6 women out of 10 total for the 2004 National Assembly election) and to impose a 25 percent quota of women on the party's central committee during the 2002 party congress. When asked why they thought President Nujoma was so supportive of women, most women MPs and politicians cited the roles played by women during the liberation struggle, most notably as combatants, but also a range of other roles; Nujoma's relationship with his mother; and his desire to utilize the skills of a range of people. Indeed, in June 2004 the chair of the sixteenth SADC Parliamentary Forum appealed to President Nujoma to include at least 30 percent women on the party's National Assembly list. She did so because over the years President Nujoma "had demonstrated the political will to address the issue of gender equality."[30]

The Impact and Experiences of Women MPs

It has been less than a decade since women have been in the National Assembly in Namibia in any significant numbers, so it is difficult to assess their impact. Yet clear gains can be identified. Since independence, remarkable progress has been made in establishing new offices and committees on women, developing a national gender policy, and passing a series of new laws that seek to undo past discrimination against women and provide new opportunities for women and girls. Effective implementation of these new policies and laws remains a much longer-term, significant challenge.

As elsewhere in Africa, an early point at which Namibian woman activists and politicians could seek to influence the post-transition gender dispensation was in the drawing up of a new constitution, a task of the Constituent Assembly (CA) elected in the country's first universal franchise elections in November 1989. Only 6 of the CA's 72 members were women; moreover, only 1 of 21 members of the standing committee that actually drafted the constitution was a woman—Pendukeni Ithana, then secretary of the SWC. Still, according to Becker, even one woman SWC officeholder on the standing committee was considered a victory for

Namibian women. Becker (1995, 239) contends that, with Ithana on the drafting committee, "the women's organization of Namibia's ruling party to be had prominent access to the final drafting process of the Constitution." According to Libertine Amathila and Michaela Huebschle, two of the six women CA members, women members played a significant role in shaping Namibia's progressive constitution.[31] Among other things, the constitution uses gender-neutral language throughout, forbids discrimination on the basis of sex and a number of other attributes, notes the special discrimination suffered by women in the past and the need to redress it with affirmative action, and states that customary law (often discriminatory toward women) may remain in effect but only to the extent that it does not conflict with the constitution or any other laws. Becker (2000, 186) argues that it is "difficult to overrate the prominent role the Namibian Constitution has played in changes which are beginning to redress gender imbalances."

Shortly after independence, a Department of Women Affairs was established within the Office of the President. After much lobbying from women officeholders in the DWA (some of whom, such as the first minister, Netumbo Nandi-Ndaitwah, were women MPs) and others, the department was upgraded to a Ministry of Women Affairs and Child Welfare in 2000 (renamed the Ministry of Gender Equality and Child Welfare in 2005). A National Gender Policy (NGP) was approved by government in 1997 and adopted by parliament in 1999. A National Gender Programme of Action was drawn up to implement the NGP, which aims ultimately to end all forms of gender discrimination and addresses ten critical areas of concern identified in the Beijing Platform of Action, including gender and economic empowerment, the girl child, and gender and legal affairs. In 1998 the cabinet gave the Ministry of Women Affairs and Child Welfare the authority to appoint Gender Focal Points in other ministries for the purpose of raising gender awareness and reviewing policies from a gender-sensitive viewpoint. In addition, successive national development plans in Namibia have addressed gender-specific sectoral objectives and strategies (LeBeau and Iipinge 2004).

In 1992 a Law Reform and Development Commission was established to oversee the bringing of new and existing laws into compliance with the Namibian constitution. The commission established a Women and Law Committee to consider law reform in those areas where gender-related legal disparities between women and men exist. Indeed, that law reform has been extensive, and women MPs have played a pivotal role in crafting and passing many of the new laws. In 1992 the Local

Authorities Act was passed, with then minister of Local Government and Housing Libertine Amathila playing a pivotal role in shaping the bill. When, during debate on the bill in August 1992, Amathila offered an amendment requiring a minimum number of women candidates at the local level, it was accepted without objection. Amathila cited that part of the Namibian constitution that refers to the need for affirmative action for women to redress past discrimination (Hubbard and Kavari 1993, 4).

Other legislative gains for women include the 1992 Labour Act, which prohibits discrimination in any aspect of employment; forbids harassment on the basis of sex, marital status, family responsibilities, or sexual orientation; and provides for maternity leave for formal sector workers, and the 1998 Affirmative Action (Employment) Act, which aims to ensure that racially disadvantaged persons, women, and persons with disabilities enjoy equal opportunities at all levels of employment and are equitably represented in the workforce. Still more important to women, perhaps, the 1996 Married Persons Equality Act made men and women equal before the law in marriage. The act invalidates marital powers that had made the husband the head of the household. It also provides for married women to have equal access to bank loans and ownership of property and for equal guardianship over minor children of a marriage. In 2000 the Combating of Rape Act, among the most progressive such bills in the world, was passed. The Combating of Rape Act prescribes minimum sentences for rape, places more emphasis on the rights of rape victims, precludes marriage from being considered a defense for rape, and expands the definition of rape to include men as potential victims. In 2002 a Communal Land Reform Bill, with two provisions particularly favorable to women, was passed. The land bill requires that at least 4 of 10 members of the communal land boards that supervise the allocation of communal lands will be women, and the bill protects women wishing to remain on their land in the event of their husband's death (Hubbard 2002, LeBeau and Iipinge 2004).

In 2003 the Combating of Domestic Violence Act and the Child Maintenance Act were passed. According to one source, the Combating of Domestic Violence Act "makes Namibia one of the very few countries in the region spearheading efforts to deal with domestic violence through legislation aimed specifically at it." In general, the law aims to make it easier for people to press criminal charges against the perpetrators of domestic violence. The law also provides for victims of abuse to secure protection against their abusers.[32] The Child Maintenance Act provides for all children, irrespective of birth order and parents' marital status, to have the same rights to their parents' resources. The law also provides mechanisms for obtaining child maintenance payments from absent fathers (or mothers), with payment in kind (for example, cattle) an acceptable form.[33] In both cases, however, "the effectiveness of . . . these laws has been undermined by problems with implementation" (Hubbard 2004). During 2004 the Children's Status Bill, which deals with the position of children born outside marriage and the guardianship of those whose parents have died, was debated in parliament. After multiple concerns were raised by women's organizations, the bill was referred back to the Committee on Human Resources, which then held more than thirty hearings on the bill around the country. Among other things, women were concerned to prevent the inclusion of automatic custody provisions counter to children's best interests (Hubbard 2004).

To what extent can these accomplishments be attributed directly to the increasing number of women—though not yet a critical mass—in the National Assembly or National Council? When asked in 2002, women MPs cited a range of accomplishments. Several felt that women MPs had definitely contributed to the aforementioned legislative gains, in particular the 1996 Married Persons Equality Act, the 1997 National Gender Policy, and the 2000 Combating of Rape Bill, as well as the more recent bills then still under consideration. According to National Council deputy chairperson Mensah, with more women in parliament, "the bills get passed faster and maybe they get polished better." Women MPs were also bringing new perspectives to the debate in parliament, according to COD MP Elizabeth Amukugo: "I find that our presence in parliament, although we are few, we make a difference in the sense that we can say, 'Wait a minute, you cannot look at this issue that way.' From the point of view of gender, engendering the legal process, I feel that we have made an impact that way, to have people look at laws from a different perspective."

Women MPs had also begun, according to Swapo MP and PWC chairperson Teopolina Mushelenga, to use "a gender lens" to analyze the annual budget. In addition, women MPs were engaged in parliament, making motions and putting challenging questions to the floor, according to COD MP Nora Schimming-Chase. As Minister Amathila put it, women parliamentarians have shown that women are "people to be reckoned with and even do better than men."

Other women MPs suggested in 2002 that they had been critical in privileging women's and children's issues, inside and outside parliament. Then minister of Labour and Swapo MP Rosalia Nghidinwa suggested that women MPs could "focus on certain areas like poverty. They can also better bring the government to the people." Then minister of Basic Education, Sport, and Culture Clara Bohitile noted that women ministers, who constantly travel to the regions to visit constituents, "are in a much better position to take care of people's problems" than are men. Woman MPs were also liaising with NGOs. Other women MPs such as Lempy Lucas and Generosa Andowa pointed out that they had established a women's caucus in parliament and an elected women's forum outside parliament, and that women were the chairs of parliamentary committees and even the deputy chairperson of the National Council. In addition, women ministers, as cabinet members, were monitoring appointments to parastatal and other boards, insisting that women be adequately represented. Other accomplishments mentioned by Swapo MP Doreen Sioka included acting as a role model to other women, especially in the regions, and encouraging them to stand for political office.[34]

Around Africa a number of constraints have been identified that are limiting the impact and effectiveness of women officeholders. These include the way in which women are brought into political office (for example, reserved seats or high-level affirmative action appointments); institutional structures of parliament that are not favorable to women and the high levels of experience and training necessary to be a legislator; continued discriminatory and demeaning treatment from male colleagues; higher expectations of women than of men MPs; and the challenges of managing career, family, and household (Goetz 2002; Britton 2001; Geisler 1995, 2000; Ferguson and Katundu 1994).

Women MPs in Namibia have been helped in meeting some of these challenges by their role in the liberation struggle and by the educational opportunities to which they had access. As I have already noted, Namibian women MPs from the third National Assembly were all shaped by the country's long struggle for independence. Almost every woman MP considered herself "born into politics" because of participating in one way or another, often beginning at a very early age, in the struggle to liberate her country from an oppressive South African rule. While almost none of them hailed from a family in which members were formally involved in politics (precluded for most Namibians until independence), many were heavily influenced by family members, most notably sisters, mothers, and grandmothers, who early on made them aware of the injustice and terror around them. One told of hearing about the Swapo fighters and even meeting them through her sisters and then leaving for exile at age twelve with an older sister. Another, "under the wing" of an older sister from an early age, followed her sister to political meetings and eventually went into exile herself. For another woman MP, whose sister went into exile (though she did not), her sister was "her sole support structure" as she became more and more involved in politics. One woman MP's grandmother, who lived through the German war on the Herero people in the early 1900s, imbued her early on with a fighting spirit.

Women MPs in Namibia have had greater access to formal education than most Namibians. Of the twenty-one in the third National Assembly, one had a Ph.D. in education, another had an M.A. in politics and linguistics, one had a B.A. in planning and another had a B.A. in journalism, one a medical degree and another a law degree (all gained overseas in exile). More than ten of the women MPs had worked for many years as teachers or nurses, with most getting their degrees in South Africa or via exile training opportunities abroad. Other previous vocations of the women MPs included trade unionist and instructor, youth leader, librarian, and tailor. Many had upgraded their skills through diploma programs completed overseas after independence—in diplomacy, gender policy, advocacy and lobbying skills, sexual and reproductive health, English as a second language, international relations, and more.

Moreover, there has been some retention of more experienced MPs. Of the 18 women in the fourth National Assembly, only 5 were serving their first term, with the remaining 13 returning for a second, if not third, term. Three of the MPs in the fourth National Assembly, including Deputy Prime Minister Amathila, had been there since the body's inception in 1990 (including Minister Ndaitwah, who was an appointed member during her first term). By contrast, of the 7 women in the third National Council, only 1, Deputy Chairperson Margareth Mensah, was in her second term, in the National Council since 1999. Over the years very few women MPs have elected not to return to parliament. A few have retired; others have simply not been placed high enough on party lists to gain a seat a second time around.

Women MPs in Namibia voice many of the same concerns expressed by women politicians around Africa. In contrast to the situation in South Africa, women MPs in Namibia have not managed to make their national legislatures more women- or parent- friendly. One woman MP, a single mother, told of sneaking out of (and back into) parliament in order to transport her children to and from school. The National Council deputy chairperson complained about the confrontational and adversarial character of parliamentary debate, which she found particularly offputting, especially at first.[35] Other women MPs reported that they continue to put up with ill-informed comments by male counterparts.[36] Many decried a lack of adequate preparation for becoming MPs and serious trepidation before their maiden speeches. At the same time, many women MPs benefited from induction workshops and training programs offered by national, regional, and international organizations and have gained confidence and skills over the years. While some pointed out the stark differences between being a community activist and a national legislator, they noted that there are ways in which the practices of the former have prepared them for the latter, and pride themselves on continuing to serve their communities.

Future Directions

A number of conclusions can be drawn from the Namibian case. Clearly, the timing of Namibia's independence has enhanced the prospects of Namibian women politicians. In strong contrast to the first wave of independence in Africa thirty years earlier, Namibia's hardwon independence came—as the minister of Women Affairs and Child Welfare noted—at a time when "gender issues were at a peak," that is, when thirty years of hard-fought struggle by women's liberation movements around the world had revealed the importance of the choice of electoral system and the use of gender-based quotas as well as the importance of influencing political parties and allying with women's organizations in bringing more women into politics. In the intervening years Namibian women, many of whom spent their formative years in exile, also had the opportunity to observe how African women around the continent had lost hardwon gains after independence as the majority of their states became increasingly authoritarian and deprived most of their citizens of the most basic rights. Indeed, Namibia's independence came at the time of Africa's "second liberation," when democratic political transitions were occurring across the continent. In many instances organized women's movements seized the opportunities offered by these political openings to insert themselves into transition processes and assure at least a basic framework for their inclusion in electoral politics. Finally, the influence of the global women's movement has been clear in the postindependence period as well, as fora such as the United Nations women's conferences have had a profound impact on national gender policies in Namibia and elsewhere.

Not only did Namibia's independence occur later than many others, but it represented the end of an enduring conflict. In the Namibian case, the conflict itself meant that many Namibian women gained training, education, and experience—political, military, and otherwise—that would have been denied them in apartheid Namibia. Whether as armed combatants, students in exile, radical mothers, or community activists, women gained the confidence and skills to allow them to stand for and serve in public office. In some respects, women's participation in the decades-long conflict, inside and outside the country, also earned them the support of key players in Namibian politics, notably the country's first president, Sam Nujoma.[37] This conclusion is certainly not intended to discount a long tradition of activism by Namibian women or of the added responsibilities that rural women especially shouldered for decades due to the migrant labor system, but the struggle experience clearly propelled some women to the political forefront.

In addition, as has been suggested for Uganda, it seems as if women's successes in elected office and in activist organizations may be reinforcing each other (Tamale 1999). Organizations such as Sister Namibia, Women's Action for Development, and the Namibia Girl Child Organization are heavily engaged in the struggle to improve the position of women in Namibian politics and society. Among other things, WAD monitors closely the economic status of Namibian women and Sister Namibia is spearheading the campaign for 50 percent women in political office. Women activists have some of their own in elected office, and in general women MPs provide points of access for the activists and their organizations. This is not to say that relations between the two groups are without problems; indeed they can be highly contentious, but in the main a synergy seems to have emerged between those women in political office and those agitating from within their grassroots organizations.

Still, enormous challenges abound. The 2004 National Assembly election, on which national and regional activists had pinned their hopes, yielded the same percentage of women in parliament as the election in 1999. Because three women MPs had been added during the third National Assembly, the election result meant an actual reduction in the number of women MPs in Namibia from late 2004 to early 2005. This change would suggest, among other things, that the formal adoption of a gender-based quota, as at the local level, is in order at the national level as well in Namibia. Clearly, relying on the goodwill of political parties and influential politicians is not enough. Without mandatory quotas, Namibian women politicians risk eroding the steady gains they have made since independence. At the same time, electing significant numbers of women and initiating and passing women-friendly legislation may not even be the hardest part. The real challenge, as yet unmet in Namibia and other countries, is the careful implementation of new and progressive legislation and offices.[38] Only then will the impact of more women parliamentarians be broadly felt.

Notes

This chapter is based primarily on research carried out in Namibia during a sabbatical leave in 2002. I would like to thank the Institute for Public Policy Research in Windhoek for hosting me as a visiting researcher. I would also like to thank very much the many women activists, woman parliamentarians, and others who allowed me to interview them and offered their keen insights into gender and politics in Namibia. Finally, I thank the University of Delaware College of Arts and Sciences for supporting this project.

1. The deputy prime minister in early 2005 was Libertine Amathila, and the deputy speaker of the National Assembly was Doreen Sioka. Women ministers appointed by the new Namibian president, Hifikepunye Pohamba, were Rosalia Nghidinwa, Home Affairs and Immigration; Saara Kuugongelwa-Amadhila, Finance; Pendukeni Ivula-Ithana, Justice; Netumbo Nandi-Ndaitwah, Information and Broadcasting; Marlene Mungunda, Gender Equality and Child Welfare. Deputy ministers were Teopolina Mushelenga, Home Affairs and Immigration; Lempy Lucas, Foreign Affairs; Petrina Haingura, Health and Social Services; Angelika Muharukua, Gender Equality and Child Welfare. "A Thumbnail Guide to President Hifikepunye Pohamba's Government," *Namibian*, March 23, 2005, www.namibian.com.na.

2. In addition to the 72 voting members of the National Assembly, there are 6 nonvoting members appointed by the president. In 1990, 1 of the 6 nonvoting MPs was a woman; in 1995, 2 were women; in 2000, none was a woman; and in 2005, 3 were women. www.ipu.org/parline-e/reports. Nonvoting members of parliament are not considered in this analysis.

3. Namibia has a bicameral parliament consisting of a 72-member National Assembly, the lower house, and a 26-member National Council, the upper house.

4. Max Hamata, "Women in the Majority," *Namibian*, April 25, 2002, www.namibian.com.na.

5. The South West Africa People's Organisation (Swapo) was the primary nationalist movement in Namibia and led the struggle for independence for three decades. The South West African National Union (Swanu) was another early liberation movement. The Democratic Turnhalle Alliance (DTA) was formed in the late 1970s as part of South African attempts to bring about an internal settlement of the independence struggle in Namibia.

6. Author interview, Nora Schimming-Chase, April 23, 2002, Windhoek.

7. Author interview, Rosa Namises, April 18, 2002, Windhoek.

8. The Local Authorities Act had been amended in 1997 as well to allow the 1998 local elections to be held under a list PR system. In proposing that

amendment, party leaders had also argued that retaining the PR system would enhance women's representation (Tjihero et al. 1998, 3).

9. "Elections '99: List of Candidates for the National Assembly Elections," *Namibian*, October 27, 1999, www.namibian.com.na.

10. Until late 2003 the COD had no women's wing or women's league; according to COD MP Rosa Namises, such a body was rejected when the party was formed as relegating women to "just a cooking-pot role." But in October 2003 the party launched Women Democrats, identifying three issues around which women in the party planned to concentrate their efforts: violence against women, HIV/AIDS awareness, and the 50/50 campaign. "COD Launches Women Democrats at Reho," *Namibian*, October 2, 2003, www.namibian.com.na.

11. Author interviews: Eunice Iipinge, April 22, 2002; Maria Lourence, May 3, 2002; Rosa Namises, April 18, 2002; Elizabeth Amukugo, April 22, 2002, Windhoek.

12. Lindsay Detlinger, "Swapo Women's Council Picks Candidates for November Polls," *The Namibian*, September 27, 2004; Tangeni Amupadhi, "At the President's Pleasure," *Namibian*, October 4, 2004, www.namibian. com.na. Personal e-mail communication, Werner Hillebrecht, National Archives of Namibia, October 7, 2005.

13. According to COD MP Rosa Namises, those women active with the disbanded Namibian Women's Voice "rebuilt ourselves" as Sister Namibia in 1988 and Women's Solidarity in 1989. Author interview, April 18, 2002, Windhoek.

14. "50/50 Campaign: Namibian Women's Manifesto Network: A Short History of the 50/50 Campaign for Women's Equal Representation in Politics and Decision Making." http://www.wedo.org/5050/namibiamanifesto.htm.

15. Liz Frank of Sister Namibia notes that Sister Namibia began to make contact with women MPs only when Rosa Namises, a member, became an MP after the 1999 election. Liz Frank, personal e-mail communication, June 1, 2003.

16. During my sabbatical leave in Namibia in 2002 I interviewed 15 of the 20 women MPs then in the National Assembly and National Council as well as 1 former woman MP, leaders of the women's wings of political parties, women activists, and members of women's organizations and support organizations for women MPs.

17. Just before the 2004 election an SADC Regional Parliamentary Caucus delegation visited Namibian prime minister Theo-Ben Gurirab to appeal for help in realizing the regional goal of 30 percent women in decisionmaking positions. "Women Join Hands in Push for Democracy," *Namibian*, September 29, 2004, www.namibian.com.na.

18. Author interview, Rumbi Nhundu, June 21, 2002, Windhoek.

19. Patience Smith, "Unity Urged as Women Aim for Greater Representation in NA." *Namibian*, September 6, 2004, www.namibian.com.na.

20. Namibia's 50/50 campaign is featured prominently on the WEDO website. See www.wedo.org.

21. Though such conventions are rarely adhered to in full, they are important because activists can use them to put pressure on their governments and attempt to hold them accountable (Pruegl and Meyer 1999, 13).

22. As West (1999, 177) argues, "women's presence at UN conferences has redefined global agendas." Through these conferences feminists have "been able to insert women-oriented concerns and agendas into international discourse and practice."

23. Author interviews: Margareth Mensah, May 7, 2002; Teopolina Mushelenga, July 12, 2002; Patricia Siska, May 13, 2002. Patricia Siska, the DTA's only woman MP, later left the third National Assembly and the DTA and joined Swapo. She was replaced by another DTA woman MP, Barbara Rattay.

24. Author interviews: Libertine Amathila and Nora Schimming-Chase. Certainly it is the case that as the UN-dubbed "sole and authentic representative of the Namibian people," Swapo received the lion's share of international support during the years of the liberation struggle. Yet Cleaver and Wallace (1990, 94) suggest that groups such as the NWV were successful for as long as they were because of their ability to generate funds from international organizations.

25. It has long been argued that despite women's involvement in revolutionary and nationalist struggles and despite the state emancipatory goals of such movements, the results for women—once liberation was achieved—were often mixed or even limited (Waylen 1996, 70–91). Similarly, studies of women involved in political transitions in Latin America found that while women played pivotal roles in initiating the breakdown of authoritarian regimes, they were often shut out of the negotiated transition process and of an active involvement in constructing the new state (Waylen 1996, 92–114; Jaquette 1994).

26. According to then minister of Women Affairs and Child Welfare Netumbo Nandi-Ndaitwah (author interview, July 17, 2002), gender equality was long a priority for many Swapo women. But the timing of Namibia's independence also worked in their favor: "We came out of the liberation struggle alert. It helped us. We also got our independence when the whole question of gender was at a high peak. So that helped us."

27. Geisler (2000, 608) observes for South Africa: "Women forced their way into political activism against male resistance on the basis of practical gender needs, namely as mothers who were to secure a better future for their children. . . . Motherhood served as a unifying factor across rural-urban, class and race boundaries . . . but also allowed for women's continued subordination to the broader nationalist project."

28. Those who went into exile included Amathila, Ithana, Ndaitwah, Kuukongelwa-Amadhila, Sioka, Lukas, Mushelenga, Schimming-Chase, Amukugo, Kamanya, and Andowa in the National Council.

29. Author interview, Elizabeth Amukugo, April 22, 2002, Windhoek.

30. "President Urged to Up Quota on Women," *Namibian*, June 2, 2004, www.namibian.com.na. This is not unlike the situation in Uganda. Tamale (1999, 19) posits that one of the reasons for the introduction of affirmative action policies in Uganda may have been women's significant contribution to the

five-year armed struggle and leader Yoweri Museveni's recognition that women could perform as well as, if not better than, men in traditionally male jobs.

31. Author interviews: Libertine Amathila, June 26, 2002; Michaela Huebschle, May 28, 2002. Huebschle also claims that she, Amathila, and Pendukeni Ithana were instrumental in ensuring that capital punishment was proscribed in Namibia's constitution.

32. Christof Maletsky, "Domestic Violence Act Signed into Law," *Namibian*, July 9, 2003. Werner Menges, "Domestic Violence: Zero Tolerance Is Now the Law," *Namibian*, December 22, 2003, www.namibian.com.na.

33. Lindsay Detlinger, "Maintenance Revolution," *Namibian,* January 6, 2004.

34. Author interviews: Clara Bohitile, July 18, 2002; National Council Swapo MPs Andowa and Mensah; COD MPs Amukugo and Schimming-Chase; and Swapo MPs Amathila, Lucas, Mushelenga, Nghidinwa, and Sioka.

35. Bochel and Briggs (2000, 67) note that women politicians "are more willing to cooperate and to negotiate as opposed to being confrontational and always playing the role of political adversary."

36. During discussion of the Children's Status Bill in the National Assembly in 2004, COD MP Schimming-Chase, exasperated by her male colleagues' comments, noted that "whenever the House discusses issues related to children and women it is treated as jokes" ("Civil Society's . . ." 2004, 2).

37. Of course there are clear pitfalls to relying on a presidential benefactor or single dominant party or movement, as Goetz (2002) warns us very clearly with reference to the situation in Uganda.

38. In their research on community perceptions of law reform in Namibia, LeBeau and Spence (2004, 27–28) find that "law reform is only the first step to women's equality, and that changing laws and government policies alone does not guarantee the protection of women's human rights or remove gender discrimination from all levels of society. . . . Law reform alone," they continue, "cannot change the realities within which women live."

5

Uganda: Agents of Change for Women's Advancement?

Aili Mari Tripp

In mid 2005 Uganda had the sixth highest percentage of women in parliament in Africa. It was one of the countries that led the way in encouraging the trends we see in Africa today to increase the number of women parliamentarians, having already increased the number of female members of parliament (MPs) to 18 percent in 1989. In 2004 almost one-quarter (24 percent) of all parliamentary seats in Uganda were held by women, a large increase from the one seat that was held in 1980. In this chapter I explore what accounts for these changes in Uganda. I also look at how female-friendly policies have been used by Ugandan authorities to serve purposes other than the advancement of women and what implications these actions have had for women in Uganda. Much of the discussion of legislative quotas and other such affirmative action measures has focused on how women have sought to increase their political representation. Less has been said of the motivations and objectives of states in adopting such policies.

This chapter explores the intersection of two sets of actors with often quite divergent goals in advocating for women's increased political representation. There are two stories about the entry of women into national politics in Uganda that need to be told simultaneously. One story is about the women's movement, and the other is about state manipulations of women's leaders. This chapter is based on over three hundred interviews conducted since 1992 with women politicians and leaders of national women's organizations in addition to scholars, politicians, and activists in Uganda in a series of studies on the political impact of the women's movement on politics. I also draw on Ugandan newspapers, publications, and unpublished papers by Ugandan scholars.[1]

Recent History of Women and Politics in Uganda

Women-friendly policies emerged in earnest in Uganda after 1986, when the new government of Yoweri Museveni and his National Resistance Movement (NRM) came to power. The women's movement that revived after 1986 had its origins in earlier forms of mobilization, but the new organizations were markedly different in a variety of ways. In contrast to earlier women's mobilization, which was frequently tied to the ruling party or the state at the national level, the new associations that flourished were independent of Museveni's government and his no-party NRM, referred to as "the Movement" (not to be confused with the women's movement in this chapter). Although the older welfare, income-generating, and domestically oriented agendas persisted in women's organizations, especially at the local level, a new emphasis on political participation emerged.

Shortly after the 1986 NRM takeover, twenty leaders of the National Council of Women (NCW), Action for Development (ACFODE), and other nongovernmental organizations (NGOs) paid a courtesy call to President Museveni with a memo in hand, requesting that women be represented in government leadership. As one of the women put it, "Fortunately we had enough contacts within the NRM, and so we began to remind them that we were there advocating for women before the NRM came to official power and therefore, we deserved to talk to the leadership."[2] Museveni asked the delegation to identify women leaders, and subsequently the leaders circulated curricula vitae and made recommendations on how to fill various leadership positions. Many of these recommendations were adopted immediately, including the appointments of nine women ministers, among them Gertrude Njuba as deputy minister of industry; Victoria Sekitoleko as minister of agriculture; and Betty Bigombe as deputy minister, prime minister's office. Eight out of 75 ministers were women in 1989. Connie Byamugisha was appointed judge of the High Court in 1988 after being promoted two years earlier to the position of acting chief magistrate. It was not long before the NRM introduced reserved seats for women in the legislature in 1989, increasing the number of women parliamentarians almost overnight. Women parliamentarians were now to be elected by an electoral college with one woman from each district. The way in which the majority of women parliamentarians are elected through this electoral college creates allegiances to the NRM which have at times made it difficult for the women parliamentarians to pursue legislation pushed by the women's movement (Tripp 2000b).

Meanwhile, the women's movement became one of the major societal forces in Uganda and has played a significant role in improving the status of women. It has also addressed more general social justice issues and worked to advance the interests and rights of the poor, the disabled, children, and other more vulnerable groups. This extraordinary growth in women's influence had in part to do with the opening of political space in Uganda in the mid-1980s and the encouragement of the Museveni regime. The transformations also had to do with changing donor strategies that emphasized nongovernmental activities to a greater extent than in the past. The flourishing of women's organizations was tied to the growth of educational opportunities for women, which gave rise to stronger female leadership. The women's movement gained added impetus from the international women's movement, especially after the United Nations women's conferences in Nairobi (1985) and Beijing (1995). It was also spurred on by the use of the Internet, cellular phones, and other forms of communication technology. When viewed from a comparative African perspective, Uganda today is a leader in advancing women's rights in spite of the continuing challenges.

New nonpartisan women's organizations formed to improve leadership skills, encourage women's political involvement on a nonpartisan basis, lobby for women's political leadership, press for legislative changes, and conduct civic education. Groups mobilized around issues such as domestic violence, rape, reproductive rights, sex education in the school curriculum, female genital cutting, and the disparaging representation of women in the media. These were concerns that had rarely been addressed by the women's movements in the past and often were considered taboo by the government and even by society.

Today, the political impact of the women's movement is being felt in a number of arenas. From 1994 to 2003 Uganda had a woman vice president, Dr. Speciosa Wandira Kazibwe, making her the first female vice president in Africa. Women hold one-third of local council seats, which makes Uganda a leader worldwide in female representation in local government. Uganda also has 18 female ministers (26 percent) out of 69 cabinet ministers. Of these only 3 are full ministers, which women's groups argue is too few. Women, however, are not relegated to the ministries of education, community development, culture, and gender. One also finds a woman minister of state for defense (Ruth Nankabirwa), a minister of state for industry (Jennifer Namuyangu), a minister of security (Syda Bbumba), a minister for parliamentary affairs (Hope Mwesigye), and a minister of state for justice and constitutional affairs (Janat Mukwaya).

Women have made inroads into other areas of government appointments. The chief government negotiator in peace talks with rebels
in the north is Betty Bigombe. Since 1996 the head of Public Service
has been Florence Mugasha, and women claim 44 percent of the positions on the Public Service Commission. For fifteen years Hope Kiven-
gere served as President Museveni's press secretary. Elizabeth Kuteesa
is the first woman to direct the Criminal Investigation Department.
Edith Sempala heads the Ugandan Embassy in the United States. The
Supreme Court has 14 percent female judges, including the Honorable
Lady Justice Laetitia Mukasa-Kikonyogo. Women hold 25 percent of
all positions in the Court of Appeals and 26 percent in the High Court
and represent 30 percent of chief magistrates (Forum for Women in
Democracy 2000, 30). Margaret Kigozi was appointed executive director of the Uganda Investment Authority in 1999 and has been helping
to push for women's investment and entrepreneurship. About 40 percent of the money allocated for private sector development has been
earmarked for women investors, who have yet to take full advantage of
these opportunities.[3]

Several key commissions have also been chaired by women. For example, the Uganda Human Rights Commission has been led by Margaret
Sekaggya, and one-third of the members of the commission are women.
The no-nonsense Honorable Lady Justice Julia Sebutinde, a judge of the
High Court, directed the Judicial Commission of Inquiry into Corruption
in the Police Force. She uncovered serious cases of abuse, brutality, and
corruption all the way to the top in a relentless investigation. Her per-
formance was so remarkable that minibus drivers pinned her picture to
their windscreens to scare off policemen seeking bribes. As the hearings
unfolded, her name became a household word: "to Sebutinde someone"
became a popular way of talking about exposing lies.

Not surprisingly, there is widespread acceptance of a political role
for women in Uganda, which is borne out in a 2000 survey carried out
by the International Foundation for Election Systems. This survey
showed that 80 percent of women are registered to vote and 75 percent
participated in the 1996 elections. At least 86 percent of women and 73
percent of men felt it was important for women to be in government;
91 percent of men and 95 percent of women felt it was important for
women to be members of parliament; and 49 percent of men and 66
percent of women thought a woman can and should be president of
Uganda (Bratton et al. 2000).

Although the changes women have experienced in Uganda over the
past two decades have been enormous, many constraints on advancing

women's rights remain, and the challenges often seem daunting. Some activists have found that the possibilities for women's advancement began to shrink after 1995 as Museveni's Movement began to experience a drop in the widespread support it had enjoyed after Museveni first took over. The broad-based and antisectarian character of Museveni's NRM had initially appealed to many women voters along with his pro-women policies. But as the Movement's base began to appear more constricted, as government corruption became more rampant, and as Museveni's treatment of dissent became more intolerant and desperate, even some of his staunchest supporters began to waver. The NRM's backing for women's causes has also increasingly come into question.

Path to Political Office: The Selection of Women to Reserved Parliamentary Seats

The growing number of women in politics has been one of the biggest changes fostered by Museveni's Movement as a result of pressure from women's associations (see Table 5.1). In 1980 there was only one woman in parliament. In 1989 the Movement introduced reserved seats for women in each district, and by 2003 25 percent of parliamentary seats were held by women (in 2005 the figure was 23.9 percent). The use of reserved seats—one seat that only women compete for in each of Uganda's fifty-six districts—has contributed to a change in political culture so that today the population by and large accepts women as public figures.

The reservation of special seats for women has been a contentious issue in Uganda, as in other countries in Africa where such measures have been taken. Opponents of this policy tend to focus on the political motivations of the measure, arguing that it is simply a maneuver by the Movement to win women's votes and ensure a solid block of female NRM supporters in parliament. However, supporters of reserved seats believe it is a necessary but temporary measure to encourage women to enter political life and to make women politically visible so that the electorate will eventually become accustomed to voting for women as leaders. Today a growing number of people would argue that both arguments hold true.

One of the most important consequences of the reserved seats was to give women the exposure, political experience, and confidence to run on their own in open electoral races. Even at the national level, where women have greater public visibility than at the local level, the

Table 5.1 Women in Elected Office in Uganda, 1962–2001

	1962	1967	1980	1989	1996	2001
MPs	90	82	126	238	276	304
Women MPs	2	0	1	42	52	75
% of women MPs	2.2	0	0.7	17.6	19.0	24.7
Women running for parliament					135	203
Women running for constituency seats	N/A	N/A	N/A		26	32
Women in district reserved seats for women	N/A	N/A	N/A	34	39	56
Women winning constituency seats	N/A	N/A	1	2	8	13
Women in youth seats (reserved)	N/A	N/A	N/A			2/5
Women in organized labor seats (reserved)	N/A	N/A	N/A			1/3
Women in seats for persons with disabilities (reserved)	N/A	N/A	N/A			2/5
Women in seats for the army (reserved)	N/A	N/A	N/A	0/10		0/10
Women ex officio (unelected cabinet ministers)	N/A	N/A	N/A			1/11
Women in seats for historic members of NRM	N/A	N/A	N/A	1/24		
Women presidential appointments				1		

Source: Cabinet Library.
Note: N/A is not applicable.

obstacles to women's full participation in the political arena are daunting. For example, female parliamentary candidates face a myriad of cultural prohibitions on political activity not experienced by their male counterparts. Married women politicians often find it difficult to find a constituency to run in: If they run in the constituency where they were born, they are told to go to the constituency where they are married. When a woman runs in her husband's constituency, she is told: "You came here to marry, not to rule."

Women candidates have to project an image of absolute devotion to their husbands and family and of being a good wife and mother, to a degree not required of men. As a woman parliamentary aspirant put it: "If you are intending to become a woman candidate to contest a seat, you can't put on shorts or trousers and go to the village. You have to wear a *gomezi* [formal women's attire], you have to look like a good girl, mommy's good girl. For the men, they can go away and drink their *malwa* [alcoholic drink] in the most unexpected place, they can run around with so many women and nobody bothers. It's patriarchal."[4]

In media interviews, journalists tend to be preoccupied with questions of whether the woman is properly married and how many children she has. Single women spend much of their time during their campaigns defending their single status. Divorcees face similar suspicions. If a woman receives assistance from a man in a campaign, almost inevitably an inference of a sexual favor will be drawn, which usually has no basis in reality (Kasente 1994). This makes it difficult for women to enter male political networks, and it also makes it difficult for men to support female candidates.

In general women candidates face greater public ridicule than men; they are labeled "unfeminine," and some even risk their marriages and public discrediting by their husbands. In one case a husband even nominated his wife's rival to run against her (Mugambe 1996, 32–33). Female politicians are attacked for being elite and building their careers at the expense of rural women, while male candidates are never berated for such reasons (Opondo 1993).[5]

Women are also at a disadvantage because they often lack the necessary resources to run. Candidates are expected to distribute beer, give small gifts, and make contributions to fund-raisers, funerals, weddings, and community projects. Women are usually not incumbents, which also puts them at a disadvantage. Incumbents have had a chance to use their positions to build roads, bridges, hospitals, clinics, schools, and churches and in this way win votes.

Once in parliament, where there are many vocal women representatives, women experience discrimination, although this situation is slowly changing as more women win parliamentary seats. In 1992 Loi Kageni Kiryapawo, women's representative of Tororo, put it bluntly: "In our case, when we are supposed to represent the interests of women, we are always shut down by the men. In most cases their reaction is negative, and since they make up the majority of the House, their decisions are always paramount."[6] Gradually these kinds of attitudes are being challenged and are changing. A study conducted by the *Monitor* newspaper of the 1996 parliamentary sessions found that in fact two out of the three most active parliamentarians were women.[7] Women have moderately good representation in the Standing and Sessional Committees (see Table 5.2), but in terms of leadership there is still an imbalance.

Table 5.2 Women in Standing and Sessional Committees

Standing Committee	Women (%)
Public Account	0
Budget	26
Rules, Privileges, and Discipline	6
National Economy	13
Commissions, Statutory Authorities, and Enterprise	26
Government Assurances	33
Local Governments Accounts	40
Business and Welfare	50
Appointments	32
HIV/AIDS and Related Matters	53
Science and Technology	27
Equal Opportunity	40

Sessional Committees	Women (%)
Agriculture, Animal Industry, and Fishery	23
Defense and Internal Affairs	—
Presidential and Foreign Affairs	35
Natural Resources	25
Public Service and Local Government	28
Tourism, Trade, and Industry	29
Works, Housing, and Communications	4
Social Welfare	46
Legal and Parliamentary Affairs	15
Finance, Planning, and Economic Development	21

Source: Hanssen 2003, 96.

Women serve as chairs of two out of twelve Standing Committees, although they are well represented in these committees (29 percent) to which they are elected. They have slightly better representation in leadership of Sessional Committees, chairing two out of ten committees.

Impact of Women in Office: Women Parliamentarians and Museveni's Movement

Many women parliamentarians feel that they owe their positions to Museveni and the existing patronage system. While the relatively large number of women in parliament has in many ways been an indication of the success of women's lobbying for greater representation, many of the elected women officials have been restrained from supporting women's issues. As one women's activist put it: "Our voice has been hijacked at the highest organs, at parliament. Our voice there has been killed."[8] Some argue that the affirmative action seats in parliament have created a group of legislators more beholden to the NRM in their loyalties than to the cause of women's emancipation (Tamale 1999). In the 2001 parliamentary elections, only two of the women elected for the women's seats were not part of Museveni's movement.

Similarly, Sylvia Tamale observed that half the women she interviewed who won the June 1996 parliamentary race had served on Museveni's campaign team in their districts. They saw allying themselves with the NRM as a way of garnering favors, and MPs were promised high positions in return for their loyalty. Women MPs made up the core of the parliamentary NRM caucus that lobbies for the NRM position in the parliament. NRM patronage politics played a role in several electoral victories of female NRM loyalists and was especially evident in the way that those who contested the outcomes of various races watched helplessly as the courts dismissed one petition after another in favor of NRM loyalists (Tamale 1999).

It is widely believed that these representatives are controlled by the Movement and that the women's seats are a gift of the Movement to women and thus an extension of government influence in parliament, even though the women ran for the seats independent of any official party endorsement (Hanssen 2003, 52).

One woman opposition leader explained: "Many of them [affirmative action women] will rather go by the position of the Government because they look to the Government as the only agency that has brought them where they are. So, in other words, we are now turning our affirmative action into patronage. That defeats the whole purpose of affirmative action" (Hanssen 2003, 68). This quid pro quo was underscored by President Museveni himself, who has implied that he regards the district women parliamentarians as being among his supporters. Museveni told journalists after the 2001 parliamentary elections: "I called to tell you how happy I am about defeating your friends the so called multipartyists. By yesterday I had counted more than 170 Movement MPs directly elected out of 214, if you add women, workers, youth and other, I have more than 230 MPs out of a house of 292."[9] It is also interesting to note that four out of the nine of the women elected in direct elections do not associate themselves with the Movement, including Winnie Byanima (Reform Agenda), Cecilia Ogwal (Uganda

People's Congress), Juliet Rainer Kafire (Democratic Party), and Proscovia Musumba Salaamu. Although this is too small a number from which to draw broad conclusions, it does suggest that these women are less likely to feel beholden to the Movement.

Role of the Electoral College

One factor that accounts for the consolidation of parliamentary loyalties is the fact that the district women representatives in parliament are elected by an electoral college whose members can potentially be manipulated through bribery and vote-buying. The electoral college that elects the women affirmative action candidates consists of councilors from the women's councils and local councils (LCs). Uganda has a hierarchical system in which all adults belong to their village LC and elect nine members to the executive committee at the first level, LC1. All LC1 executive committees in a parish form LC2. LC3 is formed similarly out of the LC2s at the subcounty level, and the LC3s form LC5 at the district level, skipping the county level. A similar structure of women's councils parallels the local council system.

According to the 1996 Parliamentary Elections Statute, women running for the reserved seats were to be elected from the councilors in LC1, LC2, and LC3 in the district and all members of the parish and subcounty women's councils rather than through universal suffrage, as other members of parliament are elected. A woman candidate is first nominated by two registered voters. She then gets a list of names signed by a minimum of ten registered voters in her constituency and pays a nomination fee of 200,000 Uganda shillings. However, unlike other parliamentarians, the women are elected on a districtwide basis rather than in their own county, which means that their constituency is potentially ten or more times larger than that of other parliamentarians (Kalebbo 1996, 16).

In contrast, other interest groups (youth, disabled, workers, and the army) with special reserved seats in parliament directly elect their own representatives through their own organizations. Women district representatives, however, are not representatives of women but rather are supposed to be women representatives for the district, which has translated into a different mode of election. People seem to be unclear as to whom the district women representatives actually represent. Opponents of the electoral college argue that universal adult suffrage would require women to campaign throughout the district in the same way that other MPs do when they seek election and feel accountable to a constituency.

Instead, the affirmative action parliamentarians are often seen as women Movement representatives rather than women representatives of the people.

It is thought that one reason women cannot be elected in the same way as other groups has to do with the strength and autonomy of the women's movement, which although it has been generally supportive of the Movement has also shown itself to take positions that are at odds with it and therefore cannot be counted on to automatically go along with the Movement (Hanssen 2003, 65). As the largest single special interest group represented in parliament it is especially important to the Movement to ensure that women parliamentarians are in tow.

Debates on the Electoral College

Activists within the women's movement have sought to implement universal adult suffrage for the women's seats. Efforts to open the election process to universal suffrage through a Parliamentary Election Bill were voted down as a result of pressure from the president, who argued that it would be too difficult and expensive for women to canvass votes around an entire district (Tegulle 2001). The vote on the electoral college came on the heels of a parliamentary election, which meant that many parliamentarians may have been swayed to vote to retain the electoral college for women's seats because they feared loss of backing by the president in their bid for reelection.

Leading up to the ill-fated legislation was considerable debate over the use of the electoral college in electing women parliamentarians. Some have suggested that an electoral college is easier to influence than an electorate, while others are convinced that the electoral college is made up of people who are better educated and informed than the citizens and are less easily bought off with little gifts of salt and sugar. They claim that the majority of people do not know what is best for them (Byanyima 1996, 15). Women already face financial limits, domestic demands, and cultural biases and therefore, according to this argument, should not be subjected to the broader electorate's vote (Kwesiga 1996, 26).

Others point out that the electoral college privileges wealthier women who have an easier time swaying a smaller electoral college. This situation lends itself more easily to corruption and the buying of votes (Waliggo 1996, 4). In the case of Kamuli District, Bugabula women were able to affect the outcome of the direct election for the women's representative for the Constituent Assembly, forcing a well-known candidate,

Rebecca Kadaga, to run in a neighboring constituency, where she lost. She had fallen out of favor for not having taken steps to pressure local authorities who had enabled a huckster to cheat a large women's organization in the area. However, when Kadaga ran for the position of women's representative for Kamuli in 1996, the women who had voted her out in the previous election had no impact.

Critics such as Father John Waliggo, secretary of the Constitutional Commission and member of the Human Rights Commission, argued that being elected by the whole district would give women representatives greater legitimacy and the capacity to challenge the member of the parliament in his or her constituency if necessary. If the candidate represented the entire district, her authority would be enhanced. In fact, some male members of parliament fear universal suffrage for the very reason that they fear the women candidates might "interfere" with their constituency.

Another critic of the electoral college system for women's representatives, former MP Winnie Byanyima, has argued that the women members of parliament cannot legitimately speak on behalf of their constituents if they represent only the views of the electoral college (Byanyima 1996, 15). She argued that women should be elected by all women in the district and not by men. This would give them a mandate to make sure that laws take women into account and promote equal opportunity for all. Moreover, as Joy Kwesiga points out, other special groups such as soldiers, people with disabilities, workers, and youth all elect their own representatives, whereas women's parliamentary representatives are elected by male and female local council representatives at the village, parish, and subcounty levels, with the implication that women are too politically immature to vote for themselves (Kwesiga 1996, 27).

Because the local councils elect the women representatives, Kwesiga points out, it is not clear whom these women parliamentarians represent. If they claim to represent the entire district, they are often told that they are representing only the women, even though they are elected by both men and women.

The other problem observers have noted is that the electoral college is susceptible to pressure because it is made up of a relatively small number people who can easily be bribed and influenced. Some men were careful to keep out candidates who explicitly took up women's causes.[10] Because there are few women on the electoral college, it is easy for more powerful men to subject the women in the college to intimidation because it is not difficult to figure out how they voted. Thus, women who were not wealthy also found themselves at a disadvantage (Okurut 1995).

Multipartyists and others raised yet another set of objections. They felt that the electoral colleges are primarily made up of Movement supporters and therefore would vote primarily for Movement representatives, even in areas made up mainly of multiparty supporters. They claimed that the electoral college is especially susceptible to corrupt methods of persuasion, making it a less democratic institution. When the electoral bill was passed, the Uganda People's Congress–Democratic Party opposition coalition, the Inter Party Cooperation, challenged the method of election in a press release that stated: "In a country where the local councils have become appendages and organs of the NRM, it would appear as if all the Women District Parliamentarians have been truly given to the NRM with both hands" (cited in Tripp 2000b, 232). In spite of these and other objections the electoral college system has prevailed.

Impact of Reserved Seats on Pro-Women Legislation

Since the electoral colleges are primarily made up of supporters of the president, it is unlikely that they will vote for anyone who would be openly at odds with the Movement even around legislation supporting women. This was evident in the lack of support among key women MPs around amendments to the 1998 Land Act as it pertained to women.

The 1998 Land Act was passed to create a system of tenure, ownership, and administration of land. It also aimed to improve land service delivery by decentralizing land administration. Women activists made sure that key clauses to protect women were included in the act. However, one key clause was omitted, so in the period leading up to the passage of the 2000 amendments to the Land Act, women's rights activists and organizations lobbied without success for the inclusion of a co-ownership clause.[11] They networked under the aegis of the Uganda Women's Network (UWONET) and the Uganda Land Alliance (ULA) and coordinated lobbying efforts.

The insistence on the co-ownership clause stems from the fact that current legislation, given customary practices, provides limited possibilities for women to own land. In patrilineal societies, which are most prevalent in Uganda, women generally do not inherit land from either their fathers or their husbands. Their fathers often do not bequeath land to their daughters because daughters marry outside the clan, and they will therefore take the land with them to another clan. Husbands often do not bequeath land to their wives for the same reason: They need to ensure that the land remains in the clan because they worry that the widow might sell the land to non–clan members. In some societies in Uganda, if the husband dies, the wife and children are inherited by the husband's brother or another family member so that he may provide for them. This practice is dying out, raising fears that if a widow remarries outside the clan, the clan land she has acquired will be lost. Thus, under customary law, which prevails in Uganda, a woman may have jointly acquired land with her husband and may have spent her entire adult life cultivating the land, but she cannot claim ownership of the property. If her husband dies, the land generally goes to the sons but may also be left to daughters. Nevertheless, the husband may still leave the wife with no land and therefore no source of subsistence.

The struggle over the co-ownership clause was a turning point in many ways for the women's movement. Until this conflict the women's movement had been fairly enthusiastic about President Museveni and his pro-women policies. They had seen his Movement as a force for change for Ugandan women. As a result of Museveni's failure to back the clause, many in the women's movement became seriously disillusioned with the government's positions regarding women's rights. In May 2003 the leading women's rights organizations held a demonstration around land rights that was led by an opposition parliamentarian from northern Uganda, Nobert Mao. The new realization forced women to rethink their strategies and allegiances. It put loyalties of key women politicians to the test and forced them to make difficult choices between support for the women's movement and a political career endorsed by the president and his Movement.

The co-ownership amendments were, in fact, passed by the parliament, but political maneuvering on the grounds of technicalities left women without the clause. MP and ethics minister Miria Matembe was about to read the amendments into the microphone for the *Hansard* (legislative record) when she was interrupted in midsentence by someone who said they were finished and that she did not need to read them. Later she was told that because she had not read the clauses into the microphone, they could not be included in the *Hansard* and hence in the amendments to the Land Act. As she explained in her book (Matembe 2002, 151): "I want to make one thing clear. If this had not been an amendment to give women their due rights, if this had had to do with things that the male MPs consider important, Parliament would have found a way to bring the matter back for more review. They would have said, this is just a technicality, and the provisions would have found their way into that law."

In February 2000, when the minister of state for lands brought the amendments to the Land Act before the cabinet, it was the president, by his own omission, who decided to pull out the co-ownership clause. He explained that he foresaw a disaster and advised his ministers to go slowly or pass the clause along for consideration with the pending Domestic Relations Bill (DRB). "When I learnt that the Bill was empowering the newly-married women to share the properties of the husbands, I smelt a disaster and advised for slow and careful analysis of the property sharing issue," Museveni said.[12] Women activists argued that moving the clause to another bill was unconstitutional because the decision should not have been made unilaterally by the executive but rather should have been put to the House. It was believed that the president's decision to shift the clause to the DRB was intended to save face so that the government would not appear antiwoman. But the effect would be to remove the issue from the agenda altogether. As the then ULA leader Jacqueline Asiimwe explained: "The DRB is already riddled with controversy over marital rape, regulation of polygamy, declaring the payment of bride price as no longer necessary in contracting a customary marriage, even the age of marriage. . . . And so we saw it as dangerous to add another clause that in essence would lock debate on the whole bill."[13]

Women activists were furious about the removal of the co-ownership clause from the amendments to the Land Act. They held protests and public days of mourning. In 2003 they launched one more unsuccessful initiative to pass an amendment to the Land Act giving all family members rights to family land. A coalition of land rights activists and women's organizations had convinced the Parliamentary Committee on Natural Resources to include a clause requiring joint registration of family land in the names of spouses and dependent children. The clause met stiff resistance in parliament, and there were strong allegations that the president had sent a directive to cabinet members and key Movement MPs warning them not to pass the Land Act amendments with the family land rights clause.[14]

Opposition to the co-ownership clause came from the then vice president and woman parliamentarian Specioza Wandira Kazibwe as well as key women ministers. Kazibwe in particular incensed women leaders of the Uganda Land Alliance when she met with them on December 7, 2000, to explain why she opposed their demand for a clause in the Land Act that would permit women to co-own land with their spouses. She told them that women need only access to rather than control of land.

In response to Kazibwe's statements at the time, UWONET had issued a communique saying:

> We cannot see ourselves being sacrificed by people who want to selfishly protect the little they have achieved through opportunities availed to them by the system that are at the expense of the majority of women in this country that are toiling to meet their daily needs. Together with the majority of members of the Uganda Land Alliance, the Women's Movement and UWONET, we would like to call upon you to rise up against the Government Position to disenable women in this country. We should make our issues political and not watch a few people grabbing and trampling over our rights.[15]

Impact of Reserved Seats for Women on Antidemocratic Legislation

The electoral college for women not only affects legislation concerning women, it also has implications for mobilizing support for antidemocratic and unpopular measures. A highly controversial Political Parties and Organizations Bill that curtailed non-Movement opposition party activities, especially at the local level, was passed on June 7, 2002, after much contestation. The act was later contested in the Constitutional Court by the Democratic Party, which in 2003 succeeded in getting its most restrictive clauses overturned. In trying to build support for this bill, women parliamentarians were targeted. The then vice president, Specioza Wandira Kazibwe, held a meeting with women MPs who were loyal to the president. According to the women who attended, she asked them to always remain loyal to the government and reminded them of how the Movement was responsible for the large number of women who came into parliament through its deliberate policy of empowering women. One of the members of parliament reported that Kazibwe tried not to anger the women, saying that it would be unfair if the women did not support the president in times of need. As one parliamentarian put it: "She indirectly told us that the Movement helped us to be in Parliament."[16] Women parliamentarians have been similarly targeted regarding matters such as the hotly debated third term for the president and other controversial legislation.

Impact of Electoral College on District Politics

The electoral college system has also influenced the selection of women candidates who adopt women's rights positions that are unpopular with local male leaders. Although this is not a conscious subversion of the affirmative action process, it may have this consequence because the majority of electoral college members can be relatively easily bribed or influenced by a few individuals to select women leaders who will not challenge the gender status quo.

The manipulations of the electoral college were evident in the 2001 elections in Kapchorwa district. For example, Makerere University sociologist Fred Bateganya suggested that the electoral college system prevented a candidate from winning the 2001 women's seat in Kapchorwa because she opposed female genital cutting. The candidate was a former minister of state and parliamentarian, Frances Kuka, who had been an active crusader in trying to abolish female genital cutting in Kapchorwa, the only district in Uganda where it is practiced. Because of the pressure brought to bear by the relatively few men who controlled the electoral college, Bateganya explained, "both the winner and loser in this election became prisoners of male norms and hegemony" (Bateganya 2002). Thus, in Kapchorwa the electoral system prevented Kuka from winning an election in a constituency where the majority opinion had turned against female genital cutting. Kuka lost her seat to Gertrude Kulany.

Interestingly, two years after claiming the Kapchorwa woman's seat, MP Gertrude Kulany, who in the past had been adamant in her opposition to abolishing the practice, succumbed to popular pressure. In 2003 she announced plans to introduce a bill to parliament that would make it a crime for someone to abet, intimidate, or force women and girls to undergo this practice.[17] Several NGOs, including the Family Planning Association of Uganda and the Reproductive Education and Community Health Project, had been working with community members to educate them about the practice, and they were planning to lobby members of parliament. The number of girls who undergo the practice has been reduced since the mid-1990s by 46 percent to about three hundred to four hundred per year in 2002.[18]

In this way the electoral college has implications both for women's issues and for broader questions of the future of democracy in Uganda. It is the mechanism that tied women parliamentarians to the Movement, and one that draws on patronage to keep women in power (Goetz 2002).

Other Influences of Women Parliamentarians

Overall, women parliamentarians' ability to use the parliament to advance women's causes has been mixed. Women have fought to change rape, sexual offense, and defilement laws and to influence the Land Act.

They tried to pass a Domestic Relations Bill, which addressed issues of inheritance and succession as well as the regulation of polygamy, payment of bride price, and the age of marriage. The bill, which was highly controversial, was not introduced in parliament for decades. The Uganda Women Parliamentary Association (UWOPA) and the Coalition on the Domestic Relations Bill initiated a new campaign in 2002 to lobby for the bill; however, it was put on the back burner by Museveni, who felt that it might not be passed into law because it was not urgent and because of the complaints from the Muslim community and from other members of the public.

Overall, the record of legislative change regarding women's concerns has been unimpressive. This can be attributed to the weakness of the legislature relative to the executive, a weak tradition of lobbying and advocacy, and the loyalties of many of the parliamentarians, which do not lie primarily with the women's movement. Moreover, parliamentarians face little pressure from constituents on gender issues, and women's organizations do not generally work directly with specific constituencies to get them to influence their parliamentary representatives.

Responses of the Women's Movement to Political Manipulation of Women Parliamentarians

Women's organizations have responded to the use of women parliamentarians by openly declaring that they will not allow manipulation by politicians in the debates over the political future of the country as Uganda began moving toward multipartyism in 2004. The head of the National Association of Women's Organizations of Uganda, Rosemary Najjemba, explained: "We shall work tirelessly to remain intact. . . . We shall not allow the misuse of our structures by hungry politicians. We shall not be divided by the political issues of the day" (Ssettumba 2004).

In 2003 President Museveni suggested that he might seek a constitutional amendment that would allow him to seek a third term. Some of the most vocal critics of Museveni's bid for a third term have come from the women's movement and have included affirmative action women parliamentarians such as Miria Matembe (Mbarara), Alice Alaso (Soroti), and Betty Amongi (Apac).

Meanwhile, Museveni's Movement has been pressuring women to support his bid for a third term. Movement officials announced in March 2005 that they would form a Women's League to advocate for a third term for Museveni and to promote Movement ideologies. Earlier, a *New Vision* article (February 18, 2004) had reported that LC5 women councilors from the twelve districts of eastern Uganda had unanimously passed the recommendation for the third term. This report met with resistance from key women members of parliament. At a UWOPA meeting the Honorable Amongi stated: "We disassociate ourselves with the resolution that the president should stand for a third term. We are principled and we want to ensure that nobody abrogates the Constitution. So the report in the *New Vision* was entirely wrong. . . . We did not discuss the third term at all. Whoever authored the story had selfish interests. For us we stand for constitutionalism." MP Alaso added: "It's wrong for legislators to make laws and later manipulate them to achieve personal interests" (Mutaizibwa and Obore 2003).

The Uganda Women's Network has rejected lifting the two-term limit on the grounds that the proposal represents a threat to democracy. UWONET member and former coordinator Jacqueline Asiimwe said: "Women in this country must make a bold and open stand for constitutionalism and should reject the present threat to democracy by those seeking the president." Various women's organizations have joined with MPs in a coalition to make sure women's interests are not sidelined with the transition to multipartyism. They are also demanding 40–50 percent representation in the cabinet and at all other levels of government (Namutebi and Ariko 2004).

Leaders of the independent women's organizations have been mobilizing to protest the proposed lifting of presidential term limits. For example, eighteen high-profile women activists went to parliament in December 2004 to express their opposition to the constitutional amendment pertaining to presidential terms, also known as *kisanja* (dry banana leaves). Over ninety-six civil society organizations that make up a Coalition on Constitutional Amendment (CCA), led by UWONET coordinator Solome Nakawesi, have opposed the lifting of presidential terms. Nakawesi said: "Lifting term limits is to ignore the lives lost and persons displaced through misrule."[19]

These are brave statements given past consequences for those who openly oppose the Movement leadership. In the 2001 parliamentary elections three prominent women candidates were singled out by President Museveni and the Movement secretariat as targets of physical and emotional violence against themselves, their agents, and their supporters. The women's association Action for Development protested the treatment of these candidates, arguing that it could "grossly undermine the future participation of capable women in Uganda's politics" (ACFODE 2001). Some groups had wanted to come out in support of one of the candidates, Winnie Byanyima, against the attacks but were fearful because they thought they would be labeled multipartyists. As one activist put it: "You can feel the fear. They will start thinking . . . that we are being used by multipartyists."[20]

Nonpartisan organizations often find themselves concerned about who should represent their association publicly and may opt for a known movement supporter so as not to be seen as antigovernmental. As one activist explained to me in 2001: "But as the years have gone by, the same mistakes from the past are being repeated. When I listen to people campaigning and mudslinging, not being tolerant with each other, we are going back to the same thing. The NRM, the Movement, has become very intolerant, which is a pity. I think people have become disillusioned, especially those who had a lot of hope that these were changes for the better. We are moving backward instead of forward. Something has happened, which is not right."[21]

The lack of a commitment to democratic reform, an antiwoman agenda, and heightened corruption have led some of Museveni's closest female supporters to break ranks, including parliamentarians Winnie Byanyima and Miria Matembe. Byanyima is a leader in the Reform Agenda party led by her husband, Col. Kiza Besigye. In 2005 Byanyima resigned from the parliament to take a new job as the African Union's director for women, gender, and development. Miria Matembe has become a leader in the movement against Museveni's pursuit of a third term. Both have been outspoken opponents of corruption within the regime.

Future Directions

By the mid-2000s Uganda was moving toward multipartyism. There were few signs that this shift was intended to further democratization, but it did serve to galvanize the women's movement, which was intent on not losing further ground. Many had become disillusioned by the lack of progress made under the Museveni regime, which started out promising so much to women and apparently being open to women's mobilization and leadership.

Instead, today women have little legislation (apart from the 1995 constitution) they can point to that suggests a sustained commitment to advancing women's status. The disappointments have been many (e.g., the loss of the co-ownership clause of the Land Act). Moreover, the presence of women parliamentarians in reserved seats has ended up serving the Movement rather than the women's movement. Those who were extremely loyal to Museveni were less likely to take up women's causes that might force them to oppose his NRM. Women who were appointed to top positions in the cabinet and ministries found themselves silenced around key women's issues, even issues that were dear to their hearts. Those who continued to be outspoken were warned, demoted, or thrown out of their positions.

The broader constraints on democratization in Uganda are closely tied to the limits on women's mobilization. Even though there is considerably more space for organizations to mobilize than under previous regimes, the continuing suspicions of autonomous collective action and the fear of political opposition bear a strong resemblance to Africa's older single-party regimes. The lack of political freedom has become the biggest constraint on women's advancement, and as long as women parliamentarians are serving the continuance of patronage politics, women are not going to make fundamental progress. The fact that there continue to be independent and outspoken voices for change in the status quo suggests that the women's movement is rising to meet some of these onerous challenges.

Notes

1. The research resulted in numerous publications, including Tripp 2000b, 2001b, 2002, 2004a, 2004b; Tripp and Kwesiga 2002.

2. Maxine Ankrah, interview by the author in Kampala, June 19, 1992.

3. "UIA in New Push for Women Investors," *Monitor* (Kampala), June 21, 2001.

4. "Politician hubby snatchers should be censored," *Monitor* (Kampala), May 8, 1996.

5. Honorable Rebecca Kadaga, interview by the author in Kampala, April 24, 1993.

6. "The Task Ahead for a Woman Legislator," *Arise* 5 (1992): 16–17.

7. "Focus on Parliament," *Monitor,* June 18, 2001, 1, 15.

8. S. K., interview by the author in Kampala, June 19, 2001.

9. *Monitor*, July 11, 2001.

10. "Who Is a Politician?" *Arise* 19 (October–December 1996): 18; "Out of the House, but Still a Politician?" *Arise* 19 (October–December 1996): 21.

11. Actually, four clauses were being contested. These included (1) an individual bringing land into the marriage can continue to own that land after marriage; (2) in monogamous marriages, home and land used for sustenance by a couple are to be co-owned.; (3) in polygamous marriage where each wife has a separate home, each woman would co-own with her husband her home and the piece of land that sustains her and her children; (4) wives living in the

same house with their husbands would co-own the single home and land together with the other women.

12. "Share Parent's Property, Museveni Tells Women," *New Vision* (Kampala), May 10, 2000.

13. Jacqueline Asiimwe, personal communication, September 27, 2000.

14. "Activists Toughen on Family Land Rights," *New Vision,* April 22, 2003.

15. "UWONET Response to Vice-President's Comments on Co-Ownership," LandWeb Features/December 2000/No7. http://www.mwengo.org/land/features-dec00.htm.

16. "Uganda: Movement Targets Women MPs to Keep Party Ban," *Monitor*, February 22, 2002.

17. "MPs to Fight Sebei Female Circumcision," *New Vision*, July 24, 2003.

18. Figures based on comments made by Frances Kuka at the 8th International Interdisciplinary Congress on Women, Makerere University, Kampala, Uganda, July 21, 2002.

19. "NGOs Oppose 3rd Term," *New Vision,* March 7, 2005.

20. M. M., interview by the author in Kampala, June 9, 2001.

21. Ibid.

6

Rwanda: Achieving Equality or Serving an Authoritarian State?

Timothy Longman

As a result of elections held in September and October 2003, Rwanda displaced Sweden as the country with the world's highest percentage of women in its lower or single house of parliament. The 48.8 percent of seats won by women in the 2003 election for the Chamber of Deputies marked the culmination of a trend of increased representation for women that had begun with the emergence of a democracy movement in the early 1990s. Since before the 1994 genocide, women have used their strong presence in Rwandan civil society as a basis for entering politics, while the specific situation for women in postgenocide Rwanda has drawn many more women into the political arena. The most significant explanation for the growth in women's representation, however, has been a strong commitment on the part of the postgenocide government to the inclusion of women and the expansion of women's rights.

While women have assumed numerous important executive, legislative, and judicial positions in Rwanda since 1994, the increasingly authoritarian nature of the Rwandan government raises serious questions about the meaning of women's participation in a nondemocratic political system. Although much of the literature on women's political participation in Rwanda, as in much of the world, waxes poetic on the greater commitment of women to peace and reconciliation (Powley 2003; Quick 2001; United Nations Development Fund for Women [UNIFEM] 2004), women politicians in Rwanda are in fact participating in the adoption and implementation of policies that are compromising individual liberties and increasing national and international insecurity.

A Brief Overview of Women's
Political Participation in Rwanda

Colonialism in Rwanda, as in many African states, undermined women's social, economic, and political power. In precolonial Rwanda, men dominated most aspects of public life, but women did enjoy several significant avenues of power. Women could hold powerful positions within the religious realm, serving as spirit mediums and priestesses in the Kubandwa cults (Berger 1981) or as traditional healers. Although men occupied most official political positions, women did have political influence. As Learthen Dorsey explains (1994, 345), the most important female political figure, the queen mother, *umugabekasi,* "was a powerful figure in her own right at the *umwami*'s court. While she lived at court, she generally had her own lands, herds of cattle, and clients." The king and the queen mother came from different clans, guaranteeing a degree of distribution of power in the kingdom of Rwanda. Queen mothers were often influential in court intrigue and played a major role in determining royal succession (Newbury 1988, 57–59).

Colonial rule effectively undermined even these limited avenues of power for women. The colonial administration centralized the political system, incorporating autonomous areas into the central kingdom and eliminating the complex system of overlapping chieftaincies that helped distribute power. The introduction of Christianity, supported by state policies that drove indigenous religions underground, undermined women's access to religious authority. Colonial laws and policies also undermined women's economic rights and opportunities. As Elizabeth Powley explains (2003, 10): "It is important to note that the dominant image of female political leadership to emerge from the colonial period is that of treacherous and illegitimate authority."

Rwanda gained independence in 1962 shortly after an ethnically based uprising by the majority Hutu group against the minority Tutsi, whom colonial authorities had used as their agents in indirect rule and given exclusive rights to economic, social, and political power. While the postindependence government articulated a revolutionary rhetoric, claiming to empower the common people who had previously been exploited, it was in many ways quite conservative, closely tied to the powerful Catholic Church. The regime took little interest in women's empowerment, and women were unrepresented in the government. The coup d'état that brought army chief Juvénal Habyarimana to power in 1973 had little impact on the position of women in Rwanda, as the new president also advanced a conservative social agenda that did nothing to improve women's specific economic, social, and political power.

The general situation for women in postindependence Rwanda, ranging from their access to political power to their position in the family, was therefore quite poor. As progressive priest and human rights activist André Sibomana explained shortly after the 1994 genocide: "Rwandan women have an unenviable status. They are completely subjected to the authority of their husband and of their community. They do the bulk of the domestic work and work on the land. They often seem to carry life on their shoulders and in their bodies like an unbearable burden" (1999, 31). Villia Jefremovas points out that difficulties for women are rooted not simply in culture but in law as well: "Legally, married women in Rwanda had severely circumscribed rights. They could vote, but their husbands' consent was required for them to engage in commerce, register a business, buy land, act as a witness, or undertake court action. . . . In principle, unmarried women had full legal status under Rwandan law; however, socially they were wards of their fathers and brothers" (2002, 98–99).

Since the 1980s women's involvement in civil society has served as a base for expanded social and political empowerment that has helped to increase women's representation in parliament and other government institutions. Postindependence Rwanda initially had a very weak civil society. The Habyarimana regime established a single political party in 1975, the National Republican Movement for Democracy and Development (MRND) that sought to subsume all political and social activity under its umbrella, including women's organizations. Women were involved in organizations sponsored by the party-state, such as the formerly independent consumer's cooperative, Trafipiro, but these provided few opportunities for women's empowerment, while the official women's group of the party promoted a conservative image of women's role in society that restricted women to the private realm and encouraged their obedience to their husbands.

In the 1980s and early 1990s Rwandans formed numerous organizations outside party-state control. Most of these organizations were not overtly political but responded to very practical social needs, yet they created a social space independent of the party-state and helped to create a thriving civil society. Women, driven by economic necessity, were a primary force behind the development of Rwandan civil society. Because of an economic downturn that resulted from overpopulation, the collapse of coffee prices, and government incompetence and corruption, much of civil society organizing focused on economic issues. Churches and other organizations sponsored development cooperatives and other economic projects both at the local and national levels, and women, who were largely neglected by government-sponsored development programs, became a major constituent of these groups (Longman 1999). During this period women founded a number of important groups focused specifically on women's interests and rights, such as Duterembere, a women's credit association; Haguruka, a women's legal aid society; and Reseau des Femmes, a network of women's development groups throughout Rwanda.

Beginning in 1989 Rwanda's civil society became active in a movement to demand democratization and political reform in the country. Women took prominent positions in more overtly political civil society organizations, such as new human rights groups. For example, after mass arrests following an attack on Rwanda in October 1990, Monique Mujawamariya organized the Rwandan Association for Human Rights and Civil Liberties and became its executive secretary.[1] Women were among the activists who pressured the government to reform, and when the MRND gave up its political monopoly in 1991 women became leaders in several of the new opposition political parties. Agathe Uwilingiyimana, a moderate Hutu official in the Ministry of Commerce and activist in the Democratic and Republican Movement (MDR), was named minister of education in the first multiparty government in March 1992, and in July 1993 she was named prime minister, making her the third female prime minister in Africa, after Elisabeth Domitien in the Central African Republic in the 1970s and Sylvie Kinigi, named a week earlier in neighboring Burundi.

Women in the Rwandan Genocide and Its Aftermath

The 1994 genocide was organized by a group of powerful government officials, military officers, and businesspeople from the Hutu majority group who sought to use violence to reverse the political reforms of the preceding years and reassert their political power. The violence they launched targeted moderate Hutu, including opposition political party leaders and civil society activists, as well as all members of the Tutsi minority group, who were considered accomplices of the invading Rwandan Patriotic Front (RPF).[2] The anti-Tutsi violence surrounding independence, which brought a Hutu majority government to power, and continuing violence against Tutsi in the early 1960s and again in 1973 had targeted primarily men while sparing women. In sharp contrast, in the 1994 genocide women were specifically targeted, and sexual violence was rampant. The violence in 1994 was much more widespread than anything known in Rwanda before, in part because of the strong ideology used to encourage it and the elimination of limits that had previously protected women, children, and the elderly. In fact, the ideology that promoted the genocide portrayed Tutsi women as seductresses who would use their sexuality to trick and entrap Hutu men, and it called Hutu who married or associated with Tutsi women traitors. Such imagery ultimately promoted sexual violence against women, which was used extensively as a weapon in the genocide (Nowrojee 1996).[3]

Christopher Taylor (1999) argues that the widespread sexual violence during the genocide represented in part a backlash against the social and political advances that women had made in the previous decade. Hence, he argues, the genocide had a clearly gendered aspect. Certainly the genocidal forces aggressively targeted women politicians and activists. Prime Minister Uwilingiyimana was among the first people sought out by the Presidential Guard, which also sought out other prominent women such as Mujawamariya, who managed to escape. The violence wiped out the leadership of many women's organizations as well as human rights and development groups.

The 1994 genocide ultimately left Rwanda devastated, with as many as 800,000 people dead from the genocide and war, millions displaced, the country's infrastructure shattered, and a new government placed in power by the victorious RPF. In the aftermath of the genocide, Rwandan women were left in a particularly difficult position. Thousands had been widowed by the violence, many left to raise children on their own. Property and inheritance laws developed during the colonial era placed the thousands of new women heads of family in legally vulnerable positions with tenuous claims to their husbands' homes and land. Many women, both Tutsi survivors and Hutu women returning from refugee camps, found their homes either destroyed or occupied. Women also faced serious social stigma because of rape during the genocide and in many cases the birth of children from those rapes. The extensive sexual violence had also left many women infected with HIV/AIDS (Nowrojee 1996; Newbury and Baldwin 2000a).

While the genocide and war devastated women's groups, with many leaders and members dead or in exile, the intense problems facing women in the postconflict period inspired women's organizations to assume an important social role. As Catherine Newbury and Hannah Baldwin explain: "In the aftermath of the conflicts, women's organizations, both new and old, took a leading role in efforts to help women reconstruct their lives through emergency material assistance, counseling, vocational training, and assistance with income-earning activities. Many organizations provided a space where women could reestablish social ties, seek solace, and find support" (2000b, 4).

Existing groups such as Duterembere, Haguruka, and Reseau des Femmes found their work substantially expanded, while a range of new organizations emerged to deal with the specific problems of women in the postgenocide period. Newbury and Baldwin (2000b, 5–6) identify the primary activities of women's groups after the genocide as providing shelter, supporting income-generating activities, providing health care and psychotherapy, and the political tasks of providing organizational and civic training and defending women's rights. An organization of widowed Tutsi genocide survivors, Avega, assumed a prominent role not only in providing assistance to genocide widows but also in pressuring the government to provide widows with services and assistance. A group of dynamic returned Tutsi exiles from Congo established Pro-Femmes/Twese Hamwe as an umbrella group for women's organizations to provide a unified lobbying voice. Pro-Femmes brings together forty member groups, including Reseau des Femmes, which is itself an umbrella group of development cooperatives, hence giving it contact with a large number of Rwandan women.[4]

These women's groups have enjoyed growing public influence, which they have been able to translate into a degree of political power. Pro-Femmes has taken the lead in lobbying the government on a series of women's issues, and it has gained concessions from both the executive and legislature. Working closely with the Forum for Women Parliamentarians, it pushed successfully for the adoption of a law banning discrimination against women as well as for an important reform of inheritance laws that granted women the right to inherit their husbands' property. The groups also pushed successfully for a law mandating harsher sentences for those found guilty of rape.[5]

The extensive involvement of women in Rwandan civil society has been a major reason for the expansion of women's representation in the Rwandan Chamber of Deputies for at least two reasons. First, experience in civil society has become an important basis for entering politics. Several people whom I interviewed complained, in jest yet expressing a true problem, that the best women in civil society keep being drawn into government, named to commissions or ministries or the parliament. Judith Kanakuze is an excellent example of how women have moved from civil society to public office. After the genocide Kanakuze became head of Duterembere, then moved over to become head of Reseau des Femmes, the umbrella women's development organization. In 2001 she was named to be one of twelve commissioners on the Constitutional Commission, charged with drafting a new constitution for Rwanda.[6] When elections were held in 2003 she was named a member of the Chamber of Deputies. Bernadette Mukarutabana, who ran as an RPF candidate in 2003 after having worked for several human rights organizations, is another example.[7] Many other women now involved in politics started in women's organizations or in other civil society organizations.[8]

The second reason that women's involvement in civil society has helped to promote women's legislative representation is that women's groups have actively promoted the legitimacy and importance of women holding office. Women's groups have promoted government policies setting aside reserved positions for women. They have also sought to encourage the population to support the candidacy of women through educational programs. Pro-Femmes, for example, held extensive public education programs prior to March 2001 local elections, October 2001 elections of *gacaca* judges, and the October 2003 Chamber of Deputies elections.[9] Women already in the Chamber of Deputies actively campaigned for the election of more women.[10] The results were impressive: Even where quotas were not in place, women won a large portion of positions. For example, approximately 27 percent of those elected gacaca judges were women.

Women and the RPF

In addition to the strong presence of women in Rwandan civil society, the substantial support within the RPF for women's representation helps to explain the growth of women's presence in parliament. The leaders of the RPF have demonstrated considerable commitment to the expansion of female representation, not only appointing women to top government posts but also establishing policies that promote the representation of women at all levels of government. Several women are in influential positions at the top of the RPF hierarchy, and the RPF has consistently articulated its support for women's rights, including the right for women to hold public office.

The Rwandan Patriotic Front was founded in Uganda in the 1980s by Rwandan Tutsi refugees. During Ugandan president Milton Obote's second period of rule in the 1980s, Rwandans in Uganda—both refugees and economic migrants—faced considerable persecution. In 1982 several thousand refugees tried to flee back into Rwanda after being attacked by the Ugandan military, but they were turned away at the border by Rwandan government troops, acting on orders from President Habyarimana, who claimed that Rwanda did not have sufficient land to welcome them home. In the face of persecution in Uganda, a number of Rwandans became involved in the National Resistance Army, the rebel group that brought Yoweri Museveni to power in 1986. When Museveni became president, he adopted policies favorable to the Rwandans, granting them citizenship, and several Rwandan Tutsis held important military posts, including Paul Kagame, who served as head of intelligence. Nevertheless, Rwandans' positions in Uganda remained tenuous, since many Ugandans did not accept their right to Ugandan citizenship and were angry over their prominence and success. Their insecure position in Uganda, nostalgia for their homeland, and a sense of empowerment that came from their participation in a movement that had successfully taken power in Uganda inspired some Rwandans from the National Resistance Movement (NRM) to form their own movement to take power in Rwanda (Prunier 1995).

The Ugandan origins of the RPF have deeply influenced its policies since taking power, including its policies on women's rights and inclusion. The organization and military tactics of the RPF and its armed wing, the Rwandan Patriotic Army (RPA), closely followed the model of Museveni's National Resistance Movement and National Resistance Army, proving as militarily successful in Rwanda as they had in Uganda and sweeping the RPF to victory in July 1994. Like Museveni's NRM, the RPF denied being a political party after taking power and instead insisted on being called a "movement," even as it dominated Rwandan political life. Also like the NRM, the RPF not only gave many women positions within its own ranks but established quota systems for women in government positions. A decentralization program instituted by the national government in 2001 reorganized local administration, creating local government committees chosen through a tiered system of voting. At each level of local administration—the cell, sector, and district—a committee of seven was selected, including one position for a women's representative, chosen through a special ballot for women, and another for a youth representative, chosen through a special ballot for youth. As part of the decentralization program, the RPF created women's councils at all levels of government (Powley 2003).

The new constitution adopted in June 2003 institutionalized the practice of reserved positions for women and youth. After a process that included a consultative period, drafting by a constitutional committee, and revisions by the Transitional National Assembly, Rwanda adopted a new constitution in June 2003 in a special national referendum. The constitution reserved 30 percent of seats in the lower house of parliament for women. Article 76 states:

> The Chamber of Deputies is composed of eighty (80) members consisting of:
> . . . twenty-four (24) members of the female sex with two per Province and the City of Kigali elected by the Councils of Districts, of Cities, and of the City of Kigali, to which are added the Executive Committees of the women's organizations at the level of the Province, City of Kigali, Districts, and Sectors.

Two seats were reserved for members elected by the National Youth Council, and one was reserved for a member elected by the Federation of Associations of the Handicapped.

The rise in women's participation cannot be attributed to quotas alone, however, since the number of women in nonreserved elected seats has also increased dramatically. For example, the percentage of women elected to cell-level councils in 1999, before quotas were in effect, was 13.7 percent. The quota system in 2001 local-level elections guaranteed 14.3 percent of seats would go to women, but nearly double that percentage won seats in the 2001 elections, with women gaining 27 percent of seats. Similarly, the constitutional quota for the Chamber of Deputies guaranteed women 30 percent of seats, but in the end women won 48.8 percent of the seats in the 2003 parliamentary elections (Powley 2003, 2). Furthermore, women have gained strong representation in elections where no quotas were involved, as in the election of gacaca judges, where women won 35 percent of seats (UNIFEM 2004).

Whatever criticisms can be made of the authoritarian practices of the leaders of the RPF (a problem discussed later in this chapter), they have nevertheless publicly demonstrated a strong commitment to expanding rights and representation for women. A number of RPF officials, including President Paul Kagame and key ministry officials, such as Protais Musoni, the main force behind important policies such as decentralization, have repeatedly articulated strong support for women's role in government and society. Furthermore, the RPF has placed women in important and influential positions at all levels of government. For example, Rose Kabuye was a lieutenant colonel in the RPA and was known to be a close confidant of RPF leader Kagame during the first years of RPF rule. She became the mayor of Kigali in 1994 and later served as a member of the Chamber of Deputies, where she chaired the Security and Defense Committee. In recent years she has reportedly fallen out of favor with President Kagame, though she has continued to hold important positions, such as serving on the Political and Judicial Commission, which oversaw reforms to Rwanda's judicial system. Another woman in the inner circle of RPF power, Soline Nyirahabimana, has seen her influence rise as Rose Kabuye's has declined. Nyirahabimana served as a member of the National Commission for Human Rights. She has become a major adviser to the president, serving first as a legal adviser and now as minister of state for the Office of the President.[11]

Although technically a Government of National Unity from 1994 until 2003, the postgenocide government in Rwanda was clearly dominated by the RPF, whose influence helped to guarantee excellent representation for women in key positions. Women have served as ministers or ministers of state in the ministries of Justice; Lands, Resettlement, and Environment; and Health as well as various others. The inclusion of women ministers in governments created by the RPF continues a trend begun during the democracy movement.

Governments named by Habyarimana in 1987, 1989, and 1990 contained no women, but the new opposition parties that formed after their legalization in 1991 pressured the government to address women's rights as a significant issue. The first multiparty government named on April 16, 1992, created a ministry of Family and Women's Promotion, headed by a woman from the MRND, and also included Agathe Uwilingiyimana as minister of primary and secondary education. The second multiparty government, named on July 18, 1993, had not only Uwilingiyimana as prime minister but a woman as minister of justice and one as minister of family and women's promotion. A government proposed as part of the implementation of the Arusha Peace Accords in 1994 but never installed would have increased the number of women ministers to five, including the ministers of commerce, industry, and artisanry and work and social affairs (Guichaoua 1995, 752–759). Although the first postgenocide government named by the RPF included only two women ministers, subsequent governments have increased the number. The new government installed after elections in 2003 included 4 women out of 17 ministers and 5 out of 11 ministers of state, with cabinet rank.

Women were also named to other key government posts in the Government of National Unity and the subsequent RPF government. Aloisea Inyumba served as governor of Rural Kigali Province and later served as president of the National Commission for Unity and Reconciliation. In 2001, Aloysie Cyanzayire was named president of the

Sixth Chamber of the Supreme Court, which was charged with over-
seeing the gacaca trials. After a 2004 restructuring of the courts, she became president of the entire Supreme Court. Another woman has
served as executive secretary of the important National Commission
for Unity and Reconciliation. Three of the twelve constitutional commission members were women.

The large number of women in prominent national positions as
well as women occupying local government posts has normalized the
involvement of women in politics in Rwanda. During the prodemoc-
racy movement of the early 1990s, empowerment of women was an important issue, but it also met with considerable resistance—in practice
if not fully articulated. The RPF's commitment to placing women in
political positions at all levels of government and administration has
meant that most Rwandans have had contact with women officials. In
the gacaca trials that I have observed, women dominated the proceedings in several communities. In this context, women's participation be
comes the norm rather than an exception, and voters are thus more willing to take seriously women's candidacy for parliament.

Women in the Rwandan Parliament

Experience in both civil society and government has served as a vehicle
for women to enter parliament. The first woman to serve in the Chamber of Deputies took office in 1965, but under both the Kayibanda and
Habyarimana regimes, the number of women parliamentarians remained fairly small. Habyarimana changed the name of the parliament
to the National Council of Development, reflecting the regime's interest
in economic development, and he did gradually increase the number of
women in office. By 1988 the Council included 12 women among its 70
members, or 17.1 percent. The democracy movement that emerged in
1990 involved a number of women, some of whom had served in the
government or civil service, many others of whom had been involved in
civil society organizations. Several of the opposition parties embraced
women's rights as an important issue. Yet this commitment to women's
rights would not necessarily have increased women's representation in
parliament. Most of the opposition politicians had previously served in
the government or administration, realms dominated by men. Each of
the opposition parties was dominated by men who were interested in
gaining power for themselves, which left few positions available for
women. The list of proposed parliamentarians put forth after the Arusha

Accords included the names of only 3 women out of 70 deputies, fewer than the number of women ministers in the proposed government (Guichaoua 1995).

The RPF, however, came into power with a strong commitment not only to women's rights but also to women's representation. After the RPF took power the Transitional National Parliament installed in November 1994 included 10 women, including 3 of the 13 RPF deputies (Guichaoua 1995, 762–767). The number of women in parliament steadily increased during the period of transition (1994–2003). By 1999 over a quarter of parliamentarians were women. Prior to the 2003 elections, women constituted 25.7 percent of parliament.

As a result of the substantial number of women who have held national office, served in local government, or served in parliament during the transition period, many well-qualified women were available to run for the Chamber of Deputies in the September–October elections held after the adoption of the 2003 constitution. The constitution guaranteed women 24 seats, or 30 percent of the 80 seats in the lower house. These reserved seats were elected through a woman-only ballot by provincial women's councils on October 2 and brought into the Chamber of Deputies primarily women active at the regional level.

Fifty-three of the Chamber of Deputies seats were chosen through a party-list system of voting. According to the constitution, these party lists "are composed respecting the principle of national unity . . . and respecting the principle of equal access for women and men to the electoral mandate and elective function."[12] While not setting any quota for women in these seats, the constitution nevertheless did encourage the inclusion of women on party lists. A substantial number of women sought candidacy in the nonreserved seats, and a number did gain positions on the party lists. The RPF and a group of smaller affiliated parties won 73.8 percent of the vote and earned 40 seats, while the Social Democratic Party won 12.3 percent and 7 seats and the Liberal Party won 10.6 percent of the vote and 6 seats (Election World 2003). Women won 15 of the nonreserved seats, for a total of 39 out of the 80 seats.

The constitution also sets a quota of 30 percent women for the Senate, the upper house of Rwanda's parliament. The Senate is an appointed body, with members appointed by provincial councils, the political parties, the universities, and the president "to ensure the representation of historically marginalized communities." Six women were named initially to the Senate in 2003 (Inter-Parliamentary Union 2003), and this number was ultimately boosted to 9 out of 26 seats. Hence, women constitute an amazing 48.8 percent of seats in the

Chamber of Deputies, 34.6 percent in the Senate, and 45 percent of the entire parliament.

The women members of Rwanda's parliament came from similar backgrounds, regardless of the method of their election. Many had already served in government posts. For example, Dr. Odette Nyiramirimo, who was appointed senator by the party forum, had formerly served as minister of state for health. Immaculée Kayuma Gahima, the senator for Butare Province, had served as a minister. Agnes Mukazibera, chosen as a deputy on the RPF list, was former secretary general of the Ministry of Youth. Many others came from civil society. For example, women chosen on the RPF party list included Bernadette Kanzayire, formerly president of the Association des Voluntiers de la Paix, a human rights group, and Bernadette Mukarutabana, head of the Collective of Leagues and Associations for the Defense of Human Rights (CLADHO), the umbrella organization for Rwandan human rights groups. Some women chosen for parliament combined experience in both government and civil society, such as Judith Kanakuze, from Reseau des Femmes and the Constitutional Commission, chosen as a women's representative from Cyangugu.

The women in Rwanda's parliament formed a caucus in the mid-1990s known as the Forum of Women Parliamentarians. Women's groups such as Pro-Femmes have worked closely with the forum on legislation such as the revision of inheritance laws and the law banning discrimination against women. Leaders of Pro-Femmes identified the presence of women in parliament as an important factor in getting their legislation passed. The women parliamentarians were open to serving as a contact for women's groups. Joining together in the forum has also strengthened the power of women parliamentarians, as they are able to act in a bloc.

Representation in an Authoritarian State

Many analysts and activists assume that increased women's representation will transform the nature of politics in Rwanda. In an interview with Women Waging Peace, Lieutenant Colonel Rose Kabuye claimed: "Women look out for their interests and those of their children; they have a vested interest in peace. . . . We want our voices to be heard. When can we be the ones to sit at the head of the table? As women gain ground in local leadership positions, we will gradually begin to get more national opportunities. And if we're there, it will make a difference—a big difference" ("Spotlight on Rose Kabuye, Rwanda" 2004). Many organizations, such as Women Waging Peace, Women's International League for Peace and Freedom, Women for Women International, and UNIFEM, have suggested that the expansion of women's representation in Rwanda will naturally or necessarily lead to a more peaceful and democratic society.

Yet the significance of women's high level of representation in parliament and in other government institutions is uncertain given the increasingly authoritarian nature of the Rwandan state since 1994. Immediately after taking power, the RPF established a multiparty government that was widely representative. This first government of national unity included moderate politicians from the Hutu ethnic group in important positions, including both the president and prime minister and the ministers of justice, interior, and foreign affairs, while a Tutsi genocide survivor was named speaker of the national assembly. In mid-1995, however, five of the most prominent Hutu in the government, including Prime Minister Faustin Twagiramungu, resigned in protest over their lack of real power, complaining that RPF officers below them in their ministries actually made decisions for the government. Over time power has been increasingly concentrated in the hands of former Tutsi refugees and the RPF, while Paul Kagame has increased his own personal power substantially. In January 2000 the speaker of the Chamber of Deputies was driven from office, and the next month, the prime minister resigned. On March 23, 2000, President Pasteur Bizimungu, a Hutu RPF member, resigned. Each of these positions was filled by someone more closely allied with Paul Kagame, while Kagame himself became the new president (Reyntjens 2004, 180–181).

The consolidation of effective political power in the hands of Kagame and a small group of his associates has been accompanied by an increasing intolerance for independent expression and political dissent. Anyone who publicly criticizes the regime risks being labeled "divisionist," or a supporter of social division and genocide. When former President Bizimungu launched a new political party in 2001, promising to unite all Rwandans, in contrast to what he called the RPF's exclusionary policies, he was accused of supporting genocide and placed under house arrest. Independent civil society organizations have been systematically bullied by the RPF, being forced either to conform to RPF directives or face dissolution (International Crisis Group [ICG] 2002). The much-promoted "transition to democracy" was in fact tightly controlled and resulted in greater consolidation of power by the RPF, even as it gave an illusion of power distribution. In the first local elections after a decentralization program in 2001, RPF officials carefully selected candidates, threatening and intimidating others who were interested in seeking office (ICG 2001). The same policy was used for presidential and parliamentary elections in 2003. Former prime minister Faustin Twagiramungu returned to Rwanda to stand as a candidate for political office, but his political party, the MDR, was disbanded and he was forbidden to campaign (Human Rights Watch 2003). In the end, official results of the August 25 presidential elections gave sitting president Kagame 95.1 percent of the vote, an outcome that belies the purported democratic nature of the vote. The European Union Observation Mission uncovered substantial harassment and intimidation and reported difficulty in observing (Mission d'Observation 2003). The researchers that I had myself hired to observe the election were not only forbidden to observe, despite having all the appropriate permissions, but subsequently harassed.

In this context of increasingly authoritarian government, parliament has itself become increasingly authoritarian. Following the resignation under pressure of the parliamentary speaker, the RPF pressured parliament to create a Forum of Political Parties, a group that would have the power of determining who was fit to serve in parliament. Members who criticized the government or took otherwise controversial positions risked being labeled divisionist and thus unfit to serve in parliament, which would force them to give up their seats. The institution of the forum had a stultifying effect on parliament, effectively quashing dissent and restricting free debate. Despite extensive criticism, the forum was written into the new constitution, making parliament operate effectively as a single-party institution.[13]

Parliament has allowed itself to be used to give a democratic sheen to distinctly undemocratic actions. In the lead-up to the 2003 elections, a parliamentary commission created at the behest of RPF leadership studied the MDR, the opposition party that had the greatest following and presented the largest threat to RPF hopes for electoral victory. The parliamentary commission published a report that was then accepted by the Transitional National Assembly that accused the MDR of supporting the 1994 genocide and continuing to support division and conflict within Rwanda. As a result of this action, the MDR was disbanded, ostensibly in the name of preserving democracy but in reality seriously undercutting the possibility of a meaningful transition.

The entrance of women into a parliament that serves more as an instrument of legitimizing and preserving RPF power is of questionable value. Elizabeth Powley, in a report praising the efforts by the RPF to include women in government, defends the regime against criticisms:

A final, more skeptical analysis of this policy decision [to include women and youth] charges that the government could be using the inclusion of women and youth as a means of diverting attention from the absence of more ethnically plural and representative government. Because the country is 85 percent Hutu, however, this argument is problematic. Decentralization and the inclusion of women and youth at every administrative level will necessitate the inclusion of the majority population. If decentralization were fully implemented, it would be difficult to maintain ethnic exclusivity in all the governing structures. (2004, 8)

Powley is right to assert that ethnic diversity in government, including parliament, is almost inevitable. Yet she is wrong to call this "representative government." Structures in both the Senate and the Chamber of Deputies guarantee diversity in membership, but with a Senate that is not popularly elected, a lower house that has a large percentage of its seats chosen through indirect election, and a Forum of Parliamentarians that monitors deputies and senators, the parliament is designed to mirror the diversity of society—except ethnic diversity—without being truly representative. With the RPF winning 40 of the 53 contested seats in the 2003 elections of questionable legitimacy (Mission d'Observation 2003) and dominating the selection of all other seats, the possibility for diversity of opinion within the parliament has been even more restrained. The only two parties outside the RPF coalition, the Liberal Party and the Social Democratic Party, present little critique of the government and have worked closely with the RPF. The parliament, thus, serves not as a forum for real debate but rather as a tool for legitimizing government policies by giving them a veneer of popularity. This is a point that many Rwandans themselves raised during my research visits in June and October 2004 and January 2005. One person told me: "The RPF focuses on diversity so that they can appear democratic even though they control all power. They put women in the National Assembly because they know they [the women] will not challenge them."[14]

The hope that the increase in women's participation in parliament after the 2003 elections would create a more democratic parliament has been swiftly shattered, as the new post-transition parliament has continued to allow itself to be used as a tool of intimidation. Following the model of the MDR study of the year before, a parliamentary commission in 2004 targeted several important civil society organizations, including League for the Protection of Human Rights in Rwanda (LIPRODHOR), the only remaining independent human rights group in Rwanda. The report produced by the commission accused LIPRODHOR and the other organizations of supporting division and having *genocidaires* among their leadership. Most of the prominent leaders and employees of LIPRODHOR have subsequently fled the country to avoid arrest or a potentially worse fate, effectively disbanding the organization. The large number of women in parliament provided no check on the use of parliament for political intimidation and repression.

Yet women's participation in parliament is not entirely without meaning. Women parliamentarians have actively promoted legislation that serves the interests of women. The Forum of Women Parliamentarians was key in pushing through revisions to the inheritance laws, a law banning discrimination against women, and a strengthening of rape laws. The larger number of women in parliament today may make it even easier to adopt legislation to benefit women—but only when it is consistent with the agenda of the RPF leadership.

The case of women parliamentarians in Rwanda thus presents an interesting paradox. On one hand, the physical representation of women does provide an important voice for women's interests and has helped to revise Rwanda's laws to make them more favorable to women. On the other hand, the nature of representation is quite limited in a highly authoritarian state. Where debate is tightly constrained, merely having women present in parliament does not mean that women's interests are truly represented. Women's role in other political institutions may be more important. Ministers have a much greater role in deciding policies, while local government plays an important role in determining how policies are actually implemented within the population.

In all levels of government, however, the lack of political freedom limits the ability of women to influence policy. The RPF regime certainly has a commitment to improving women's participation and opportunities, but the regime's conception of women's rights is highly constrained because it does not tolerate the broader range of human rights. Freedom of speech, assembly, and press are just as relevant for women as they are for men, and the restriction of these rights seriously undermines the meaning of women's representation. The growing constraints on civil society will have particularly serious consequences for women since women have been so active in this realm. Women's groups are likely to find that they are able to challenge the authorities only in limited ways and will ordinarily be able to work only on issues consistent with the regime's agenda. Until the Rwandan government shows greater tolerance for human rights in general, the impressive representation of women in Rwanda's parliament and other government institutions will have only a limited impact on the lives of Rwandan women.

Notes

1. Interview by the author with Monique Mujawamariya, Boston, November 1994.

2. The best sources on the genocide are Des Forges (1999) and Prunier (1995).

3. I participated in the research for this publication while head of the Human Rights Watch office in Kigali in 1996.

4. Based on interviews conducted by the author, particularly in March and April 1996 and September and October 2002.

5. Interview with Odette Kabaya and Suzanne Ruboneka of Pro-Femmes/ Twese Hamwe, Kigali, September 9, 2002.

6. Interviews with Judith Kanakuze, March 2001–October 2003.

7. Interview with Bernadette Mukarutabana, Kigali, January 18, 2005.

8. Based on multiple conversations with Judith Kanakuze, March 2001–October 2003.

9. In 2001 the Gacaca Law was adopted in Rwanda to establish gacaca courts throughout the country. The courts constitute an alternative justice system for handling the tens of thousands of Rwandans accused of taking part in the 1994 genocide.

10. Based on multiple conversations with Judith Kanakuze, March 2001–October 2003.

11. Based on numerous interviews and Women Waging Peace's Rwanda page, www.womenwagingpeace.net/content/conflict_areas/rwanda.asp.

12. Constitution, Article 77.

13. Based on research conducted under the auspices of the US Agency for International Development in September 2002.

14. Interview with civil society activist, Kigali, January 12, 2005.

7

Senegal: Contending with Religious Constraints

Lucy Creevey

Twenty-three women were elected to the National Assembly in Senegal in 2001. This meant that 19.2 percent of the members were female, a 5 percent increase over the 1998 parliamentary election. Yet the gains women have made in National Assembly membership over the past twenty years have hardly been spectacular. In 1981 there were thirteen women in parliament, and the increase of ten women delegates over that period hardly represents a major gain in political power for Senegalese women, especially when contrasted with some parliaments in Eastern and Southern Africa.

In this chapter I look at the factors that have contributed to women's slow infiltration into national electoral politics in Senegal. Although economic development and the spread of formal education are extremely important in the movement of women into politics, I focus on three other factors that deserve exploration. Perhaps the most important of these is culture and religion. Though Senegal is a secular state, Islam is heavily entwined in national and local politics. Because Senegalese voters have been strongly influenced by Muslim leaders, women have had a harder time gaining access to political power. This is true despite the fact that rural Muslim leaders (known as *marabouts*) have generally not behaved as radical fundamentalist Muslims, resisting modernization and the education and economic and political participation of women.

The second factor is the organization of the electoral system and the use of electoral quotas. Senegal utilizes a mixed electoral system for its National Assembly election, and that mix has changed over the years. More recently a number of parties have adopted gender quotas, if somewhat minimal, for their candidate slates. Finally, Senegalese women's

151

political organizations—their membership, goals, and achievements—are an important third factor in determining the current political position of women. National-level women's organizations in Senegal have tended to be elite groups without a mass following. Further, they have had to adapt to the changing political culture as Senegal becomes increasingly influenced by the anti-Western perspective of much of the Islamic world. Current campaigns led by women's organizations must tread a careful line between asserting women's need for more equality (including in politics) and not appearing too confrontational (De Diop 2000b; Callaway and Creevey 1994).

A Brief History of Women in Senegal

Senegal has a population of 9.5 million, of whom 51.6 percent are women. More than 69 percent of the population lives in the rural areas, and 77 percent of those engage in agriculture for a living (Government of Senegal 2001). Senegal is still a poor country. In 2001 the annual per capita gross national income was US$480. More than one-third of the total population lived below the national poverty line, and more than 40 percent of rural residents lived below this income level (World Bank 2003, 235, 237).

Senegal has been at least a quasi-democracy since independence in 1960, but power is heavily concentrated in the hands of the president and his close advisers. The president appoints the prime minister and names the chief ministers in the government, although technically the prime minister chooses his cabinet. Traditionally in Senegal the prime minister is dismissed if he begins to acquire too much power or in any way threatens the authority of the president. Abdoulaye Wade, elected president in 2000, had named four prime ministers by late 2004. One of those prime ministers was a woman, but she had little political power in her own right and since her dismissal has more or less faded from political view.

The National Assembly has had little or no power, and none of the body's major political leaders—either in government or in the opposition—have been women. The government in Senegal is composed of a prime minister and cabinet of ministers and subministers, a National Assembly, and a judiciary. The national legislature is unicameral, although for a brief time, from 1999 to 2001, there was an indirectly selected senate as well. There are 120 members in the National Assembly. As previously noted, however, power in Senegal resides in the presidency. Indeed, the National Assembly has been called (not too affectionately) *la chambre d' applaudissement* (the applause chamber) (Beck 1994, 101). Like the president, members of the National Assembly are elected every five years. Following the 2000 presidential election that brought a new party, the Democratic Socialist Party (PDS), to power for the first time since independence, a new constitution was adopted; a legislative election was held in 2001, only three years after the previous legislative election.

Women in Senegal have a fair amount of freedom, but they do not have the same access to economic resources or political power as men. Girls are less likely to be educated than boys. Seventy-three percent of Senegalese women are illiterate as compared to 55 percent of men. Fifty-eight percent of school-age girls are in school as compared to 73 percent of school-age boys. This difference increases in some of the rural areas such as Tambacounda and Kolda and narrows in the Muslim centers of Diourbel and Kaolack, where few children of either sex attend state-sponsored public schools—31 percent of girls and 40 percent of boys in Diourbel, and 35 percent of girls and 45 percent of boys in Kaolack. Aside from less education, women in Senegal also face other disadvantages relative to men. Because of less training and greater domestic obligations, women are less able to get formal sector jobs and, if they do, to get equivalent jobs and equivalent pay. Indeed, fewer than 20 percent of women are wage workers in the public or private sectors. Over 60 percent of women are "self-employed," usually working in petty commerce, grain processing, or agriculture and fishing (Canadian International Development Agency 2001). Moreover, Senegalese women are less able than men to obtain loans because of a lack of collateral.

At the same time, women in Senegal are not cloistered, that is, they move freely from the household to the fields or the marketplace and elsewhere. A growing percentage of educated women have adopted more conservative dress, including head scarves (Villalón 2004b, 10; Augis 2002, 1–23), and there is increasing pressure on Senegalese women from conservative Muslim groups to adopt the veil (Sow 2003, 75). But most Senegalese women are not veiled and wear Western clothes or, more typically, bright-colored wraps with blouses or *boubous* and turbans. Although women have generally not held important political positions, they can and do speak out and are increasingly named to political office. Women's organizations have proliferated, organized around a variety of specific goals and topics. One woman (Marieme Wane Ly) has headed her own political party and ran for president in 2000 (De Diop 2000b, 7). Another (Mame Madior Boye) served as prime minister from March

2001 to November 2002. It is common to see articles or opinion pieces in newspapers and journals written by women. In recent years the high rate of domestic violence against women (and the lack of retribution for it) has attracted widespread attention, and women have reacted openly and publicly to it. In September 2001 the wife of the president, Vivian Wade, led women through the streets of Dakar to protest the high rate of domestic violence (US Department of State 2002).

Religion and Culture and the Political Power of Women

Aside from less access to education, the factor assumed here to be a, if not the, principal force restricting the political power of Senegalese women is the importance of Islamic institutions and leaders in Senegalese politics. Senegal's constitution establishes secular authorities and laws. The 2001 revision of the constitution follows the postindependence tradition of assuring equal rights to all citizens of Senegal, but it places an even greater emphasis on gender equality than did earlier versions of the constitution (Sylla 2001, 81).[1] Nonetheless, Islam and Islamic leaders heavily influence the government in Senegal. The unique (or at least unusual) alliance of conservative rural Muslim leaders (marabouts) with Western-trained politicians is a replication of a pattern that was established during French colonial rule. The French, pushing in from the coast, weakened the power of the traditional nobles and kings. Marabouts, heads of *sufi* mystical orders, emerging in the wave of Islamicization from the East in the mid- and late 1800s, replaced the traditional leaders as the rural authorities (Behrman 1970). The colonial leaders feared potential uprisings led by Islamic leaders. Their fears may have been deliberately exaggerated by the traditional upper-caste leaders who resented losing their power to the marabouts (Searing 2002). In any case, by the early 1900s the French administration had moved from attempting to suppress the Islamic brotherhoods to recognizing that one way to control the large territories they had conquered was to collaborate with the Muslim leaders—allow them to proselytize and control their disciples, give them gifts, and support them in their leadership struggles in return for their keeping their followers quiescent under French rule (Robinson 1999, 193–194). This shift was a change in policy for the French and ended up establishing a pattern that has dominated politics in Senegal to the present day, although not without some major changes (especially in recent years).

    The traditional school of thought is that the conversion to Islam reduced the social and political power that women in Senegal had previously held. In pre-Islamic Senegal, among the central ethnic groups, the Wolof and Serer, the wife and mother or sister of the ruler had specific political roles and powers. These public roles disappeared when marabouts became the leaders of the community. Although Islamic law did give women certain rights that they had not had previously (for example, inheritance rights and the right to keep their bride price) (Diop 1985, 15–30), it also appears to have institutionalized a subservient role for women. As Fatou Sow notes (1985, 566), it "loosened women's control on society" by reinforcing the patriarchal system. The situation, however, is more complex than that. Senegalese traditions allowed women to play important economic, political, and social roles, and most Muslim leaders have not attempted to fully eradicate these traditions (Sow 2003, 71). Thus, Senegalese sufi brotherhoods emphasize the disciples' membership in the order and their obedience to its leader, the marabout, and women do not take the vow to become disciples. Practically, however, women also show their obedience to the marabouts and call on the Muslim leaders' support when needed. They interact in brotherhood affairs and often assume very important roles, at least behind the scenes and sometimes publicly (Creevey 1996, 282–284). A 1999 survey indicated that most women in Senegal see themselves as members of a brotherhood or the social organizations that support these, the *dahira* (Creevey and Magala 2002, 14). Women are indeed central to the core of sufi Islam in Senegal and make their contributions to the orders by their work, their money, and their support of maraboutic leadership (Rosander 2003).[2]

There are five principal brotherhoods in Senegal. The largest is the Tidjaniyya, whose principal leaders, called *khalifs* or caliphs, descend from Al Hajj Malik Sy (d. 1922) and have their major headquarters in Tivaoune in the Thies region (slightly north and east of Dakar). A second and smaller branch of the Tidjaniyya, which has also been politically significant, has leadership descended from Abdoulaye Niasse (d. 1922) and headquarters in Kaolack, the peanut-processing capital in the Sine Saloum region to the south (but north of Gambia). The second-largest brotherhood, the Muridiyya, founded by Ahmad Bamba (d. 1927), has been most notable for its direct collaboration first with the founding president of Senegal, Leopold Senghor (a Catholic), and then with his successor, Abdou Diouf (a Muslim). The latter was defeated in the 2000 presidential election by his rival, Abdoulaye Wade (a Muslim and direct disciple of the Mourides). The two other major brotherhoods in Senegal are much smaller and less significant in Senegalese national politics. The Qadriyya (from which the Muridiyya originally derived) are found along the Senegal River and in the southern part of Senegal.

The Layenne, which is primarily found among the Lebou ethnic group in the Dakar region (especially around the town of Rufisuqe), has an interesting political history (it was a mahdist movement) but is not currently a major force in politics. It is also originally derived from the Qadiri brotherhood.[3]

In the past Muslim leaders, and in particular the Mouride caliphs, expected their followers to abide by government policies and vote for their candidates of choice in national and local elections. In turn government leaders gave the Muslim leaders gifts and economic privileges and carefully respected their pronouncements on Islam and their dealings with their disciples. Commentators suggested that by the time the Socialist Party (PS) (which had held power since independence) was defeated in the 2000 election, the close alliance between the Mouride leaders, in particular, and the president had slackened, and Muslim brotherhood leaders were no longer as involved in the political process as in the past.

The reasons for this shift were complicated. Splits in the formerly tightly and hierarchically organized Mouride brotherhood deriving from succession struggles were cited as one factor. The Tidjanis also faced succession struggles in both the Sy and Niass branches (Villalón 1999; Villalón and Kane 1998). In addition, former President Diouf's regime seemed ineffective, especially after the adoption of structural adjustment policies in 1994. The economy was stagnant, and marabouts had less to gain from collaboration. Increased education and the growing urbanization of Senegal also suggested a less subservient population, less ready to be told what to do politically. Indeed, there were signs that disciples would no longer sit quietly by and let marabouts dictate what would happen to them (Beck 2001). Added to this was the rise of dissident young radical leaders within the brotherhoods who took distinct political positions of their own (such as Atou Diage in the Mouride order and Moustapha Sy in the Tidjaniyya) (Beck 2001; Villalón 2004b). But, to the surprise of some, the new president of Senegal, Abdoulaye Wade, celebrated his 2000 win by traveling to Touba to show his fealty to the caliph of the Mourides, which act he repeated when his party also won the 2001 National Assembly elections. Although Wade did not shift his policy to favor the Mourides—indeed, his Family Code put through further reforms equalizing the position of women against the strong objection of the leading marabouts—the old pattern of collaboration seems to have endured. As Leonardo Villalón observes, "The core understanding of the mutuality of relations between the religious and the political elite in the country remains intact" (2004b, 7–8).

A major additional factor in the influence of Islam on politics in Senegal is the rise in importance of Islamist groups. These groups differ somewhat among themselves in their goals and ideology, but they share the desire to reform and purify Islam in Senegal, and they reject Western modernization. These groups do not have a broad following in the countryside, where the populace remains avowed disciples of the sufi brotherhoods, but they do have influence—even on the brotherhood leadership. The four principal reformist groups in Senegal since the 1990s have been the Al-Falah movement, the Jamaatou Ibadou Rahman Association, the Organization for Islamic Action, and the Association of Muslim Students of the University of Dakar (Piga 2002). In the early postindependence period, radical reformist groups such as the Muslim Cultural Union at the University of Dakar were highly critical of the marabouts and the "corruption" of Islam that they represented (Behrman 1970, 157–170). But in Senegal in 2004, the equivalent groups seem to have arrived at a détente with the brotherhoods. Although still calling for a purification of Islam, they are less inclined to attack the marabouts. In turn, the brotherhood leaders seem to have been influenced by the reformist groups' emphasis on purifying Islam, and there appears to be a greater concern with preserving and protecting Islam as the country develops (Villalón 2004b, 13–15; Piga 2002).

What then does the increasing influence of Islamist groups imply for the position of women in Senegal? The brotherhoods were and are principally led by men, although there have (rarely) been women who emerged as marabouts within both the Mouride and Tidjani orders.[4] Women are not passive members; they are even central to the sufi orders' hold on the countryside (Rosander 2003). But they do not make the major decisions within the brotherhoods and do not decide the policies that the orders pursue. And the brotherhood leadership is by and large conservative, much less inclined than educated secular urban businessmen to tolerate Western dress or morals or any deviation from their interpretation of the code of life put forth in the Koran and the *sharia*. Certainly the pattern of collaboration between the brotherhoods and government leaders meant that the latter tolerated a very slow acceptance—or nonacceptance—of some of the reforms put through to equalize the position of women. Thus, one observer pointed out sarcastically after the first wave of reforms to the civil code (the Family Law) that while women in urban areas might enjoy some of the benefits, women in the rural areas did not even know the code existed: "The Senegal of the Code still lives this paradox, which consists of seeing a law applied—sometimes with extreme rigor—in urban centers where women use at will, often in an immoderate fashion, this new weapon given them by the legislator, while [the Code] is virtually ignored in the countryside where the great majority of the women are not even sure of its existence" (Magassouba 1985, 114).

This disparity inevitably continues despite increased education for both boys and girls and slow but persistent economic development. Recent surveys of a sample of the population (1999) and of Muslim leaders (2004) show that marabouts are considerably less likely than the overall population to endorse women's groups that advocate reforms to help women improve their lives. The surveys also show that men are much less likely than women to approve of feminist groups, but the contrast with the marabouts is as significant. Whereas 47 percent of the overall population surveyed completely approved of feminist groups, only 1 percent of the leaders surveyed had full confidence in them. Although 35 percent of the Muslim leaders had little or no confidence in feminist groups, only 18 percent of the general respondents—mostly male— either disapproved or disapproved strongly of feminist groups.

The increased influence in the early twenty-first century of educated Islamists who are highly critical of the West might be expected to restrict Senegalese women even further than the more tolerant, if still conservative, marabouts have done, at least in terms of women's public political roles. But in fact, the reality is more complex. As noted earlier, Senegalese women are able to be active in the public sphere, and it is not necessarily in the interest of the Islamist groups to restrict them from this access. Indeed, it may be consistent in their view for women to be very politically active as long as they are supporting the "just cause." It is noteworthy that in her in-depth study of women in politics in Senegal, Aissata De Diop (2000b, 5) shows that women are 51 percent of the registered voters. She writes: "Women seem more mobilized than men in terms of political militancy." She also points out that women are more likely to register to vote in rural than in urban areas and suggests that this may be because religious authorities are more visible in the rural areas and may tell women how to vote.

As for the Islamists in general, although some Senegalese scholars express apprehension at the new insistence on veiling and its implications for women's freedom (Sow 2003, 75), others suggest that educated women choose to join Islamist groups and adopt the veil because it gives them personal satisfaction and even power. Veiling gives women a way of taking a stand against tradition, often in defiance of their relatives and friends who are themselves constrained by a highly patriarchal society (Augis 2002, 251–264). Women who take the veil (whom Erin Augis calls "Sunnite") voluntarily submit themselves to a variety of restrictions in dress and behavior, but this does not mean that they have no influence within the movements they have joined or that they are silenced. It remains to be seen, however, if a spread of this Islamist influence among educated women will reduce the ability of Senegalese women's groups to speak for political reform and improved living conditions for women.

The growing importance of the Islamist perspective is incontrovertible. Villalón estimates that 5 percent of female students were veiled in the late 1990s (which would have been unheard of ten years before). He also observes that even women who are explicitly members of brotherhoods have begun to adopt the practice of veiling (Villalón 2004a, 12; Villalón 2004b, 13). Further, there is a clear change in the language of these groups. They are less openly feminist in the Western sense and more moderate in their language and their goals. What this implies for Senegal is not clear, however. Moderation could lead to a higher rate of success in goal attainment or it could simply imply admitted defeat.

The Electoral System and the Representation of Women

The electoral system in Senegal has changed over the years, setting rules sometimes restricting, then expanding, the number of parties that may compete and moving between larger and smaller percentages of members chosen from single-member districts versus those selected by proportional representation (PR). The electoral system characteristics that appear to be the most significant include having greater numbers of deputies chosen by proportional as opposed to single-member district representation, greater numbers of representatives per district (greater numbers of seats a party expects to win), and the existence of a threshold (the percentage of seats that a party must win in order to have any representatives) (Vengroff et al. 2000, 200). In all of these cases, the party is more likely than in the converse situation to feel it can afford to risk a seat on a potentially less attractive female candidate (except in the rare case where the woman has her own national political following).

In Senegal in 1983 and 1988 a mixed electoral system was used, with 60 seats elected on a PR system and 60 by plurality block vote at the departmental level. Party electoral alliances were not permitted, thus favoring the dominant PS and preventing opposition coalitions. In

1993 the PR seats were increased to 70, thus decreasing the plurality seats to 50. In 1998 the number of seats was increased to 140, of which half would be PR and half plurality. In 2000 the opposition, the PDS, finally defeated the PS in the presidential election, and Abdoulaye Wade took office. Ironically, although Wade had called for more proportionality (and therefore greater representativeness) in the electoral system, once in office he chose a less equitable alternative. The number of National Assembly seats was reduced back to 120, with 65 chosen by plurality and 55 by PR. Indeed, the electoral system disproportion between the allocation of seats and votes cast was higher than it had been under the PS (Creevey et al. 2005, 488).

Just as significant, in 2002 fourteen political parties (urged on by the US National Democratic Institute) agreed to reserve at least 30 percent of their candidate lists for female candidates (National Democratic Institute 2003; Niang 1998). Interestingly, however, the party that elected the most women to the 2001 National Assembly, the PDS, did not utilize a quota for the number of women candidates (De Diop 2002). At the time of the 1998 election eleven political parties had some form of gender quota in place. Two had quotas mandating that up to 6 percent of candidates be women. Five, including the PDS and PS, had a quota requiring between 10 and 13 percent women candidates, and four had quotas ranging from 20 to 27 percent (Cisse et al. 1999, 14).

Several striking points emerge when the election lists from 1998 and 2001 are compared. Clearly, despite the fact that 46 percent of the seats in the 2001 National Assembly were elected by proportional electoral rules, there is a "winner-take-all" mentality. Because the SOPI (Wolof for "change") coalition (in which the PDS is the dominant party) was in power through its success in the 2000 presidential election, voters turned out to support SOPI candidates for the National Assembly. Where the PS dominated in 1998, SOPI swept the boards in 2001, winning 89 out of 120 seats. This is not a new development. Senegal has often been portrayed as "clientelist," as the earlier discussion about the power of Muslim brotherhoods indicates. Senegal is a political system in which the political leader garners votes and in return hands out political positions and other privileges to his followers, a type of patron-client system (Villalón 1999; Beck 1997; Young and Kanté 1992, 57–74; Fatton 1987). Voters identify with their leader and do not consider the receipt of money, position, and power in return for votes as a sign of corruption. They flock to the leaders who accrue the most power, abandoning those who have less to give. In addition, there is cultural striving for consensus rather than conflict. Democracy in Wolof *(demokaraasi)* for the broad base of the electorate means coming to a broad agreement or consensus (Schaffer 2000, 116–138). Thus, once Wade had won, it was inevitable that voters would shift to support his party for the National Assembly.

Moreover, women are elected to the National Assembly on the coattails of their parties. Since there is no national female leader in the coterie of major "patrons," the women who are elected to office do not have power in their own right (Sylla 2001, 72). It is not, therefore, surprising that only Awa Diop, the head of the women's wing of the PDS, the governing party, was elected both in 1998 and in 2001. Diop has a certain distinction and certainly name recognition in Senegal, as she achieved the post of *questeur-adjointe* in the treasury in the 1998–2001 National Assembly, but her political position depends on the success of President Wade and his close advisers (Sylla 2001, 74).

It appears that the PR system does favor women in Senegal in contrast to the plurality electoral system. In 1998 women were elected on the proportional list as opposed to the plurality list by a margin of 14 to 2. Women won 20 percent (14) of the PR seats and only 3 percent (2) of the plurality seats. Furthermore, there were significantly more female candidates on the proportional side than on the plurality side (Vengroff et al. 2000, 212). In 2001 what can be observed is a less strong but still convincing positive impact of PR on the likelihood of women being elected. Seven of the 30 (23 percent) SOPI candidates elected through the PR system were women, and 10 of the 59 (17 percent) SOPI candidates elected under the plurality system were women. The 3 women elected by the former ruling party, the PS, were elected through the PR system, as were the 2 women who won seats for two smaller opposition parties, the Alliance Jef-Jál/African Party of Senegalese Democracy (AJ/PADS) and the Alliance of Forces for Progress (AFP). A certain caution is needed in drawing this conclusion, however. A larger percentage of the elected delegates to the National Assembly were female after the 2001 elections than ever before. This was true despite the fact that the electoral system shifted so that there were more plurality seats than in 1998.

Perhaps it can be said that, all other things being equal, evidence suggests that the plurality system does not favor the election of women in Senegal as much as the PR system does. However, all things are never equal. In this case two other major political factors need to be considered. One is the political views and attitudes of the leadership of the dominant parties. Abdoulaye Wade was a reform candidate, and in other matters he has shown a tendency to be more supportive of women's issues than his long-serving and undoubtedly more change-resistant predecessor, Abdou Diouf. Both men are elderly, and both are devout Muslims, but Wade is associated with a move toward modernizing Senegalese society away from some of the stagnation and rigidity of the past. And, through the Family Code, the new constitution, the prominent role of his wife in the antiviolence campaign, and the appointment of Mame Madior Boye as prime minister, Wade has signaled his support of women's issues. Indeed, as Seynabou Ndiaye Sylla points out (2001, 71), Wade has publicly asserted his belief that women are inequitably treated in Senegal and that this is wrong. He said in a speech on the International Women's Day in 2001: "I am far from satisfied by the situation of women. Go forward to gain your rights, I am with you!"

More women are indeed holding office under Wade's regime, but the question remains of how much influence they exert on the policies and programs that are adopted. It appears that at least publicly they do not act as leaders in decisionmaking, whatever their influence behind the scenes may be. The most direct evidence of this is Seynabou Ndiaye Sylla's 2001 study of women and politics in Senegal. She points out that most women delegates (chosen in 1998 or earlier) do not contribute much to parliamentary debates. This, she argues, is because most women delegates are not well trained professionally. She notes that they are often housewives, secretaries, or seamstresses and that intellectual women tend to avoid politics and the illusions associated with it (Sylla 2001, 74).[5]

Although Sylla has a close perspective on women in Senegalese politics, her view seems too derogatory. According to data provided by the National Assembly (2004), numerous professional women were elected to the national legislature in 2001, including three university professors, two teachers, a lawyer, a midwife, and two secretaries. Moreover, although there are undoubtedly more men than women professionals, not all the male delegates could be so classified. More important, the National Assembly to date has had very little power, and the real debates about what happens in Senegal take place outside the chamber. Insofar as the National Assembly does have authority, women parliamentarians in Senegal have not been leading forces within it.

Sylla also points out that more women are being appointed to ministerial posts in government now than in the past and that they are no longer being assigned only to traditional women's positions. The first woman minister was Caroline Faye Diop, widow of Demba Diop, who was assassinated in 1967. She was elected to the National Assembly in

1963, was twice reelected, and then withdrew to take on the post of minister of the Feminine Condition in 1978 (Sylla 2001, 63, 75). In 1995 three women ministers held the posts of Education, Science and Technology, and Women, Children, and Family (Creevey 1996, 307). In the last Diouf government there were five female ministers, four of whom held nontraditional posts (the ministries of Budget, Communications, Employment, and African Integration) (De Diop 2000b, 3).

In the 2000 Wade government, there are eight women ministers. Three hold traditional female posts while five others hold much more technical posts. Indeed, Awa Gueye Kebe (Trade) and Soukeyna Ndiaye Ba (Decentralization and Regional Planning) lead ministries that have considerable power and influence over policies and practice within their areas. Moreover, as Table 7.1 indicates, all of these women ministers are highly qualified.

The increase in the number of women ministers and the increasing importance of the positions they are given is a strong indication of

Table 7.1 Women Ministers in the Wade Government (2004)

Name	Ministry	Profession/Training
Aminata TALL	Local Collectivities and Decentralization	Teacher in teacher training school (Ecole Normale Supérieure)
Awa Gueye KEBE	Trade	M.A. in family studies (*economie familiale*)
Soukeyna Ndiaye BA	Decentralization and Regional Planning	B.A. in sociology, founder of FDEA, a savings and loan scheme for women
Aida MBODJ	Family and National Solidarity	Teacher (*institutrice*)
Aminata DIALLO	Health, Hygiene, and Prevention	Doctor
Safietou Ndiaye DIOP	Culture	University professor in literature (*lettres*)
Maimona Sourang NDIR	Small and Medium Enterprises and Women's Entrepreneurship and Microfinance	Professor of family studies (*economie familiale*)
Oumou Khairy Guèye SECK	Cattle Breeding	Veterinarian, formerly minister of Agriculture and Animal Husbandry

Source: Aissata De Diop, personal e-mail communication, 2004.

women moving toward the center of the political stage. Even here, though, Sylla notes that qualified women are often not chosen for political positions and that President Wade himself has occasionally carelessly selected unqualified women. For example, in 2000 he appointed Marie Lucienne Tissa Mbengue as head of the Department of National Education, Technical and Professional Training, and she had to resign within the first week because of "incompetence and inexperience" (Sylla 2001, 73). At the same time, there are many qualified women active in local and international businesses and nongovernmental organizations (NGOs), and some of these women are beginning to be appointed or elected to significant political office. Finally, Mame Madior Boye, the former prime minister, was not a political power in her own right and certainly not in her governmental role. She was, however, a qualified professional, a former judge and legal adviser to the West African Bank (Williams 2001, 39).

The Power of Women's Groups in Senegal

In fact, the increased numbers of qualified and trained women in Senegal and the interest of many of them in forming political action groups around specific matters relating to women is a very positive indicator that women are beginning to move more centrally into politics. The context and language of these groups is curious, though, because, as mentioned before, the tenor of their discourse is more moderate and less directly confrontational than that of earlier Senegalese women's groups. At the same time, they draw in more members than the earlier groups and are better organized.

The first national women's groups in Senegal preceded independence. The Senegalese Women's Union, for example, publicly celebrated International Women's Day for the first time in 1954. This group, made up of the wives of Senegalese politicians of the day, was strongly nationalist and anticolonialist (Sylla 2001, 64). Other women's groups succeeded the union and began to advocate for the advancement of women specifically. In the 1980s the most prominent women's group was Yewwu Yewwi (Wolof for "raise consciousness for liberation"). Yewwu Yewwi was headed by Marie Angelique Savané, a scholar and consultant to many international organizations. The goal of the group was social reform: "We are all intellectuals with a strong consciousness of the hardly enviable and certainly unjust fate reserved for women and who commit themselves to . . . act as a spark which will provoke a crisis of conscience and a mobilization to transform the situation of women and the relations between them and men" (quoted in Callaway and Creevey 1994, 166).

Yewwu Yewwi fought on many fronts, but probably its best-known battles were for reform of the Family Code. Passed in 1972, the code spells out the specific rules and obligations of marriage, divorce, and inheritance. Although Senegal is a secular state, the government permitted a variation of the general law for those who declared themselves Muslims, a variation that was close to the specific family laws spelled out in the Koran and *sharia*. Yewwu Yewwi rejected the code because it allowed the continuation of Muslim traditional law, which limited the rights of women, at the same time that conservative Muslims rejected the code because it interfered with Muslim law. Fundamentalist groups of the era and marabouts were unified in their opposition to the code. Leaders of Yewwu Yewwi spoke against the code in national forums, on the radio, and in newspaper and journal articles. They were heavily criticized by conservative Muslim leaders for doing so. Ultimately neither side was a complete victor. But pressure from Yewwu Yewwi was a significant factor in moderating some provisions and making them more favorable to women. (Pressure from foreign donors and NGOs and the government's need to modernize the economy also played a role.) In 1989 the code was reformed to give a woman more rights; among other things, to decide if and where she worked (her husband's right before) and to establish her own place of residence (Creevey 1996, 292–301; Callaway and Creevey 1994, 176–181).

Since the mid-1990s the political scene has changed in Senegal. There are many more women's groups, most focused on a specific issue or concern for women.[6] The leaders of Yewwu Yewwi have replaced it with a group called Reseau Siggel Djigeen (Wolof for "women advance") that is more moderate in its tone. As Khady Sakho (2003), a close observer of women's groups in Senegal, noted recently:

> The first feminist movements (too radical) were pitched against a society still too feudal and patriarchal and resistant to all innovation especially Western ones. Unfortunately these movements have little by little lost their visibility and their actions and demands have become less specific. In the meantime the emphasis on equality of men and women is progressively subverted to the emphasis on gender in all areas of life—socio-economic, administrative and political. This approach is better received (although its precise definition is still unclear) because it is directed to the equality of choice and opportunity for men and women; for boys and girls.

Women's groups no longer see themselves as radical feminists but rather emphasize "the dignity of women with social, political and cultural emancipation, while being rooted in women's positive cultural values" (Sumarée 2002). Yet many of the goals of current groups are strikingly similar to the older groups, although their demands appear less strident to those who dislike Western feminism. And the Family Code is still a concern. For example (among others) there are three articles under debate: 152, 153, and 277. Article 152 declares: "The Husband is head of the family. He exercises that position in the interest of the household and the children" (Sakho 2003). Previously this article referred to the "power" rather than to "position," implying the husband's control. Despite this improvement, some Senegalese women activists such as Professor of Law Amatou Sow Sidibé argue that the notion of family head should be removed altogether, as it has been in some other Muslim African countries (Sakho 2003). Article 153 states: "Husband and wife must choose their common residence together." In the past it said that the choice of household residence belonged to the husband. Nonetheless, this provision can still lead to conflicts if there is disagreement on the choice of residence and is an object of concern for Senegalese women (Sakho 2003). Article 277 substitutes the notion of parental authority for the previous provision that referred to paternal authority over children. Here the complaint of some women observers is that the law is unclear and imprecise as it is written (Sakho 2003).

Alongside the actions of women to simplify and to diminish the subordination of women in some of the code provisions are the quite opposite efforts of some of the Islamists in Senegal. By and large, Muslim leaders in the brotherhoods and reformist groups continue to oppose the code as a violation of Muslim law. In a survey of Muslim leaders in Senegal conducted in 2004, most leaders (more than 58 percent if the Qadiri are excluded[7]) were opposed or strongly opposed to the Family Code. The most strongly negative were the Mouride marabouts (58 percent strongly opposed) and those with no brotherhood affiliation, which included Islamists (60 percent strongly opposed).

Some of the Islamists propose that the Family Code be scrapped in favor of a Code of Personal Statute that would mean that every Muslim would be judged under pure Islamic law as set down in the *sharia*. Women's groups in Senegal other than the Sunnites, whatever their purpose or organization, are united in their opposition to this effort, which to date does not appear to be making any substantial headway (Sakho 2003).

Finally, while the fight for a more liberal code continues, other women's organizations target other issues and problems. There is, for example, a women's organization that focuses on violence against women, an Observatory on Gender Relations in the National Education of Senegal, and a working women's network (Sakho 2003). Many of these are grouped under an umbrella organization that was founded in 1995, the Senegalese Council of Women (COSEF). COSEF combines the various women's action groups into one organization with a general shared theme: to fight the "judicial, cultural, political and social marginalization of, and discrimination against, Senegalese women" (Cisse et al. 1999, 11). Its first big national campaign was to mobilize women around the country to be involved in local and national politics. COSEF's 1998 manifesto, used during its campaign to increase women's participation in the National Assembly elections, clearly states the group's orientation:

> Considering that, conforming to the plan of action of Beijing, a better representation of women in decision making positions is essential for the deepening of democracy.
>
> Decide to launch a campaign for the elections of May 1998:
>
> **Democracy, Where are you?** Through meetings with political leaders, a press campaign, advertisements . . .
>
> Invite political parties to increase and improve the investiture of women on their (electoral) lists. . . .
>
> Call on the electorate to take into account a gender perspective in their choice (of candidate) so that women should be more and better represented in the National Assembly. . . .
>
> Call upon (all) the different candidates to take into account women's hopes and needs in the elaboration and formulation of their programs.
>
> March 1998 (Cisse et al. 1999, 53)

Conclusion

More women were elected to the National Assembly in 1998 (20) than had been elected in 1993 (8), and, as stated before, the number and percentage of women in the National Assembly rose again in the 2001 election, when 23 women were elected. In addition, more women were chosen as ministers in ministries with significant power in the Wade government. How much of this success was due to COSEF and how much to President Wade cannot be determined here. However, it is clear that under the Wade administration there is a favorable context for women's groups, at least as long as they do not take on the persona of militant Western feminists. Islam is still very important in Senegalese politics, and there is a dangerous undercurrent represented by the more militant Islamists. They do not have widespread support or membership, but they have a wider influence than just membership. The language of the women's movement is somewhat muted as a result. There is more consciousness of the need to purify Islam and more criticism of the West and Western lifestyles among educated Senegalese than existed formerly. Simultaneously, Wade is choosing to emphasize economic development and modernization, and his sources of support are principally in the West. Dakar is filled with offices of international organizations and aid agencies and foundations such as the United Nations (and its women's organization, UNIFEM), US Agency for International Development, the Friedrich Ebert Foundation (which supported COSEF), and many others. These groups openly support the work of the various women's organizations in Senegal.

Most women in Senegal do not belong to these issue-based organizations, but many rural women do belong to women's promotional groupings that were originally sponsored by the government in a Women's Promotion Program in 1982. By 1987 there were 2,500 of these women's associations (Creevey 2004, 67–68). These groups were organized hierarchically into a Senegalese National Federation for the Advancement of Women Groupings in 1987 (Sy 2002, 134). These groups have multiple purposes. They can receive loans from the government (or other agencies), they can act as social gatherings, and very frequently they have an economic purpose (Creevey 2004, 65–66). They are also political forums. Certainly the Diouf government used them to promulgate support for the president's policies and programs. But they must also be seen as arenas through which COSEF and other women's groups can reach uneducated rural women. The existence of these promotional groups provides a base for the spread of new ideas about women's rights and political roles. Aissata De Diop asserts that more women than men vote in rural areas in Senegal. She suggests that Muslim leaders may tell these women to vote and, of course, how to vote. Undoubtedly this is so, but it is also the case that rural women in Senegal are relatively mobilized to take political action and, as COSEF and others begin to broadcast their messages widely, Senegalese women are increasingly able to be reached.

Increasing women's representation in the National Assembly does not appear to be the priority for most Senegalese women's groups. They are focused instead on decreasing domestic violence, ending female circumcision, equalizing economic opportunities for women, and mobilizing women to be involved in politics more broadly. Some women leaders have now sought election to the National Assembly, and as there are more women in the upper ranks of the political parties, this will become more of an issue. There is certainly fairly widespread support for assuring that political parties set minimum percentages of women candidates. But, until the National Assembly becomes more than an audience for the decrees of the government, election to it will not be the highest priority for Senegalese women.

Notes

1. Seynabou Ndiaye Sylla cites Marie Pierre Sarr Traoré, legal scholar and professor at University Cheikh Anta Diop, on the greater emphasis on guaranteeing women's rights in the newest constitution (Sylla 2001). One of the new constitutional provisions gave women the right to own land in agricultural communities (Sumarée 2002).

2. Rosander's (2003) article about the female cult of Mam Diarra, mother of Ahmadou Bamba (founder of the Mouride brotherhood in Senegal), makes the general point as well that most scholars mistakenly see women in the sufi brotherhoods as passive and insignificant.

3. There are numerous analyses of the influence of the brotherhoods on politics in Senegal. Some major works include Copans 1980, Coulon 1981, Cruise O'Brien 1971, and Villalón 1995. My citations come from a book that I wrote under my former name (Behrman 1970).

4. See the discussion of the Mouride marabout Sokna Magat Diop of Thies (Coulon and Cruise O'Brien 1988). As Rosander (2003) points out, however, there are few such female marabouts: "Mouridism, like most of the other Sufi orders, is thoroughly male-dominated in its public, religious manifestations."

5. According to Aissata De Diop (2002), in the 1998 National Assembly women delegates were professors, teachers, secretaries, nurses, civil servants, and traders. Only one woman was classified as a housewife.

6. Some examples include the Collective for the Defense Against Violence Done to Women, headed by Oulimata Gaye Du; the Observatory for the Study of Gender Relations in National Education in Senegal, led by Mame Bineta Ndiaye Mbodj and Awa Fall Diop; and the African Network of Working Women, headed by Awa Wade and Amsatou Sow Sidibé.

7. Exclusion warranted because of the little influence that this brotherhood currently has in politics in Senegal.

8

The Virtuous Circle of Representation: Women in African Parliaments

Shireen Hassim

This book is testimony to the vibrancy of feminist political activism and intellectual debate on the African continent. The demands for greater representation of women in parliaments, articulated within the context of larger processes of democratization over the past twenty years, reflect robust women's movements that are alert to the opportunities presented by transitions. Women's movements have thus seized on opportunities for redesigning political institutions—parliaments, political parties, and electoral systems—in ways that produce fairer outcomes, particularly for marginal groups. As the chapters in this book show, there have been varying degrees of success in different countries, although the overall impact of women's movements has been to irrevocably break the association between maleness and political office. Women's movements have signaled decisively that there is room for women's agency to shape politics and that formal political rights are an important precondition for advancing equitable social policies.

Although the most visible strategy for increasing women's representation is the demand for quotas to break through ideological and institutional barriers, the case studies show that there is a multiplicity of ways in which women can gain political access. All of these strategies recognize that the formal institutions of democracy, even in postcolonial countries that avow a commitment to participatory democracy, are constituted in an exclusionary manner. Quota demands are based on the assumption that increasing the representation of women is a democratic good in itself. As Bauer and Britton argue in the introduction, the glaring absence of women in legislatures exposes a democratic deficit at the core of political systems. "Normal" processes of electoral competition cannot be seen as fair or just if they persistently produce the underrepresentation of the same subordinate groups in society. The consequences are significant even for the thinnest forms of democracy that focus on formal equality. For democrats committed to substantive and not merely procedural democracy, women's underrepresentation also limits the range of strategic possibilities. Without representation in legislatures, women citizens have a diminished ability to hold governments accountable.

In this chapter, I aim to take the debates on representation further by reflecting on a question raised by many of the authors in this volume: How can women's representation advance the agenda of gender equality? Although the chapters carefully detail the gains that have been made with regard to institutional access, they also show the enormity of the struggles that lie ahead, first in transforming institutions and second in developing the forms of political mobilization and constituency-building that will enable representational politics to be successful. The authors challenge us to consider the conditions under which women's access to political office can be directed toward the goal of reducing social and economic inequalities of gender. In this chapter I argue that in thinking about an effective feminist parliamentary politics we need to consider critically the relationship between representation, participation, and gender equality outcomes—what I will refer to as the virtuous circle of political representation.

The idea of a virtuous circle of representation refers to the assumption that women's political participation and mobilization will increase the number of women in decisionmaking office and, consequently, will enable women to have influence over decisionmaking in regard to national budgets, policy priorities, and the ideological direction of government policies, skewing these in ways that would redress inequalities. This assumption has become rhetorically common, particularly in campaigns for quotas. Note, for example, the Women's Environment and Development Organization argument that Bauer and Britton refer to, which claims that increasing women's representation will enhance the likelihood that issues such as child care, violence against women, and unpaid labor will become policy priorities. It also underpins many women's movements' views that achieving higher levels of representation will extend political activism into the state and allow them policy leverage. Yet the question of when and how shifts in policy outcomes are achieved is rarely examined, and demands for representation can easily become detached from the more difficult questions of political process and equality outcomes. In this chapter I will deal with each of the "drivers" of the virtuous circle—participation, representation, and gender equality—in turn in order to offer a modest theoretical framework within which to push the debate on women and parliaments further. In each instance I offer a "thin" (or weak) definition of the term as opposed to a "thick" (or strong) definition, arguing that for transformations in gender relations, feminists need to focus on advancing strong definitions. The central questions that I pose in this chapter are: What forms of participation, underpinned by what kinds of ideologies and in which arenas, are most likely to facilitate a gender equity agenda? How can effective representation be secured in the context of considerable institutional bias against women's presence in the public sphere? And finally, what kinds of policy outcomes are desirable from the point of view of different constituencies of women?[1]

Participation

Increasing women's participation in decisionmaking is a key part of the virtuous model. However, there are differing views on what constitutes participation. The thinnest definition (which is often evident in discussions of quotas) is that the mere presence of women in parliaments shifts "the patriarchal demeanor of political institutions" (www.gender.ac.za/50/50) and forces institutions to recognize women. Anne Marie Goetz and I distinguish this definition from that of effective participation, where the emphasis is on more effective interest articulation and representation—that is, to make the "voice" of particular constituencies louder in processes of policymaking (Goetz and Hassim 2003). However, as Goetz (2003, 34) points out, we should be careful not to assume that the amplified voice "will automatically strengthen the moral and social claims of the powerless on the powerful and produce better accountability to that group." Institutional norms and procedures and the nature of processes of deliberation can undermine the extent and impact of women's voice in the public sphere. The chapters in this volume all demonstrate the enormous difficulties women face in being taken seriously within institutions that are historically and culturally male. These more subtle patterns by which power hierarchies are upheld, even when new groups are included in institutions, are hard to make visible as well as hard to change. Women's participation as individuals in institutions of decisionmaking is generally limited—women are less likely to participate in parliamentary debates than men and are more likely to feel intimidated by the demands of public speaking, even when the women elected are highly skilled professionals.

Participation should also be understood in a "thicker" sense as an activity that encompasses collective mobilization through associational vehicles over which women have control. A strong social movement has the capacity to articulate the particular interests of its constituencies, to mobilize those constituencies in defense of those interests, and to develop independent strategies to achieve its aims while holding open the possibilities of alliance with other progressive movements. This definition suggests that a strong social movement requires a degree of political autonomy in order to retain its relative power within any alliance. Arguing for the importance of independent women's organizations is a thorny issue in African feminist debates (Tripp 2000b). Although autonomy was highly valued in Western women's movements—and in many was seen to be a condition of existence—in postcolonial countries autonomy is less highly valued. Because women's political activism in postcolonial contexts was enabled by larger struggles against colonial and class oppression, the result is a more highly developed politics of alliance rather than autonomy.

It is important to note that social movements do not merely "activate" preexisting identities and consciousness; they also *create* consciousness. Solidarity associations such as these often provide the arenas in which women develop collective consciousness that can be mobilized when the survival of communities is at stake. In many cases collective consciousness developed within these arenas forms the bedrock of indigenous feminist mobilization. As Temma Kaplan (1997) has pointed out, although the activities within these forms of organizations are "unspectacular" and may seem politically insignificant, they can be important sources for the emergence of social movements (not only women's movements). Thus, definitions of women's movements should not be so prescriptive or inelastic that they exclude the kinds of organized activities that involve the majority of poor women. Nevertheless, a critical factor in shaping whether women's movements aim to transform society is the existence of feminism as a distinct ideology within the movement, emphasizing the mobilization of women in order to transform the power relations of gender. Feminist ideology is pivotal in women's movements, as its relative strength determines the extent to which collective action is directed to democratic ends.

These difficulties have shaped the divergent forms that women's movements have taken in different contexts. Women's movements are not homogeneous entities characterized by single and coherent sets of demands. Rather, by their nature they tend to be diverse, embracing multiple organizational forms, ideologies, and even at times contradictory demands. Despite these diversities, it is possible to name and loosely bind together organizations that mobilize women collectively on the basis of their gender identity. Like other social movements, women's movements wax and wane in the context of particular political, economic, and social crises. What needs to be understood is why and when women's organizations act in a coordinated way—that is, defining at what moment disparate groups within the movement coalesce in such a way that they act as a movement, distinct from other political forces. This moment has been referred to by some analysts as "tipping" (Baldez 2002, 5). Tipping—the point at which disparate acts of protest cascade into a mass movement—occurs "when people come to believe that their participation becomes necessary or even required" (Baldez 2002, 6).

To what extent has women's participation—understood not just as referring to individual women's participation in institutions such as parliaments but as the collective mobilization of women—been advanced in the past twenty years? Can we understand the "quota fever" that has gripped the continent as a moment of tipping? This question has to be answered within the context of nationalism, as women's participation in national liberation struggles was very important in laying the basis for contemporary feminism. Although women have always been politically active, especially when the definition of activism is widened to include private acts of resistance to injustice and the modes of song and storytelling through which women have articulated their political visions, nationalism enabled mass-based collective action. Women's participation in these movements resulted in relatively rapid shifts from their roles as the foot soldiers of male-dominated movements to demands for women to be recognized as full citizens. In several countries, such as Mozambique, Namibia, and South Africa, women activists demanded that postindependence political platforms include commitments to gender equality. Nevertheless, gender politics was constrained by the paternalistic framework of nationalism: Women relied on the movement or party as the primary vehicle for articulating their citizenship claims and rarely developed autonomous political movements of their own. Women's incremental gains within nationalist movements did not obliterate the fundamental character of the politics of national liberation, in which women were mobilized primarily for the purposes of nationalism and as secondary subjects within the nation (and within subordinate women's organizations).

Contemporary strategies for institutional inclusion have a different character, as women are more firmly in control of their strategic aims, ideological forms, and organizational vehicles. In many ways this shift represents not so much a break with nationalist politics as a growing sense of agency and the flowering of indigenous forms of feminism that emerged out of women's participation in national liberation struggles. It also reflects disillusionment with postindependence nationalist governments, and particularly with the tendency to close spaces for independent political organization. As Mahmood Mamdani (1998) has pointed out, although nationalist movements derived their strength from popularly based social organizations (including those of women), the postcolonial period is characterized by the reduction of this diversity to a single movement that claimed to represent the entire nation. Consequently, all political mobilization outside the boundaries of the movement was delegitimized, and women's organizations—along with those of workers, peasants, and youth—either located themselves as subordinate to the movement or were driven to the margins. Contemporary women's movements seek to force open political space and have been important in enabling democratization. Among the earliest of these was the Ugandan women's movement, which used the transition to democracy in 1986 to develop associations that were independent of government and political parties (Tripp 2000b). Against this analysis, it can be argued that in many African countries women are in the moment of tipping, and that the demands for institutional inclusion can galvanize and reinforce women's movements—although the extent to which this will happen depends on whether strong relationships can be maintained between women in parliament and women's organizations in civil society. In part this extent will be determined by the nature of representation, that is, by whether electoral systems are designed to foster strong relationships between elected representatives and their constituencies.

Representation

The idea of representation has gained new currency around the world in the wake of campaigns for electoral quotas. For some feminists, women's exclusion (or at least marginalization) from the political arena as conventionally understood is the most stable interest, cutting across the range of differences between women (Phillips 1995; Baldez 2002). They argue that regardless of race, class, or ethnicity, women are consistently defined as political outsiders or second-class citizens whose entry into the public sphere is either anachronistic and short-term or conditional upon their maternal social roles. In my view, this constitutes a thin definition of representation, emphasizing women's interest in obtaining access to arenas of public power rather than debating the policy outcomes of such engagements. The task of feminism, in this more constrained approach, is to challenge exclusion. The political projects associated with this approach are, for example, women's enfranchisement, struggles around women's representation in national parliaments, and the emphasis on electoral systems, quotas, and other mechanisms for breaking political-systemic blockages. This form of feminism is crucial in creating some of the necessary conditions for the removal of gender inequalities, but it is limited by its reluctance to tamper with the structural basis of inequalities.

There are two quite different reasons why women's movements might avoid issues of structural inequality. The first stems from a strategic imperative to maintain minimal conditions for unity among women. Thus, for example, the South African Women's National Coalition, while recognizing that formal equality was a limited political goal, nevertheless maintained that inclusion in formal institutions was a common interest that would hold together a wide range of women's organizations and that questions of policy content would be dealt with separately once women were in parliament. The second reason, less widespread in Africa, is advanced by liberal feminists, who regard family and market as lying outside the realm of state action (Baldez 2002). It is far more likely, as the Mozambican and Rwandan case studies show, that women parliamentarians adopt the implicit view that policy directions should be developed by party elites in the first instance.

A thicker understanding of representation locates interest articulation and interest representation through parties and civil society organizations as central, and is more clearly tied to a politics of transformation. Interest articulation has a checkered history in African governments, as it has been associated most closely with the idea of national machineries for women, which have treated women's interests as narrow and "special" and as in need of patronage. Creating a set of specialized institutions for the consideration of gender shifted the issues of gender inequality out of the realm of politics and into the technical realm of policymaking. As Banaszak et al. (2003, 6) point out, this is increasingly a problem with national machineries around the world: "Women's movements have been presented with an increasingly depoliticized and remote set of policy-making agencies at the national level. . . . The relocation of responsibility to nonelected state bodies eventually reduces social movement influence." In the administration, gender equality concerns have fallen hostage to a range of institutional hierarchies and systemic blockages that are hard to deal with from outside the bureaucracy. In advancing the importance of interest articulation, I want to point to a bottom-up politics in which different constituencies of women identify and define policy demands that can be advanced as part of a horizontal coalition of interests (for example, poor urban women linking up with housing movements) as well as through policy-focused alliances with (or where necessary pressure on) women parliamentarians. The emphasis on building a constituency-based politics recognizes that not all women have the same interests, that women's organizations might conceive of their interests differently from women politicians, and that strong organizations of women at the local level enhance the virtuous circle of representation.

Quota demands tend to emphasize the creation of collective identity; they rest on the successful articulation of women's group–based interest in entering arenas of power. Quotas are a means of achieving recognition; indeed, they are best understood as a form of symbolic politics, as there is no predictable relationship between the greater number of women in decisionmaking and feminist outcomes. Interest representation, by contrast, may shatter the notion of women as a homogeneous group as the resource claims of some women based on their class and/or race disadvantages may come into conflict with the interests of other women, or require privileging the building of alliances with other social actors.

Of course, as many of the case studies show, the aims of inclusion and transformation are not mutually exclusive. Rather, they need to be seen as part of a continuum of women's struggles for full citizenship, which may take a linear historical form (that is, a shift over time from inclusionary demands to transformative demands) or may be present within a single movement at a given moment, with some sectors pursuing alliances with political elites for inclusion and others pushing toward a more radical set of demands. As the preceding chapters show, both of these approaches have been used in order to advance gender equality claims, at times (as in South Africa) with striking synergy. However, although these approaches may coexist within women's movements, there are many ways in which they are in tension with one another. It is important to note that each approach has long-term implications for what kinds of political alliances are built, which may in turn affect internal relations within the women's movement. Those arguing for remaining focused on inclusion cite the need for women's movements to gain access to political power to pursue the interests of representation effectively. Although they can gain this access through effective mobilization, they also need links with power brokers within political parties in order to ensure ongoing attention to the political system. Consequently, there is a tendency for such politics to become increasingly elite-based. Transformatory feminism, by contrast, is more likely to be conducted in alliance with other social movements aiming at structural transformation, such as social movements of the poor. This kind of politics may bring certain sections of the women's movement into contestation with elite and party-oriented members, as it is likely to take a more confrontational approach over party manifestos and state policies. The outcome of such alliances may be a marginalization of these actors from the state and political parties.

I would argue that recognition through quotas is a deceptively easy strategy. A transformative demand for representation (that is, that women need access to decisionmaking in order to advance a project of eliminating gender hierarchies of power) is reduced to a simple mechanism for institutional access as an end in itself. Although it is generally accepted in feminist literature that a combination of factors is responsible for women's increased access to political office—the nature of the political system and the organization of political competition, the nature of civil society and especially of the feminist lobby within it, and the nature and power of the state—all too often actual political strategies are collapsed into a demand for a quota. This is not surprising; it is without doubt more difficult to reshape the nature of the political system except, as the South African case demonstrates, during periods of major transition. Quotas are seen as a fast-track mechanism to cut through more intractable institutional blockages, to at least get "a foot in the door" of the political system.

There is enormous strategic sense in pushing for quotas in Africa, as they are politically cheap (and therefore politically salable) in political systems where there is a single dominant party; extending a quota to women does mean that some men will not get onto party lists, but with sufficient power such a party can exert control over the women it places on party lists. Advancing women into prominent positions is also relatively costless electorally when you have the combination of an electoral system of proportional representation (PR) and a dominant party. Yet processes of representation also matter from the perspective of effective representation. Electoral systems play a key role in determining the nature of the relationship between elected representatives, political parties, and constituencies. As Bauer and Britton point out, PR systems are now commonly assumed to be the most favorable for women, but the system carries costs that are less frequently detailed. On one hand, a PR system allows progressive parties to bypass customary and cultural objections to women's election—no small factor in societies where conservative religious forces dominate civil society. On the other hand, they also allow parties to establish mechanisms of control over elected leaders. PR systems breed loyalty to party rather than constituency: Disney shows how in Mozambique this can undermine the effectiveness of women members of parliament (MPs) as they simply "say yes" to the party. Similar concerns have been expressed in the South African case, where women MPs have found it difficult to establish a set of priorities for feminist intervention.

These concerns take us back to the dilemma of party paternalism that was inherited from the national liberation era. The ability of women representatives to mobilize within their parties and their willingness to challenge party hierarchies is an important determinant of the extent to which women will be effectively represented, yet individual women MPs often find it difficult to develop the confidence and political base from which to push for gender equality platforms. In many countries parliamentary women's caucuses have been mooted as a strategy for setting priorities and building support and confidence. However as Disney and Britton show for Mozambique and South Africa, respectively, these caucuses have not been successful precisely because of the electoral system. Women are after all elected to represent the party rather than women as a constituency. The challenge is therefore whether and how women's gender interests can be articulated in a way that is distinct from their party interests and identities. Uganda is an intriguing example in this respect. There women are elected to seats reserved for women, by an electoral college made up of women and men councilors, but rather than unambiguously representing women are required to represent the district as a whole. This means that women MPs remain beholden to the movement as the primary political force and that the election of women MPs who might challenge movement policies in parliament is as unlikely as in a multiparty PR system. As Tripp argues, this situation has led women's movement activists to seek to change the electoral process so that the women's seats are elected by universal adult suffrage—unsurprisingly, a move opposed by the president.

Senegal, with its mixed electoral system, also offers an interesting counterpoint to the conventional PR system. Although more women are elected to parliament through the PR than through the plurality system, Creevey points out that an increasing number of women are elected through the plurality system. She shows the role that political leadership and a modernizing party can play in shifting attitudes toward women—showing what possibilities there are for feminist politics even in constituency-based systems. Similarly, Longman writes that in Rwanda it would be erroneous to attribute the massive gains in gender representation to quotas alone, as the number of women in nonreserved elected seats has also increased dramatically—with women winning nearly half of all the seats in the National Assembly in the 2003 elections (against a guaranteed 30 percent of seats). Similarly, Longman points out, women won offices where quotas did not apply, as in the election of judges. The involvement of women in previous governments and particularly in the democracy movement appears to account for the rapid increases in the number of women in elected seats. In addition, as in Senegal, strong support for women's rights and women's political representation from the president of the leading party (the Rwandan Patriotic Front) played a key role.

Yet both the Senegalese and Rwandan cases show the potentially ugly side of presidentialism and single-party dominance, with Creevey and Longman both warning of rising authoritarian tendencies in the ruling party. Indeed, Longman argues that because the parliament "serves more as an instrument of legitimizing and preserving RPF power," the increase in women's representation is of questionable value. This statement might be overly strong, yet it suggests that democratic women's movements need to move quickly to buttress the openings allowed in transitional periods to build strong movements outside parliament that will sustain women's representational gains. These examples suggest that women cannot rely on political parties as their only vehicles for representation, particularly when parties are less vehicles for interest articulation and more instruments of ethnic mobilization. The examples reinforce the importance of independent representative organizations in the women's movement that may have relationships with political parties but also have an independent existence. This ensures that women are mobilized not only for their votes but as electoral constituencies with clearly articulated policy interests.

The case studies also implicitly highlight the importance of linking representation to accountability, not least to guard against women parliamentarians becoming co-opted by male party elites. Here women can benefit from multipartyism, even though the innate democratic potential of multipartyism is often overrated. As Disney shows for Mozambique, there is a distinction between a women's organization representing all women and one representing a distinct constituency of women. In the former instance we see a reflection of the nationalist assumption that the nation is a singular homogeneous entity with one legitimate representative party. In the latter, political constituencies are not a given; there is a socially and politically constructed relationship between citizens and political parties that needs to be constantly nurtured. Multiparty systems can also assist constituencies of women to push parties into supporting gender equality because of the threat that they can vote for other parties. In Sweden, for example, feminists successfully advanced the argument that they would switch their allegiances from the Social Democratic Party if women's views on party policies (such as nuclear weapons) were not taken into account. In South Africa, feminist gains within the African National Congress have produced a contagion effect; virtually all parties now formally support gender equality, thus democratizing the party system as a whole.

The relationship between women parliamentarians and the women's movement is as difficult as the relationship between women activists and leaders within political parties. In some respects there are organic political ties within these spheres; many women parliamentarians cut their political teeth in women's organizations. As a result, the relationship between party/parliament and civil society can often be fluid, as women activists can move back and forth between state and civil society. This fluidity solidifies policy influence but can also have negative impacts in countries with small political elites. Close personal and political relationships can breed a sense of loyalty to comrades that undermines criticism. Yet even if political elites were a much larger segment of the population, there are inherent tensions in this relationship. Anne Summers (1986) has characterized this as the tension between missionaries (activists in civil society) and mandarins (politicians), with each expecting relationships of support and accountability that may be hard to provide. In South Africa, for instance, there has been a growing gap between women in the national machinery and women in civil society (Hassim 2003; Gouws 2004). Britton suggests that the gap is recognized and that attempts are being made for closer cooperation between different sections of the national machinery and women's organizations in civil society. However, the structural tension between "femocrats" inside the state, accountable to bureaucratic hierarchies, and women's organizations with more radical demands is likely to persist.

Gender Equality Outcomes

Looking finally at the nature of policy outcomes, it is important to consider the meanings attached to gender equality in different contexts. In this debate, the central concern is what can be achieved through the state—that is, how to use openings in the formal decisionmaking process to advance equality. As Disney (along with other contributors to this volume) notes: "There is a gap between the quantitative representation of women . . . and the qualitative capacity of women to effect change on behalf of women's political, economic, and sociocultural rights and interests." Representation is a necessary condition for policy effectiveness, but it is not a sufficient condition by any means.

Although this argument is easily recognized, debates about quotas and other mechanisms have been more or less separate from debates about what interests women politicians ought to represent once in parliament. Throughout the continent, women's movements have historically struggled for forms of liberation that included but were not restricted to the achievement of equal rights and opportunities. This is not to deny the importance of formal political and civil rights, especially in contexts where there is tremendous resistance to the idea of women's equality. Yet poor women's movements have consistently held out for an understanding of liberation that would include economic transformation and (to a lesser extent) social reordering of gender relations. Definitions of equality need to be grounded in the particular context in which claims are being made, and I would guard against specific policy prescriptions that should be applied to all African contexts. Nevertheless, some kind of broad definition of equality seems necessary as a framework in which to locate a politics aimed at policy outcomes that would benefit poor women. I would argue that a strong notion of equality would rest on the extent to which overall poverty is reduced; the degree to which women have autonomy and are able to make choices free of the constraints of care work within families and communities, as well as free of the pressure to remain in oppressive and violent relationships (Orloff 1993);[2] and the extent to which women feel safe in society. This notion of equality has specific implications for social policy, as it would require that resources be directed not only to address the needs of the poorest women but also to be part of an incremental process of enhancing the recognition of women's personhood and their full participation in political and economic processes. This would entail considerable debate about the relationship between the public and private sphere and the cultural recognition of women's unpaid work, and at the very least a public debate about how to negotiate women's individual rights against those of the communities to which they belong.

If the particular content of gender equality ought to be left to women's organizations themselves to define, in their particular socio-economic and cultural contexts, the argument for collective mobilization of women and the building of electoral constituencies as the under-girding of representational politics is strengthened. Disaggregating representation from the debate about desirable policy directions and policy outcomes—however strategically useful such a strategy might be in the short term—carries the danger that political party elites (albeit with a gender-neutral face) will continue to determine the content of liberation.

Conclusion

In this chapter I argue that the form of women's democratic inclusion needs attention—that is, how women are included can have effects on how they aggregate as a political power bloc, and on the kinds of political and policy outcomes that are possible through increased representation. I also argue that quota mechanisms can result in demands for representation being disembedded from processes of constituency formation. This has a significant impact on the feminist ambitions to shift the nature of gender power relations. Rapid inclusion in political institutions through mechanisms such as quotas has many advantages. However, if these are unlinked from processes of collective mobilization on one hand, and intensive debate about the meanings of equality and the desirable outcomes of policy for women on the other, it can act as a brake on more transformative feminist ambitions.

Returning to the idea of a virtuous circle, I have taken as a starting point the evidence that there is not an automatic relationship between women's increased political representation and the erosion of gender equalities. Rather, I have shown that a far more complex discussion is required of the relationship between participation, representation, and equality. A schematic view of this discussion might appear as shown in Table 8.1. In this framework the virtuous circle of representation is best achieved, from a feminist perspective, when the drivers of the circle are pursued in their strongest form. The outcomes of weak formulations of the virtuous circle are likely to be the achievement of formal liberal democracy that is procedurally fair but does not substantially erode gender inequalities in the lives of the majority of the poor. At the same time, stronger conceptualizations of the nature of strategies to achieve gender equality, while relatively harder to pursue politically, are likely to have the long-term effect of democratizing the whole of society, not just the political system.

I have, of course, oversimplified the distinctions between these approaches; in practice many women's movements move between these

Table 8.1   Representation, Participation, and Equality: A Schematic Picture

	Weak Conceptualization	Strong Conceptualization
Participation	Women's participation in formal political institutions (parliament and political party)	Women's collective mobilization, including parliament and parties as well as civil society
Representation	Increased number of elected women	Parliamentarians represent particular interests and are accountable to constituencies of women
Gender equality outcome	Formal legal equality	Substantive transformation of political, social, and economic relations of inequality

strategies depending on the particular campaign. Nevertheless, as a heuristic device this characterization of different tendencies in current debates about representation lays open the underlying assumptions of particular strategies and aims to shift debate away from quotas to more challenging questions of accountability and equality outcomes.

Notes

1. The alternative, a vicious political circle, can also be posited, in which there is a numerical increase in women representatives without a concomitant impact on policy outcomes, resulting in women citizens exiting from formal political participation or mobilization through political parties.

2. Orloff (1993, 319) takes this argument much further in suggesting that social policies should aim at decommodification of gender relations by enabling women to form and maintain autonomous households. I am hesitant to apply this notion to women in the African context, given the particular cultural attachments and support systems that women value within family and communities. It could be argued that the high number of women-headed households in South Africa suggests that women are indeed free to form autonomous households, but this has patently not empowered women to become full and equal citizens.

Appendix: Interviews with Four African Women Parliamentarians

Rwanda

This interview was conducted by Timothy Longman in Kigali, Rwanda, on January 18, 2005. The interview was conducted in French and translated by the interviewer.

Bernadette Mukarutabana was elected a Rwandan Patriotic Front (RPF) deputy in the Chamber of Deputies of the Rwandan Parliament in October 2003. A native of Karaba Commune in Gikongoro, Rwanda's poorest province, she has been a longtime human rights activist.

TL: *Could you tell me a little about your background? I know that you were previously active in civil society.*

BM: It has been a while since I left civil society, but I have a long history in civil society, working in human rights groups. I served as president of the LDGL, the League of Human Rights Organizations in the Great Lakes Region. Before that I was in LIPRODHOR [League for the Protection of Human Rights in Rwanda], where I also served as president. I was with CLADHO [Collective of Leagues and Associations for the Defense of Human Rights], the umbrella organization for human rights groups in Rwanda. And now I am on a committee in parliament that deals with human rights.

How did you get involved in politics? How did you end up running for office?

Working in civil society, I understood the need for political involvement. In civil society, we participated in various forums of civil society organizations, such Reseau des Femmes [Women's Network]. As women, we had the ambition to participate in politics, even before the war. We say here that "when a woman speaks, the nation speaks." But women have not had political power. After the war there were so many widows, so many women survivors, so many women taking care of children alone, and their issues needed to be addressed. We saw that if women were involved in politics more, then there were many things in society that could be changed.

We have tried to have an influence on the laws, especially those affecting us directly as women. The most important of these has been inheritance. Women were left without husbands to raise their families alone, and yet they couldn't inherit the land and goods of their husbands. Widows were being thrown out. Their husbands' families simply cast them aside, and they had no rights. Even after changing the laws, we saw that men were continuing to ignore the rights of women. And women couldn't get credit, which is very serious. If a woman is alone, it is she who has to pay the school fees for her children. Women have gone through all of these terrible things, but life continues afterward, and women have to go on. So we wanted to participate in elections to promote the interests of women.

The Forum of Women [Parliamentarians] supported women candidates. But personally, I am a member of a political party. I am a member of the RPF.

So you were elected on the party list?

Yes, I was elected on the party list of the RPF. They put my name forward. But I was also supported by the forum. So I was supported by both the party and the Forum of Women [Parliamentarians].

And how have you found conditions for you as a woman in parliament? Is there resistance to the women parliamentarians?

There was resistance in the past. But the women now are so many, and they stand up for themselves. After all, they vote on the issues. The women parliamentarians stay very active. And we continue to work on our issues. Women can now get credit. They now have their own bank. Many things have changed for women. In the future I don't think that there will be as much concern for the issue of women in office; there may not be a need to have seats for women. But for now, there is no discrimination. In fact, men are now complaining that if things continue like this, we will take over everything. [Laughs.]

Is there any difference between women elected as women's candidates and those elected on the party lists? Are they treated any differently?

No, once they are elected there is no difference. We have the same votes, and we are treated the same.

What is the role today for the Forum of Women Parliamentarians?

The forum continues its work because despite the existence of laws, there are still problems for women in society. For example, there is still a lot of polygamy, especially in places like Ruhengeri, even though monogamy is required in the constitution. We have been thinking about how to develop appropriate punishments for the continuation of the practice, since it is now against the law. But it continues.

What is the policy for those who are already in polygamous marriages? Do the men have to leave their wives? What happens to the women?

Well, the law expects the men to take responsibility for all of their children, but they have to have a single wife. They have to choose, for example, from among their five wives which one they want to stay with and liberate the others. It is really a problem when they take so many wives and have so many children and then can't support them. Or sometimes a man has his formal wife back home but other wives on the side who are not official. In these cases, we make him take just the legal wife and leave the others. If these men are public officials, well, they have to show a good example, so there are consequences.

So what is the work of the forum?

I think that the forum needs to continue to sensitize. The laws are there, but people do not always follow them or understand them, so we have to raise awareness. There is also a ministry for women that works on these issues, sensitizing people about the rights of women. We have to continue to work on the rights of children, the right for women to keep their husband's property, so that people accept the law.

Are there more laws that need to be passed to protect women's rights?

No, the laws already protect women, but it is the putting them in application that needs to be developed.

As someone who came out of civil society, what is your relationship now with the civil society?

I have stayed very active with civil society. Really we have a privileged relationship [as parliamentarians] with civil society. We are often together at meetings and conferences. We are often together. We work on common issues. I am now on a committee in parliament for human rights. As someone who was involved in human rights organizations, as someone who was president of a human rights organization, I continue.
. . . I have recently been elected vice president of an organization of parliamentarians that struggles against corruption throughout all Africa: African Parliamentarians Network Against Corruption. This has also become an important issue here for parliamentarians.

So we *have* to work with the civil society because we are working on the same issues. For example, we have to work with civil society on AIDS if there is a project dealing with AIDS. Sometimes the rights of those who have AIDS are denied, and we have to work for their rights, and this needs help from civil society. So we have to work together.

Also, I forgot to add the very important fact that when we have legislation, we have to consult civil society in the process. When we have the consultation process for a new law, we have to pass it by civil society for consultation. When a new law is adopted, we need civil society to sensitize the population, because they deal directly with the population.

Namibia

This interview was conducted by Gretchen Bauer in Windhoek, Namibia, on July 8, 2002. The interview has been shortened and edited.
Saara Kuukonwgelwa-Amadhila was first elected to Namibia's National Assembly in 1999 from the Swapo party list when she was the director general of the National Planning Commission; she was reelected to the National Assembly in 2004 and is now the minister of finance.

GB: *What motivated you to become involved in politics?*

SKA: I believe that I was born into politics because I was born the year after the armed struggle for independence was launched in Namibia. Growing up, I could see that things were not normal—the segregation, the discrimination, the restrictions. The thing that really opened my eyes was the restrictions. When I shared my dreams with my parents, I noticed that there were certain things that I could not do because I was black. And then as I progressed in school and I was taught history, I came to learn that we were a nation, living in a country, as opposed to just an ethnic group, living in a tribal reserve. That is when I started asking questions: I live in a nation. I am a Namibian. I am not just an Ovambo girl. All of Namibia, including Windhoek and Oranjemund, is my country. Why is it I don't have the right to go there any time I want to? Why is it I cannot become a doctor if I want to?

Later on when I was about eleven, the South African forces of occupation became more visible. They were deployed even in the villages; I started to feel afraid, seeing them beat and murder people. Then I started hearing about the liberation movement. It was actually the strategy of the South Africans themselves which motivated Namibians to join the liberation movement. They made up things—that the Swapo leaders were half animals, they killed people, they were cannibals, and so on. We then turned to our parents and our teachers to ask them about this. We also turned to the older kids, especially the ones who lived in areas where Swapo militants had established bases. They would come and tell us stories about the militants, what they were fighting for, what other systems existed around the world, how other people in Africa were independent, and how they could aspire to become whatever they wanted to become.

When I was just twelve years old I was introduced to some Swapo fighters by my older sister. Not physically; I never came to see them. I came home for a weekend and I was told that they were there, and my sisters were telling me about it. So I became interested. I thought that what was happening was wrong and maybe I should become part of the process of changing things. And so in 1980 when I was twelve years old I left home with my older sister and crossed into Angola [to the Swapo camps]. So I actually grew up in Swapo. I joined Swapo in Angola, and because I was too young for military training I was sent to an education center where I finished my primary school. Then I got a scholarship with the UNHCR to complete my secondary schooling in Sierra Leone. When I finished I returned to Angola and joined the military wing of Swapo. I was trained and deployed for a short while. Then it was 1989, and we returned to Namibia for elections. So that is how I was introduced into politics. And the main motivation was just that I found it objectionable that one people should subject another people to the kind of brutality that the South Africans did, that one people should deprive another of their basic rights. I thought that I had an obligation to be part of the process to change that.

After returning from exile you left Namibia again to study at Lincoln University in the United States. After finishing your degree you returned to Namibia, and in 1995 you were appointed the director general of the

National Planning Commission. When you were elected to the National Assembly in 1999, did you feel fully prepared?

I did not really find it extremely difficult because I had worked as the DG of the NPC, which is a semipolitical position as well as a technical position. It has a ministerial rank, and so I attended cabinet meetings and I was considered to be a politician. And even though I was not an MP, I followed parliamentary issues and I was able to gather some small experience that helped me when I became a member. And also we were put through a one-week [National Democratic Institute] orientation program. Maybe it was not enough, but I think we were introduced to the basic things that we would experience there in parliament; I think it did help to a degree. I think it was becoming DG that was more difficult for me. That is where I had the most difficulty because I just went from being a low-level civil servant who never really worked very closely with politicians and other senior civil servants. And when I became DG I didn't have a deputy, and my permanent secretary was also new. So that was more difficult than becoming an MP.

What do you think is needed to elect more women to public office in Namibia?

I think one of the things that is needed is legislation that requires that all political parties nominate a certain number of women. And secondly, we need to educate our colleagues because it is one thing to make sure a minimum number of women are nominated and another thing to not take them seriously when they make a contribution just because they are women. When you talk about maternity leave, people laugh. Then when you get offended, they say, "Oh, I was only kidding." When we were talking about equality between black and white, nobody thought it was funny, but when you talk about equality between men and women, people think it is funny and they make jokes about it. And it is the education not only of men, but also of women that is needed. A lot of times we think we are marginalized because men don't accept us, but sometimes it is also because we have come to believe that we are inferior, that we ourselves are reluctant to grab opportunities even when they are there. So I think there should also be the education of women, you know, to be aggressive in a political way, look out for opportunities, and grab them when they are there.

And then we also need legislation that would provide for the full participation of women in an array of economic opportunities. Some of the legal barriers that existed in this country in the past were incredible.

Women were considered minors; they couldn't take a certain job without their husband's permission; they couldn't have a bank account. Those kinds of barriers should also be removed. A supportive legislative environment should be created so that women can realize their potential. And also things like the educational empowerment of women and the removal of stereotypes. Because you realize that our girls at school think that boys should study engineering, and their teachers encourage boys to do that and girls to study other things like home economics. So I think it is a whole lot of things that we need to do simultaneously and persistently.

Do you feel solidarity with other women MPs across party lines? Does gender ever supersede party?

Yeah, I think that there are certain issues that we are united around. We have, for example, established a women's caucus in parliament. We have decided to put in place a program to educate fellow women and to encourage them to participate in political life. And I think all of us also are fully behind the realization of at least 30 percent participation of women in all SADC parliaments and we are all working toward that. Also, when there are appointments made or endorsed by parliament we always try to question why there is not adequate representation of women if there is none. We want to make sure that women are included, even though sometimes, being that we are a new nation, this is a struggle. It is a difficult one. There are areas where there are differences. But what we try to do is to emphasize more those issues that unite us. We can emphasize things over which we differ on other platforms. We have our political parties; if we disagree on political issues we should address those through our parties—we shouldn't try to make them part of the agenda of our women organizations. That is one sure way to bring about division.

What do you think you and other women MPs have accomplished in parliament?

First of all, speaking from the side of being a government official, I would say that what we have achieved is that government programs impact women's lives. We are also ensuring that issues like rural development receive priority in government. These are areas in which women are active: issues like the economic empowerment of women where we have made sure that the women's community-based organizations are given due attention by government and are provided with whatever support they would need, whether financially or technically.

Also, we have made sure that gender equity is considered in the appointment of boards, for example, of parastatal boards. There have been instances where we have held up the approval of a board because there were no women. So we have done that.

In parliament I think we have been successful in that we have agreed to unite across political lines and meet certain objectives, for example, the establishment of a parliamentary women's caucus. We are united in our commitment to promoting objectives that would result in the improvement of the lives of women. We have established our women's caucus, and it does meet, it does have a program. And we are also promoting the women's organizations in parliament by ensuring that when they bring petitions forward to parliament, the petitions are considered and are responded to. And we are making sure that we support legislation that seeks to undo discriminatory laws against women and to make it possible for women to realize their potential. And we are considering ourselves as colleagues even though we are political foes, recognizing that we have our differences but we also have similarities. So I think those are achievements, and we are determined to build on those successes. Finally, hopefully in the future we will realize a 50 percent representation of women in parliament and other important structures.

How would you describe relations between women MPs and women's organizations in Namibia?

There are a number of women's organizations in Namibia, and we do have interactions with them. Sometimes we organize joint meetings with those organizations and parliamentarians. It is a matter of concern for some of us that we have a host of women's organizations in a small country like Namibia. I think we should have been able to have a single women's organization with unified objectives. I think that you will observe that sometimes the differences are things that relate to things like homosexuality. Nobody can deny that that is a significant issue to discuss, but my view is always that homosexuality is not an exclusively women's thing. You have gays and lesbians. So one does not necessarily have to put it in there because the moment you do, then those that are opposed will not support you. I think the very important issue that we have to resolve is to identify common issues and try to concentrate on those and then establish different platforms where we can address those issues. Because otherwise we have political differences, we have religious differences, we have cultural differences, and the only way that we have managed to maintain unity, even for example in Swapo, is to focus on one thing—such as in the past, the most important thing was to liberate Namibia. If you wanted to become a communist, if you wanted to become a capitalist, if you wanted to become an atheist, no problem. You could pursue that after independence. Those other issues were never part of the agenda. Because of that we got the unity that we wanted and the strength that we needed to bring about our independence. And I think maybe that is what we have to consider amongst women, so that we can really achieve the unity that we need and make the progress that needs to be made.

How important do you think an international women's movement has been to women's participation in politics in Namibia?

Well, I think that there have been some positive influences. First of all, we try to liaise with other organizations. We attend international platforms and forums like the Beijing conference, for example; we were there. We acceded to the protocols and instruments that came out of those forums. And we learn from the experiences of other women, being that we are a new nation. Things like reaching certain benchmarks. We don't want to push them too much into people's faces, but we want to sensitize people and make sure there are clear yardsticks or goalposts by which progress can be measured. So we have learned from that. And then we have exchanges through which we build our own women's organizations' capacity. So I think all of those are positive things. We need to consider liaising with international organizations as an important strategy for promoting our gender equality and equity strategy here in Namibia.

South Africa

This interview was conducted by Hannah Britton in Cape Town, South Africa, on May 29, 2003. The interview has been shortened and edited.

Usha Roopnarain is a member of the Inkatha Freedom Party (IFP) who was elected to the South African parliament in 1999. At the time, she was finishing her Ph.D. in political science and working for the IFP Caucus as a researcher. She was also a member of the Joint Monitoring Committee on the Improvement of the Quality of Life and Status of Women. Roopnarain was reelected in 2004 and currently serves on the Joint Monitoring Committee on the Improvement of the Quality of Life and Status of Children, Youth, and Disabled Persons; the Portfolio Committee on Public Enterprises; and the Portfolio Committee on Public Service and Administration.

HB: *Would you tell me how you became involved in politics and how you came to parliament?*

UR: You know, I have been asked this question so many times. I actually started off in academia. I was doing my Ph.D. on women in politics. The title of my dissertation was "Women in the Political Process in a Comparative Context." And I was dealing with India and the environmental movement, Brazil and the women's movement there, and South Africa. I was trying to draw the link of how women were using the spaces or avenues that were available to them, how they mobilized and how they got their voice heard. Little did I know that this was actually going to be preparing me for my life in politics.

And it so happened that while I was completing my Ph.D. in political science that I applied for a job as researcher for the IFP's Caucus. . . . And when I started I was told that researchers always get usurped into parliament: They are writing their own speeches. It was almost a prophetic word over my life because I didn't want to be a politician. I liked working in the background, writing their speeches, doing their press statements. And you have this perception of a politician. It is a very negative one.

But it so happened that I was nominated by my constituency, and I was put on the list, and I was put on as number seven on the list. And that was an automatic guaranteed seat. Everybody was calling me and asking me how I felt about being number seven on the list. I think my research work was preparatory ground for being an MP. It wasn't even in my career choice to be an MP. I thought that really I would be an academic, be involved in one of these institutes or lectureships or something like that. And I thought I would be working in women's equality projects and that sort of thing. Little did I realize that I would be an MP.

Can you map how those skills have translated into your new career?

Absolutely. Essentially my job as a researcher was to write speeches and research the party policies and things that were really close to my heart: women's issues, children's issues. I like environmental issues, those kinds of things. I have passion for these issues—especially women's rights. If you know about women's rights, you are able to lobby and use particular skills. . . . If you are able to read the constitution, you know what your legal rights are and how to access those rights. For example, if you know about the Chapter 9 institutions, then you know about the Commission for Gender Equality; you know there is the Public Protector and there is the Youth Commission.

So academia molds you into becoming a better politician. You realize you come equipped with all these skills that most women don't have. I was directly from that experience. And research skills are especially helpful in speeches. If you are able to quote research and facts, it makes the speech all the more powerful, and people listen. And they say, "I didn't know all these figures," and so you learn how to access those figures.

Politics reinvents you. You have to become tougher and be able to withstand all the darts and criticism. You become built a certain way, and especially with women. We are much more compassionate. We tend to serve on the softer portfolios. And I have opted to serve instead on Public Service. So you break the stereotypical mold.

So you have found that there is the perception that women should serve on the softer portfolios. Yet if you said that you want to serve on another type of committee, would your party let you?

Absolutely. I find that in most of the portfolios, like health and social development, the bulk of the members there are women. That needs to change. And we keep asking, "Where are all the women?" We need to be equipping ourselves to take over. Some of my new portfolios are Public Enterprises and very male-dominated portfolios. And that is how we take charge. And all the women are always serving on the Joint Monitoring Committee on the Quality of Life and Status of Women.

How have the men perceived you in these male-dominated portfolios?

Well, in my caucus, whenever there is a women's issue or whenever I put up my hand, they say, "She is going to be talking about women!" That is their response. In one of my speeches, I remember, in caucus, I addressed the men, and I used a quotation by Nancy Reagan that "women are like teabags—you only realize how strong they are when you put them in hot water." And most of the time you want to bring up a feminist issue or a gender-sensitive issue—they are always at the bottom of the agenda, something [we get to] just before we close. . . .

Just the other day, we were discussing the electoral law. Most political parties are lobbying for, and justly so, the 30 percent representation, [or] like a zebra system, one male and one female, that kind of thing. Our party is still in the process of deciding where they stand. So issues like that. And even with debates related to women, most of the time we have a male and a woman to speak, so it is not only that a woman's issue needs to have a woman speaking . . . because gender involves both men and women.

. . . Essentially, our party has always tried to promote women. I think if I weren't a woman, I wouldn't be put number seven on the list. . . . I think being a woman also helps in a way. We haven't reached that place where we can say we have adequate representation of women. But we are going in that direction. We have a deputy chief whip who is a woman, Mrs. Seaton. Our deputy leader of our caucus, Mrs. Mars, is a woman. We have whips who are women, like Mrs. Mbuyazi. At one stage we had a minister who was a woman. She is now ambassador. And so our party certainly has made progress. And they are always trying to mold me and groom me and mentor me to take over positions and take over in the portfolio.

So this grooming and mentoring is an alternative to a party quota? Even if your party does not adopt the quota system, it is using affirmative action measures—like mentoring and recruitment?

And merit also. If you look at a woman—she shouldn't be there just because she is a woman. That kind of thing. But if she is competent and able to perform her duties even better than a man, then she should be there.

What sort of obstacles or challenges have you faced in your new role?

The biggest one initially was that I was in the province, and I came to the National Assembly. And I came from a very traditional Indian family, and I was at home all the time with my parents. And the biggest challenge was having to leave my home and come here and live on my own. Personally that was a huge challenge for me, and it really teaches you a lot of resilience, and you realize you have such greater strength within yourself. I was able to draw on that.

The other thing was that the provincial government, it was a microcosm of parliament, and national parliament itself is like a macrocosm. So the provincial legislature also trained me and groomed me for bigger fora, and that was the good thing about it. But there were lots of changes: yourself, your personality, you have to be tough, you have to be a public figure, you have to have a public image to address all these meetings. I never could quite deal with the image factor as well.

You know this title "honorable member," and I prefer to be called by my first name, and those kinds of things, and the status that went with that. . . . But essentially when the shiny shoes are off and the designer suits are away, you are a public servant, so you have to realize that you are a public servant.

What are your main goals as a member of parliament?

Even if my term comes to an end next year, there is a lot I would like to see happen. For one, there are so many things we are trying to put forward. From a party point of view, especially from the province from which I come, KwaZulu Natal, the political violence there, the infighting between political parties. You hope that there would be some sort of peace development, nation-building, reconciliation in all provinces I think, amongst all people.

And secondly, you know in parliament we end up fighting over so many issues. At times it takes so many of us to make a bill into law. And most of the time, most people do not know what legislation is. I will be happy when it becomes a practical reality for every human being, when they will be able to live their life with a sense of worth and dignity, and say, "I am glad to be a South African, and the constitution affords me this right as a human being." I think that will be the greatest thing for me.

Those are strong goals, and I really respect them. Specifically, are you also talking about political education and the pride that can come with that education?

Absolutely. You find that if you look at the demographics of South Africa, there is this great urban/rural divide, the gap between the literate and the illiterate, the gap between the women who know where they are going and the women who don't know at all. We talk about fantastic pieces of legislation: the Maintenance Act, the Domestic Violence Act, and women don't know about these things. They don't even know what the constitution is. Those kinds of things. Today we are going to be talking about children's rights in parliament, and there are still those innocent children who are being raped, abused, and neglected. So maybe it is a very idealistic goal, but that is my vision. That is the way I would love South Africa to be, for everybody to have this freedom from fear.

I would love to follow up on implementation. Now that you have the legislation, how do you translate that into a changed reality for women and children around these issues and also this reconciliation in KwaZulu Natal? How do you manifest that?

In terms of legislation and getting it down to women. We are in the National Assembly; we are MPs. You have to use women's groups; you have to use NGOs, the coalitions, the networks. They are sort of the vehicles that saturate it to women. Organizations actually take away the legalistic jargon and make it more accessible, but it needs to go beyond that.

Mozambique

This interview was conducted by Jennifer Leigh Disney in Maputo, Mozambique, on July 2, 2004. The interview has been shortened and edited.

Ana Rita Sithole has been a Frelimo MP in the Mozambican Assembly of the Republic since the first multiparty parliament in 1994. She was reelected in 1999 and served a second term until 2004. Since this interview she has been reelected to a third parliamentary term. Sithole has been and continues to be a member of the Permanent/Standing Commission of the Assembly of the Republic. She is also a presiding member of the African, Caribbean, and Pacific/European Union (ACP/EU) Joint Parliamentary Forum.

JLD: *You are one of the only MPs I interviewed five years ago whom I am interviewing again. I wonder if you wanted to reflect on the changes that have taken place for women in parliament in the last five years.*

ARS: Well, this is my second term as an MP for Frelimo in parliament. Our term has almost reached its end. We are having general elections in December. I will run on behalf of my party again for another term. The number of women parliamentarians increased a lot this term. We are almost seventy-five, both from Frelimo and the opposition. I think there are changes in terms of women's participation if you take account of the quality of debate women have been involved in. We have one vice speaker who is a lady. We have women presiding in permanent committees. We have women in the Standing Committee of the Assembly, and we have more [women] than the last term. We have women in all national groups. We call "national groups" those groups which participate in other parliamentary forums internationally, such as the IPU [the Inter-Parliamentary Union] and ACP/EU. I am the presiding person [of the ACP/EU]. This is a joint parliamentary forum composed of African, Caribbean, and Pacific MPs and EU MPs. We also have our ordinary sessions of the joint parliament in Brussels two times every year, and I am presiding there. Then we have the SADC [Southern African Development Community] Parliamentary Forum. We have the Commonwealth Forum. In all these groups, women are there. And of course, there is the Pan-African Parliamentary Forum. The most important thing is that in every group women are there. I think this is a big change in our political behavior.

You also mentioned the quality of the debate in parliament.

Yes. It is much more in favor of women's development. I know many parties are trying now to do so. In Frelimo, of course, it is a question of status. There are quotas for women and youth. That is why you find in every election more women coming through. And I hope for these next general elections the group will improve a lot. I just feel that there will be a day when we will be 50 percent. We still have to look at the question of quality, capacity, training, but I think according to Frelimo's plan, we might get there, 50/50.

Mozambique has international acclaim for having 30 percent women in parliament. This is the big question everyone wants to know: Given those numbers, does it matter? Does it make a difference having women in parliament? When I asked Zelma Vasconcelos, she said, "No, No, No! It's just numbers! It doesn't matter!" I was shocked to hear a woman parliamentarian say it doesn't matter, so I asked her more about what she meant. And she said, "Women in parliament are simply spokespersons for their parties. They do not operate as women." I wonder how you would respond to that.

I think it's her point of view. I think talking in a broader way, this is the second term Frelimo has been in power since independence. I can assure you of the impact of women parliamentarians. They are the ones who are politically clear in terms of the development of the country. Among the OMM [Organization of Mozambican Women], we are clear-minded in terms of what actually should be done in terms of influencing debates for the bills which are brought to parliament by the government, or initiatives that come through parliament. I can see both Frelimo and the opposition women are trying to have influence. Now, there is a handicap, in terms of the low levels of training for most of the women in the parliament, but this is the situation if you talk about the whole nation. The level of illiteracy in Mozambique is high, and women are the biggest group. So, we have to do both. At once, we are trying to get access to politics, but we have to look ourselves for our training. There is no way to separate these issues.

That's a good point. Let me just ask you one other thing. I heard there was an attempt to create a women's caucus, that there were three members of Frelimo and three members of the opposition coalition who came together to talk about the creation of a women's caucus in the parliament. I was told they decided it was impossible, that is, was too difficult because the party divides were too great. Do you know anything about the caucus? What happened from your perspective?

I know from the last term until now, there is a need to create this women's caucus because in all the international parliamentary forums, in the agendas there is always a meeting of women. Every, every, every [forum]. The first day of the [forum], it's the women's meeting. This means that Mozambican women parliamentarians have to go to participate in these forums with ideas of what is going on among women parliamentarians in Mozambique. But, as Zelma said, there is this big issue of trying to politicize these structures. But that's not easy because, you know, in Mozambique, until now, we are too much influenced by our parties. There is no other way. The rules and procedures of the parliament are according to the procedures of each parliamentarian group. It will be very difficult for any MP to do something unrelated to the rules of procedure. That's why you have to reflect on what, first, are the objectives of your parliamentary group, in my case Frelimo. And I don't find it difficult because women's organizations in Frelimo are very well structured. Once you are a member of that organization, you know everything about the development, social politics in Mozambique. But I feel that for the next term, we have to make sure that we create that caucus. There's no other way. Within our own parliamentarian groups, we have to raise the discussion with our leaders that we need to create this group regardless of party. Otherwise, we do not have a way to communicate with others in other parliaments.

You said earlier, "We in Mozambique are too much influenced by our party." By "we," do you mean women or Mozambicans in general?

To be able to get access to political discussion, you have to be integrated in a party. This is the situation. There is no other way women can get involved in politics, the debates, without being in a party. OMM is the party league, Frelimo's women's league. So from that beginning, you find there's no other orientation than the party itself. And the other parties—of course—they follow the same [pattern]. They all have their women's league. And when we meet for discussion, there is a problem with the dialogue because we keep on trying to keep our parties on the safe side, not just talking generally as women. We don't talk as women. We have to try to do so, to say, "Look, this is a women's problem. We have the same things, the same feelings, the same problems, and then why don't we sit and discuss them in terms of development and not in our parties only?" One has to discuss these things. But I feel, in my own point of view, I have to start to discuss this within my own party. I think we have to open our minds and stop just accepting [things the way they are]. It is something we have to do among ourselves. I'm not a skeptic.

I think we will succeed. You find women now more open-minded than before.

How would you describe the women's movement in Mozambique today?

There is a sense that women have the support among themselves to get access to the decisionmaking process, to the political process. And then, if that happens, you will find that we have women who are capable both professionally and socially. You find the increasing consciousness of women in that sense. But, still there is this problem. You find a woman becomes the prime minister like we have now, and most women feel that she keeps aside women's problems, that she becomes a man in terms of development. This is part of the public debate. . . . This is the fear. They will never be straightforward when they talk about women. I feel a few women make sure they know the difference between women's problems and the problems in general in society. We have to do so. The most prestigious women I know in the world, even Hillary Clinton—I appreciate her so much for what she went through, her own status of first lady. But then, you could still see she's a woman, in terms of her fight for her rights. We have Graça Machel here in Africa. She fights for development as a whole, for women's access in terms of development. She says, look, it is impossible to develop a country without the involvement of women . . .

Do you think women MPs did more to get the Family Law passed, or was it pressure from NGOs in civil society, or both?

Mostly civil society and NGOs. Women parliamentarians represent civil society, but through parties. At the end of the day, we are all called the people's representatives in the parliament. The easiest way to participate in political debate is to be an MP in Mozambique. You see? And then, when you are in the parliament, you are free to discuss the whole range of problems which affect the society. So we represent the people. But then, since we are MPs belonging to different parties, we can never be against the objectives of our own party.

Acronyms and Abbreviations

ACFODE	Action for Development (Uganda)
ACP/EU	African, Caribbean, and Pacific/European Union
ADOCA	Association of Housewives (Mozambique)
AFP	Alliance of Forces for Progress (Senegal)
AJ/PADS	Alliance Jef-Jál/African Party of Senegalese Democracy
ANC	African National Congress (South Africa)
AWEPA	European Parliamentarians for Africa
AZAPO	Azanian People's Organization (South Africa)
CA	Constituent Assembly (Namibia)
CBO	community-based organization
CCA	Coalition on Constitutional Amendment (Uganda)
CEDAW	Convention on the Elimination of Discrimination Against Women
CGE	Commission for Gender Equality (South Africa)
CLADHO	Collective of Leagues and Associations for the Defense of Human Rights (Rwanda)
COD	Congress of Democrats (Namibia)
CODESA	Convention for a Democratic South Africa
COSEF	Senegalese Council of Women
DP	Democratic Party (South Africa)
DRB	Domestic Relations Bill (Uganda)
DTA	Democratic Turnhalle Alliance (Namibia)
DWA	Department of Women Affairs (Namibia)
Frelimo	Front for the Liberation of Mozambique
GAC	Gender Advisory Committee (South Africa)

GDP	gross domestic product
ICG	International Crisis Group
IDASA	Institute for Democracy in South Africa
IPU	Inter-Parliamentary Union
JMC	Joint Monitoring Committee on the Improvement of the Quality of Life and Status of Women (South Africa)
LC	local council (Uganda)
LIPRODHOR	League for the Protection of Human Rights in Rwanda
MDR	Democratic and Republican Movement (Rwanda)
MP	member of parliament
MRND	National Republican Movement for Democracy and Development (Rwanda)
MULEIDE	Women, Law, and Development Organization (Mozambique)
NA	National Assembly
NAWA	Namibian Women's Association
NCOP	National Council of Provinces (South Africa)
NCW	National Council of Women (Uganda)
NGM	national gender machinery
NGO	nongovernmental organization
NGP	National Gender Policy (Namibia)
NRM	National Resistance Movement (Uganda)
NWMN	Namibian Women's Manifesto Network
NWV	Namibian Women's Voice
OMM	Organization of Mozambican Women
OSW	Office on the Status of Women (South Africa)
PAC	Pan-Africanist Congress (South Africa)
PDS	Democratic Socialist Party (Senegal)
PR	proportional representation
PS	Socialist Party (Senegal)
PWC	Parliamentary Women's Caucus (Namibia)
PWG	Parliamentary Women's Group (South Africa)
Renamo	Mozambique National Resistance
Renamo-UE	Renamo–Electoral Union (Mozambique)
RPA	Rwandan Patriotic Army
RPF	Rwandan Patriotic Front
SADC	Southern African Development Community
SOPI	Change coalition (Senegal)
SSA	sub-Saharan Africa

Swapo	South West Africa People's Organisation (Namibia)
SWC	Swapo Women's Council (Namibia)
ULA	Uganda Land Alliance
UN	United Nations
UNIFEM	United Nations Development Fund for Women
UWONET	Uganda Women's Network
UWOPA	Uganda Women Parliamentary Association
WBI	Women's Budget Initiative (South Africa)
WEDO	Women's Environment and Development Organization
WLSA	Women and Law in Southern Africa
WNC	Women's National Coalition (South Africa)

References

Abreu, Alcinda. 2004. "Enhancing Women's Participation in Electoral Processes in Post Conflict Countries. Experiences from Mozambique." United Nations Office of the Special Advisor on Gender Issues and the Advancement of Women (OSAGI).

ACFODE. 2001. "More Women Joining Uganda's Parliament but the Rules of the Game Remain Unjust." *Monitor* (Kampala), August 20.

Amadiume, Ifi. 1997. *Re-inventing Africa: Matriarchy, Religion, and Culture.* New York: Zed Books.

Assembly Debates Radical Change in the Family Law. 2003. Mozambican Information Agency (AIM). Maputo. April 29.

Assembly Passes Revised Family Law. 2004. Mozambican Information Agency (AIM). Maputo. August 21.

Augis, Erin Joanna. 2002. "Dakar's Sunnite Women; the Politics of Person." Ph.D. dissertation, University of Chicago.

Baden, Sally, Shireen Hassim, and Sheila Meintjes. 1999. *Country Gender Profile: South Africa.* Prepared for the Swedish International Development Agency (SIDA). Pretoria. http://womensnet.org.za/links/genderpr.htm.

Baldez, Lisa. 2001. "Coalition Politics and the Limits of State Feminism in Chile." *Women and Politics* 22(4): 1–28.

———. 2002. *Why Women Protest: Women's Movements in Chile.* Cambridge: Cambridge University Press.

Ballington, Julie. 1999a. "Gender Considerations in Electoral System Reform." *The Election Bulletin,* 6th ed. Women's Net1: August. http://womensnet.org.za/election/eb6-esysreform.htm.

———. 1999b. "Party Representation—The Women's Profile." *The Election Bulletin,* 6th ed. Women's Net1: August. http://womensnet.org.za/election/eb6-esystem.htm.

———. 1999c. "The Participation of Women in South Africa's First Democratic Elections." Johannesburg: Electoral Institute of South Africa.

―――. 2002. "Political Parties, Gender Equality and Elections in South Africa." In Glenda Ficks, Sheila Meintjes, and Mary Simons, eds. *One Woman, One Vote*. Johannesburg: Electoral Institute of South Africa.

―――, ed. 2004. *The Implementation of Quotas: African Experiences*. Quota Report Series no. 3. Stockholm: International Idea.

Banaszak, Lee Ann, Karen Beckwith, and Dieter Rucht, eds. 2003. *Women's Movements Facing the Reconfigured State*. Cambridge: Cambridge University Press.

Bateganya, Fred. 2002. "The Female Genital Mutilation Phenomenon in the 2001 Women Parliamentary Elections in Kapchorwa District." Paper presented at the 8th International Interdisciplinary Congress on Women, Makerere University, Kampala, Uganda. July 21.

Bauer, Gretchen. 2004. "'The Hand That Stirs the Pot Can Also Run the Country': Electing Women to Parliament in Namibia." *Journal of Modern African Studies* 42(4): 479–509.

Beck, Linda. 1994. "Advancing Beyond Semi-Democracy in Senegal: A Fair Electoral Code Does Not a Democracy Make." Paper presented at the Democratic Challenge in Africa Seminar, Emory University, Governance in Africa Program, Atlanta, GA.

―――. 1997. "Patrimonial Democrats: Incremental Reform and the Obstacles to the Consolidation of Democracy." *Canadian Journal of African Studies* 31(1): 1–31.

―――. 2001. "Reining in the Marabouts? Democratization and Local Governance in Senegal." *African Affairs* 100: 601–621.

Becker, Heike. 1995. *Namibian Women's Movement 1980 to 1992: From Anticolonial Resistance to Reconstruction*. Frankfurt, Germany: IKO.

―――. 2000. "Striving for Change: The Struggle for Gender Equality in Namibia." In Eunice Iipinge and Marlene Williams, eds. *Gender and Development*. Windhoek, Namibia: Pollination Publishers.

Behrman, Lucy Creevey. 1970. *Muslim Brotherhoods and Politics in Senegal*. Cambridge, MA: Harvard University Press.

Berg, Nina, and Aase Gundersen. 1992. "Legal Reforms in Mozambique: Equality and Emancipation Through Popular Justice?" In Kristi Anne Stolen and Mariken Vaa, eds. *Gender and Change in Developing Countries*. Oslo: Norwegian University Press.

Berger, Iris. 1981. *Religion and Resistance: East African Kingdoms in the Precolonial Period*. Butare, Rwanda: Institut National de Recherche Scientifique.

Bochel, Catherine, and Jacqui Briggs. 2000. "Do Women Make a Difference?" *Politics* 20(2): 63–68.

Bowen, Merle. 2000. *The State Against the Peasantry: Rural Struggles in Colonial and Postcolonial Mozambique*. Charlottesville: University of Virginia Press.

Bratton, Michael, Gina Lambright, Kimberly Ludwig, Jacqui True, and Robert Sentamu. 2000. "Democracy, Economy and Gender in Uganda: Report of a National Sample Survey." Washington, DC: International Foundation for Election Systems.

Britton, Hannah. 2001. "New Struggles, New Strategies: Emerging Patterns of Women's Political Participation in the South African Parliament." *International Politics* 38: 173–200.

———. 2002a. "Coalition Building, Election Rules, and Party Politics: South African Women's Path to Parliament." *Africa Today* 49(4): 32–67.

———. 2002b. "The Incomplete Revolution: South African Women's Struggle for Parliamentary Transformation." *International Feminist Journal of Politics* 4(2): 43–71.

———. 2005. *Women in the South African Parliament: From Resistance to Governance*. Champaign: University of Illinois Press.

Budlender, Debbie. 1998. *Women and Men in South Africa*. Pretoria: Central Statistics Office.

Byanyima, Winnie. 1996. "A Fresh Vision for Women MPs!" *Monitor* (Kampala), January 26–29, 15.

Bystydzienski, Jill. 1992. "Influence of Women's Culture on Public Politics in Norway." In Jill Bystydzienski, ed. *Women Transforming Politics: Worldwide Strategies for Empowerment*. Bloomington: Indiana University Press.

Callaway, Barbara, and Lucy Creevey. 1994. *The Heritage of Islam: Women, Religion, and Politics in West Africa*. Boulder, CO: Lynne Rienner Publishers.

Canadian International Development Agency. 2001. "Gender Profile: Senegal." September. http://www.acdi.

Carroll, Sue. 1992. "Women State Legislators, Women's Organizations, and the Representation of Women's Culture in the United States." In Jill Bystydzienski, ed. *Women Transforming Politics: Worldwide Strategies for Empowerment*. Bloomington: Indiana University Press.

Casimiro, Isabel. 1990. *A Mulher em Mocambique*. Maputo: CEA/NORAD.

Castles, Francis. 1981. "Female Legislative Representation and the Electoral System." *Politics* 1: 21–27.

Caul, Miki. 1999. "Women's Representation in Parliament: The Role of Political Parties." *Party Politics* 5(1): 79–98.

———. 2001. "Political Parties and the Adoption of Candidate Gender Quotas: A Cross-National Analysis." *Journal of Politics* 63(4): 1214–1229.

Childs, Sarah, and Mona Lena Krook. 2005. "The Substantive Representation of Women: Rethinking the 'Critical Mass' Debate." Paper presented at the Annual Meeting of the American Political Science Association, Washington, DC. September 3.

Cisse, Katy, Aminata Diaw, and Aminata Faye. 1999. *Démocratie où es-tu? Campaigne du Conseil Legislatif des Femmes (COSEF), Legislatives 1998*. Dakar, Senegal: Fondation Friedrich Ebert.

"Civil Society's Liveliest Campaign Issue: Children and Women's Rights." 2004. *LAC News*, no.14. Windhoek, Namibia: Legal Assistance Centre.

Cleaver, Tessa, and Marion Wallace. 1990. *Namibia Women in War*. London: Zed Books.

Cock, Jacklyn. 1991. *Colonels and Cadres: War and Gender in South Africa.* Cape Town, South Africa: Oxford University Press.

Copans, Jean. 1980. *Les marabouts de l'arachide: La confrérie mouride et les paysans du Sénégal.* Paris: Sycomore.

Coulon, Christian. 1981. *Le Marabout et le prince: Islam et pouvoir au Sénégal.* Paris: A Pedone.

Coulon, Christian, and Donal Cruise O'Brien. 1988. *Charisma and Brotherhood in African Islam.* Oxford: The Clarendon Press.

Creevey, Lucy. 1996. "Islam, Women and the Role of the State in Senegal." *Journal of Religion in Africa* 26(3): 268–307.

———. 2004. "Impacts of Changing Patterns of Women's Association Membership in Senegal." In Bandana Purkayastha and Mangala Subramaniam, eds. *The Power of Women's Informal Networks; Lessons from Social Change in South Asia and West Africa.* Lanham, MD: Lexington Books.

Creevey, Lucy, and Michael Magala. 2002. "Gender and Changing Political Values in Senegal." Unpublished manuscript. University of Connecticut.

Creevey, Lucy, Abdou Ndoye, and Richard Vengroff. 2004. "Islam and the Transition to Democracy in Senegal." Unpublished manuscript. University of Connecticut.

Creevey, Lucy, Paul Ngomo, and Richard Vengroff. 2005. "Party Politics and Different Paths to Democratic Transitions." *Party Politics* 11: 471–493.

Croucher, Sheila. 2002. "South Africa's Democratisation and the Politics of Gay Liberation." *Journal of Southern African Studies* 28(2): 315–330.

Cruise O'Brien, Donal. 1971. *The Mourides of Senegal: The Political and Economic Organization of an Islamic Brotherhood.* Oxford: Clarendon Press.

Dahlerup, Drude. 1988. "From a Small to a Large Minority: Theory of Critical Mass." *Scandinavian Political Studies* 11: 275–298.

———. 2002. "Using Quotas to Increase Women's Political Representation." In International Idea. *Women in Parliament: Beyond Numbers.* Stockholm: International Idea.

———. 2004. "Quotas Are Changing the History of Women." In Julie Ballington, ed. *The Implementation of Quotas: African Experiences.* Quota Report Series No. 3. Stockholm: International Idea.

De Diop, Aissata. 2000a. "Elections Legislatives 98—Investiture des Femmes." In A. Diaw, K. Cisse, and K. Kasse. *Démocratie ou-es tu?* Dakar, Senegal: COSEF.

———. 2000b. *Femmes, enjeu électoral: des chiffres qui parlent!* Institut Africain pour la Democratie. Dakar, Senegal: Editions Democraties Africaines.

———. 2002. Personal e-mail communication.

Department of Women Affairs (DWA). 1999. *Namibia National Progress Report on the Implementation of the Beijing Platform for Action.* Windhoek, Namibia: DWA. Office of the President, Republic of Namibia.

Des Forges, Alison. 1999. *Leave None to Tell the Story: Genocide in Rwanda.* New York: Human Rights Watch.

Diop, A. Bara. 1985. *La Famille Wolof.* Paris: Karthala.

Disney, Jennifer Leigh. 2002. *The Theories and Practices of Women's Organizing: Marxism, Feminism, Democratization and Civil Society in Mozambique and Nicaragua.* Ph.D. dissertation, City University of New York Graduate Center.

————. 2004. "Incomplete Revolutions: Gendered Participation in Productive and Reproductive Labor in Mozambique and Nicaragua." *Gender and Globalization: Marxist-Feminist Perspectives*, a special edition of *Socialism and Democracy* 18(1) (Winter/Spring).

Documentos da 2 Conferencia da Organização da Mulher Mocambicana Realizada em Maputo, 10 a 17 de Novembro de 1976. Imprensa Nacional de Mocambique, 1977.

Dorsey, Learthen. 1994. *Historical Dictionary of Rwanda.* Metuchen, NJ: Scarecrow Press.

Duverger, Maurice. 1955. *The Political Role of Women.* Paris: United Nations Economic and Social Council.

Election World. 2003. "Elections in Rwanda." www.electionworld.org/rwanda.htm.

Fatton, Robert. 1987. *The Making of a Liberal Democracy.* Boulder, CO: Lynne Rienner Publishers.

Ferguson, Anne, and Beatrice Liatto Katundu. 1994. "Women in Politics in Zambia: What Difference Has Democracy Made?" *African Rural and Urban Studies* 1(2): 11–30.

Forum for Women in Democracy (FOWODE). 2000. *From Strength to Strength: Ugandan Women in Public Office.* Kampala, Uganda: FOWODE.

Frank, Liz. 2004a. "Call for Zebra-Style Lists: Open Letter to Political Parties." *Namibian*, August 6.

————. 2004b. "Far From 50/50!" *Sister Namibia* (Windhoek) 16(5 and 6).

————. 2004c. "Working Towards Gender Balance in Elected Positions of Government in Namibia." In Julie Ballington, ed. *The Implementation of Quotas: African Experiences.* Quota Report Series No. 3. Stockholm: International Idea.

Friedman, Elisabeth. 2000. "State-Based Advocacy for Gender Equality in the Developing World: Assessing the Venezuelan National Women's Agency." *Women and Politics* 21(2): 601–613.

Geisler, Gisela. 1995. "Troubled Sisterhood: Women and Politics in Southern Africa." *African Affairs* 94: 545–578.

————. 2000. "Parliament Is Another Terrain of Struggle: Women, Men and Politics in South Africa." *Journal of Modern African Studies* 38(4): 605–630.

————. 2004. *Women and the Remaking of Politics in Southern Africa: Negotiating Autonomy, Incorporation and Representation.* Uppsala, Sweden: Nordic Africa Institute.

Goetz, Anne Marie. 1998. "Women in Politics and Gender Equity in Policy: South Africa and Uganda." *Review of African Political Economy* 76: 241–262.

————. 2002. "No Shortcuts to Power: Constraints on Women's Political Effectiveness in Uganda." *Journal of Modern African Studies* 40(4): 549–575.

————. 2003. "The Problem with Patronage: Constraints on Women's Political Effectiveness in Uganda." In Anne Marie Goetz and Shireen Hassim, eds. *No Shortcuts to Power: African Women in Politics and Policy Making*. London and New York: Zed Books.

Goetz, Anne Marie, and Shireen Hassim. 2003. "Introduction: Women in Power in Uganda and South Africa." In Goetz and Hassim, eds. *No Shortcuts to Power: African Women in Politics and Policy Making*. London and New York: Zed Books.

Goldblatt, Beth, and Sheila Meintjes. 1998. "South African Women Demand the Truth." In Meredith Turshen and Clotide Twagiramariya, eds. *What Women Do in Wartime: Gender and Conflict in Africa*. New York: Zed Books.

Gordon, April. 1996. *Transforming Capitalism and Patriarchy: Gender and Development in Africa*. Boulder, CO: Lynne Rienner Publishers.

Gouws, Amanda. 2004. "The Politics of State Structures: Citizenship and the National Machinery for Women in South Africa." *Feminist Africa* 3. http://www.feministafrica.org/2level.html.

Govender, Pregs, Debbie Budlender, and N. Madlala. 1994. *Beijing Conference Report: 1994. Country Report on the Status of South African Women*. Pretoria, South Africa: Office of the President.

Government of Senegal. 2001. *Rapport National sur le Developpement Humain au Sénégal; 2001—Gouvernance et Developpement*. Dakar.

Gray, Tricia. 2003. "Electoral Gender Quotas: Lessons from Argentina and Chile." *Bulletin of Latin American Research* 22(1): 52–78.

Guichaoua, André. 1995. *Les Crises Politiques au Burundi et au Rwanda (1993–1994)*. Lille, France: Université des Sciences et Technologies de Lille.

Guy, Jeff. 1990. "Gender Oppression in Southern Africa's Precapitalist Societies." In Cherryl Walker, ed. *Women and Gender in Southern Africa to 1945*. Cape Town, South Africa: David Philip.

Hanssen, Kari Nordstoga. 2003. *Can You Really Fail to Support the One Who Feeds You? An Analysis of Female Representation in the Ugandan Parliament*. M.A. Thesis, Department of Comparative Politics, University of Bergen, Norway.

Hassim, Shireen. 2003. "The Gender Pact and Democratic Consolidation: Institutionalizing Gender Equality in the South African State." *Feminist Studies* 29(3): 505–529.

Hubbard, Dianne. 2001. "50/50: Options for Namibia." Paper prepared for the Namibian Women's Manifesto Network. Windhoek, Namibia: Legal Assistance Center.

————. 2002. "Gender and the Law Scorecard 2002." *Namibian,* December 20.

————. 2004. "Gender Scorecard 2004." Windhoek, Namibia: Legal Assistance Center Gender Research and Advocacy Project.

Hubbard, Dianne, and Kaveri Kavari. 1993. *Affirmative Action for Women in Local Government in Namibia*. Windhoek, Namibia: Legal Assistance Center.

Hubbard, Dianne, and Colette Solomon. 1995. "The Many Faces of Feminism in Namibia." In Amrita Basu, ed. *The Challenge of Local Feminisms: Women's Movement in Global Perspective*. Boulder, CO: Westview Press.

Human Rights Watch. 2003. "Preparing for Elections: Tightening Control in the Name of Unity." Briefing Paper. New York: Human Rights Watch.

Hyland Byrne, Lesley. 1997. "Feminists in Power: Women Cabinet Ministers in the New Democratic Party Government of Ontario, 1990–1995." *Policy Studies Journal* 25(4): 601–613.

Ibrahim, Jibrin. 2004. "The First Lady Syndrome and the Marginalisation of Women from Power: Opportunities of Compromise for Gender Equality?" *Feminist Africa* 3. http://www.feministafrica.org/2level.html.

Iipinge, Eunice, and Debie LeBeau. 1997. *Beyond Inequalities: Women in Namibia*. Windhoek: Gender Training and Research Programme, Social Sciences Division, University of Namibia.

Iipinge, Eunice, F. A. Phiri, and A. F. Njabili, eds. 2000. *The National Gender Study,* vols. 1 and 2. Windhoek: University of Namibia.

International Crisis Group (ICG) 2001. "'Consensual Democracy' in Post-Genocide Rwanda: Evaluating the March 2001 District Elections." *Africa Report No. 34*. Nairobi and Brussels: ICG. October 9.

———. 2002. "Fin de Transition au Rwanda: Une Liberalisation Politique Necessaire." Rapport Afrique No. 53. Nairobi and Brussels: ICG. November 13.

Inter-Parliamentary Union. 2003. "Rwanda Leads World Ranking of Women in Parliament." Geneva. October 22.

Jaquette, Jane. 1994. "Introduction: From Transition to Participation—Women's Movements and Democratic Politics." In Jane Jaquette, ed. *The Women's Movements in Latin America: Participation and Democracy*. Boulder, CO: Westview Press.

Jefremovas, Villia. 2002. *Brickyards to Graveyards: From Production to Genocide in Rwanda*. Albany: State University of New York Press.

Jones, Mark P. 1996. "Increasing Women's Representation Via Gender Quotas: The Argentine Ley de Cupos." *Women and Politics* 16(4): 75–98.

———. 1998. "Gender Quotas, Electoral Laws and the Election of Women: Lessons from the Argentine Provinces." *Comparative Political Studies* 31(1): 3–21.

Kadalie, Rhoda. 1995. "Women in the New South Africa: From Transition to Governance." In Sandra Liebenberg, ed. *The Constitution of South Africa from a Gender Perspective*. Cape Town, South Africa: David Philip.

Kalebbo, Geoffrey Denye. 1996. "How to Make It to Parliament." *Women's Vision* (Kampala), April 30, 16.

Kaplan, Temma. 1997. *Crazy for Democracy: Women in Grassroots Movements*. New York: Routledge.

Kasente, Deborah. 1994. "Women in the Constituent Assembly in Uganda." Paper presented at public forum on African Women and Governance Seminar and Training Workshop, Entebbe, Uganda. July 24–30.

Khaxas, Elizabeth. 2002. "Analyzing the Impact of the 50/50 Campaign in Namibia." www.wedo.org/5050/namibia.

Kwesiga, Joy C. 1996. "Electoral Colleges for District Women Representatives to Parliament: A Test for Maturity or a Half-hearted Act." *Arise*, 26.

Lakeman, Enid. 1970. *How Democracies Vote: A Study of Majority and Proportional Electoral Systems*. London: Faber.

Launch of the Southern African Development Community (SADC) Regional Women's Parliamentary Caucus: Voice of Women Parliamentarians in SADC. 2002. Luanda, Angola, April 11–12.

LeBeau, Debie, and Eunice Iipinge. 2004. "Namibia's Progress Towards Gender Equality: Post-Beijing Policies and Programmes." In Justine Hunter, ed. *Beijing + 10, the Way Forward. An Introduction to Gender Issues in Namibia*. Windhoek: Namibia Institute for Democracy.

LeBeau, Debie, and Grant Spence. 2004. "Community Perceptions on Law Reform: People Speaking Out." In Justine Hunter, ed. *Beijing + 10, the Way Forward. An Introduction to Gender Issues in Namibia*. Windhoek: Namibia Institute for Democracy.

Liebenberg, Sandra, ed. 1995. *The Constitution of South Africa from a Gender Perspective*. Cape Town, South Africa: David Philip.

Lindberg, Staffan. 2004. "Women's Empowerment and Democratization: The Effects of Electoral Systems, Participation, and Experience in Africa." *Studies in Comparative International Development* 39(1): 28–53.

Longman, Timothy. 1999. "State, Civil Society, and Genocide in Rwanda." In Richard Joseph, ed. *State, Conflict, and Democracy in Africa*. Boulder, CO: Lynne Rienner Publishers.

Lovenduski, Joni. 1997. "Gender Politics: A Breakthrough for Women?" *Parliamentary Affairs* 50(4): 708–719.

Lovenduski, Joni, and Azza Karam. 2002. "Women in Parliament: Making a Difference." In International Idea. *Women in Parliament: Beyond Numbers*. Stockholm: International Idea.

Lovenduski, Joni, and Pippa Norris. 1993. *Gender and Party Politics*. London: Sage.

———. 2003. "Westminster Women: The Politics of Presence." *Political Studies* 51: 84–102.

Mabandla, Brigitte. 1994. "Choices for South African Women." *Agenda* 20: 22–29.

Machangana, Keboitse. 1998. "Emang Basadi Women's Association and the *Women's Manifesto:* Advocating for Women's Rights in Botswana." In Phiroshaw Camay and Anne Gordon, eds. *Advocacy in Southern Africa: Lessons for the Future*. Johannesburg, South Africa: Cooperative Research and Education.

Magaia, Lina. 1988. *Dumba Nengue: Run for Your Life: Peasant Tales of Tragedy in Mozambique*. Trenton, NJ: Africa World Press.

Magassouba, Moriba. 1985. *L'Islam au Sénégal; Demain les Mollahs?* Paris: Karthala.

Mamdani, Mahmood. 1998. "Africa: Democratic Theory and Democratic Struggles." In Manoranjan Mohanty and P. N. Mukherji, with Olle Tornquist, eds. *People's Rights: Social Movements and the State in the Third World*. New Delhi: Sagse.

Matembe, Miria. 2002. *Gender, Politics and Constitution Making in Uganda*. Kampala, Uganda: Fountain Publishers.

Matland, Richard. 1993. "Institutional Variables Affecting Female Representations in National Legislatures: The Case of Norway." *Journal of Politics* 55(3): 737–756.

———. 2002. "Enhancing Women's Political Participation: Legislative Recruitment and Electoral Systems." In International Idea. *Women in Parliament: Beyond Numbers*. Stockholm: International Idea.

Matland, Richard, and Donley T. Studlar. 1996. "The Contagion of Women Candidates in Single-Member District and Proportional Representation Systems: Canada and Norway." *Journal of Politics* 58(3): 707–733.

Matland, Richard, and Michelle Taylor. 1997. "Electoral System Effects on Women's Representation: Theoretical Arguments and Evidence from Costa Rica." *Comparative Political Studies* 30(2): 186–211.

Mazrui, Ali. 1976. "Ghandi, Marx, and the Warrior Tradition: Towards Androgynous Liberation." *Journal of Asian and African Studies* 12(1–4): 179–196.

Meintjes, Sheila, and Mary Simons. 2002. "Why Electoral Systems Matter to Women." In Glenda Flick, Sheila Meintjes, and Mary Simons, eds. *One Woman, One Vote*. Johannesburg: Electoral Institute of South Africa.

Mikell, Gwendolyn. 2003. "African Feminism: Toward a New Politics of Representation." In Carole McCann and Seung-Kyung Kim, eds. *Feminist Theory Reader: Local and Global Perspectives*. New York: Routledge.

———, ed. 1997. *African Feminism: The Politics of Survival in Sub-Saharan Africa*. Philadelphia: University of Pennsylvania Press.

Minter, William. 1994. *Apartheid's Contras: An Inquiry into the Roots of War in Angola and Mozambique*. Trenton, NJ: Africa World Press.

Mission d'Observation Electorale de l'Union Europeenne. 2003. "Election Presidentielle 25 Aout 2003; Elections Legislatives 29 et 30 Septembre, 2 Octobre 2003: Rapport Final."

Molyneux, Maxine. 1985. "Mobilization Without Emancipation? Women's Interests, State, and Revolution in Nicaragua." *Feminist Studies* 11(2): 227–254.

Morna, Colleen Lowe, ed. 2004. *Ringing Up the Changes: Gender in Southern African Politics*. Johannesburg, South Africa: Gender Links.

Mugambe, Beatrice. 1996. "Are Women Afraid of Seeking Elective Office?" *Arise*, 32–33.

Mutaizibwa, Emma, and Chris Obore. 2003. "No Third Term—Women MPs." *Monitor* (Kampala), February 19.

Namutebi, Joyce, and Charles Ariko. 2004. "Women Form Coalition." *New Vision* (Kampala), May 13.

National Democratic Institute (NDI). 2003. "Senegal." NDI newsletter. Washington, DC: NDI.

Newbury, Catherine. 1988. *The Cohesion of Oppression: Clientship and Ethnicity in Rwanda, 1860–1960*. New York: Columbia University Press.

Newbury, Catherine, and Hannah Baldwin. 2000a. "Aftermath: Women in Postgenocide Rwanda." Working Paper no. 303. Washington, DC: Center for Development Information and Evaluation, USAID. July.

———. 2000b. "Aftermath: Women and Women's Organizations in Postgenocide Rwanda." USAID Evaluation Highlights no. 69. Washington, DC: USAID.

Niang, Setta. 1998. "Women and Democracy in Africa." *Courier* 171: 66–68.

Norris, Pippa. 1996. "Legislative Recruitment." In L. Leduc, R. Niemi, and Pippa Norris, eds. *Comparing Democracies: Elections and Voting in Global Perspective*. Thousand Oaks, CA: Sage.

Nowrojee, Binaifer. 1996. *Shattered Lives: Sexual Violence During the Rwandan Genocide and Its Aftermath*. New York: Human Rights Watch.

Okurut, Mary Karooro. 1995. "Of 'Sweet' Things at Women's Elections." *Monitor* (Kampala). March 24.

Opondo, Ofwono. 1993. *Sunday Vision*. October 3.

Organization of Mozambican Woman (OMM). 1980. *Informative Bulletin*. Maputo: OMM.

Orloff, Ann Shola. 1993. "Gender and the Social Rights of Citizenship: The Comparative Analysis of Gender Relations and Welfare States." *American Sociological Review* 58(3): 303–328.

Oyewumi, Oyeronke. 1997. *The Invention of Women: Making an African Sense of Western Gender Discourses*. Minneapolis: University of Minnesota Press.

———. 2003. *African Women and Feminism: Reflecting on the Politics of Sisterhood*. Trenton, NJ: Africa World Press.

Pankhurst, Donna. 2002. "Women and Politics in Africa: The Case of Uganda." In Karen Ross, ed. *Women, Politics, and Change*. Oxford: Oxford University Press.

Parpart, Jane L., and Kathleen Staudt. 1989. *Women and the State in Africa*. Boulder, CO: Lynne Rienner Publishers.

Phillips, Anne. 1991. *Engendering Democracy*. University Park: Pennsylvania State University Press.

———. 1995. *The Politics of Presence*. London: Polity Press.

———. 1998. "Democracy and Representation: Or, Why Should It Matter Who Our Representatives Are?" In Anne Phillips, ed. *Feminism and Politics*. Oxford: Oxford University Press.

Piga, Adriana. 2002. "Neo-traditionalist Islamic Associations and the Islamist Press in Contemporary Senegal." In Thomas Bierschenk and Georg Stauth, eds. *Yearbook of the Sociology of Islam*, vol. 4. Muenster, Germany: Lit Verlag.

Pitkin, Hanna. 1967. *The Concept of Representation*. Berkeley: University of California Press.

Powley, Elizabeth. 2003. "Strengthening Governance: The Role of Women in Rwanda's Transition." Women Waging Peace. October.

———. 2004. "Strengthening Governance: The Role of Women in Rwanda's Transition: A Summary." United Nations Office of the Special Adviser on Gender Issues. January 26.

Pruegl, Elisabeth, and Mary Meyer. 1999. "Gender Politics in Global Governance." In Mary Meyer and Elisabeth Pruegl, eds. *Gender Politics in Global Governance*. Lanham, MD: Rowman and Littlefield.

Prunier, Gérard. 1995. *The Rwanda Crisis: History of a Genocide*. New York: Columbia University Press.

Quick, Diana. 2001. "Redefining the Roles of Women in Post-genocide Rwanda." *Forced Migration Review* 11. http://www.fmreview.org/text/FRM/11/04.htm.

Ranchod-Nilsson, Sita. 1998. "Zimbabwe: Women, Cultural Crisis, and the Reconfiguration of the One-Party State." In Leo Villalón and Phil Huxtable, eds. *The African State at a Critical Juncture: Between Disintegration and Reconfiguration*. Boulder, CO: Lynne Rienner Publishers.

Reynolds, Andrew. 1995. "Constitutional Engineering in Southern Africa." *Journal of Democracy* 6(2): 86–99.

———. 1999. "Women in the Legislatures and Executives of the World: Knocking at the Highest Glass Ceiling." *World Politics* 51(4): 547–572.

Reyntjens, Filip. 2004. "Rwanda, Ten Years On: From Genocide to Dictatorship." *African Affairs* 103: 177–210.

Robinson, David. 1999. "The Murids: Surveillance and Collaboration." *Journal of African History* 40(2): 193–213.

Rosander, Eva Evers. 2003. "Mam Diarra Bousso—the Mourid Mother of Porokhane, Senegal." *Jenda: A Journal of Culture and African Women Studies* 4. http://www.jendajournal.com/issue4/rosander.html.

Ross, Karen, ed. 2002. *Women, Politics, and Change*. Oxford: Oxford University Press.

Rule, Wilma. 1987. "Electoral Systems, Contextual Factors and Women's Opportunity for Election to Parliament in Twenty-three Democracies." *Western Political Quarterly* 40: 477–498.

Rule, Wilma, and Joseph F. Zimmerman, eds. 1994. *Electoral Systems in Comparative Perspective: Their Impact on Women and Minorities*. Westport, CT: Greenwood.

Russell, Diane. 1989. *Lives of Courage: Women for a New South Africa*. Oakland, CA: Basic Books.

Sainsbury, Diane. 2004. "Women's Political Representation in Sweden: Discursive Politics and Institutional Presence." *Scandinavian Political Studies* 27(1): 65–88.

Sakho, Khady. 2003. E-mail response to list of questions from author sent to Abdou Ndoye (November 3).

Saxonberg, Steven. 2000. "Women in East European Parliaments." *Journal of Democracy* 11(2): 145–158.

Schaffer, Frederic C. 2000. *Democracy in Translation: Understanding Politics in an Unfamiliar Culture*. Ithaca, NY: Cornell University Press.

Searing, James F. 2002. *"God Alone Is King": Islam and Emancipation in Senegal: The Wolof Kingdoms of Kajoor and Bawol, 1859–1914*. Portsmouth, NH: Heinemann.

Seidman, Gay. 1999. "Gendered Citizenship: South Africa's Democratic Transition and the Construction of a Gendered State." *Gender and Society* 13(3): 287–307.

Sibomana, André. 1999. *Hope for Rwanda: Conversations with Laure Guilbert and Hervé Deguine*. London: Pluto Press.

Sister Namibia. 1999. *Words into Action: The Namibian Women's Manifesto*. Windhoek: Sister Namibia.

Situation of Women in Mozambique, The. 1994. Report by the Women's NGOs to the NGO Forum taking place concurrently with the African Preparatory Conference for Beijing in Dakar, Senegal, November 12–15. Maputo, Mozambique: Forum Mulher.

Soiri, Iina. 1996. *The Radical Motherhood: Namibian Women's Independence Struggle*. Research Report no. 99. Uppsala, Sweden: Nordiska Afrikainstitutet.

Southern African Development Community (SADC) Gender Unit. 1999. *Women in Politics and Decision Making in SADC: Beyond 30 Percent in 2005*. Report of the Proceedings of a Conference Held in Gaborone, Botswana, March 28–April 1, 1999. Gaborone: SADC Gender Unit.

Sow, Fatou. 1985. "Muslim Families in Contemporary Black Africa." *Current Anthropology* 26(5): 563–570.

———. 2003. "Fundamentalisms, Globalization and Women's Human Rights in Senegal." *Gender and Development* 11(1): 69–76.

"Spotlight on Rose Kabuye, Rwanda." 2004. Women Waging Peace. www .womenwagingpeace.org

Ssettumba, Samuel. 2004. "We Will Not Be Used—Women." *Monitor* (Kampala), January 8.

Staudt, Kathleen. 1998. "Women in Politics: Mexico in Global Perspective." In Victoria E. Rodriguez, ed. *Women's Participation in Mexican Political Life*. Boulder, CO: Westview Press.

Steininger, Barbara. 2000. "Representation of Women in the Austrian Political System 1945–1998: From a Token Female Politician Towards an Equal Ratio?" *Women and Politics* 21(2): 81–106.

Stetson, Dorothy McBride, and Amy G. Mazur, eds. 1995. *Comparative State Feminisms*. Thousand Oaks, CA: Sage Publications.

Steyn, Melissa. 1998. "A New Agenda: Restructuring Feminism in South Africa." *Women's Studies International Forum* 21(1): 41–52.

Sumarée, Bamby. 2002. "Being a Woman in Senegal." *International Viewpoint* 4. www.3bh.org.uk/IV/Issues/2002/IV341/IV341%2013.htm.

Summers, Anne. 1986. "Mandarins or Missionaries? Women in the Federal Bureaucracy." In Norma Grieve and Alisa Burns, eds. *Australian Women: New Feminist Perspectives*. Melbourne, Australia: Oxford University Press.

Sy, Mouhamadou. 2002. "Factors Inhibiting the Participation of Peasant Organisations in the Democratisation Process in Senegal." In Mahmoud Ben Romdhane and Sam Moyo, eds. *Peasant Organisations and the Democratisation Process in Africa*. Dakar, Senegal: Council for the Development of Social Science Research in Africa.

Sylla, Seynabou Ndiaye. 2001. "Femmes et Politique au Sénégal; Contribution à la réflexion sur la participation des femmes sénégalaises à la vie politique de 1945 à 2001." Memoire de D.E.A. Paris: Université de Paris.

Tamale, Sylvia. 1999. *When Hens Begin to Crow: Gender and Parliamentary Politics in Uganda*. Boulder, CO: Westview Press.

———. 2000. "Point of Order Mr. Speaker: African Women Claiming Their Space in Parliament." *Gender and Development* 8(3): 8–15.

Taylor, Christopher. 1999. *Sacrifice as Terror: The Rwandan Genocide*. Oxford: Berg.

Tegulle, Gawaya. 2001. "Electoral College: A Shield for Non-Performing MPs." *The Other Voice*. April 15, 2.

Thiel, Hermann. 2003. "Elections, the Electoral System and a Gender Quota: Views of Namibians." Institute for Public Policy Research (IPPR) Briefing Paper No. 17. Windhoek, Namibia: IPPR.

Thomas, Sue. 1991. "The Impact of Women on State Legislative Policies." *Journal of Politics* 53(4): 958–976.

Tjihero, Kapena, Doufi Namalambo, and Dianne Hubbard. 1998. *Affirmative Action for Women in Local Government in Namibia: The 1998 Local Government Elections*. Windhoek, Namibia: Legal Assistance Center.

Tremblay, Manon. 2005. *Femmes et Parlements: Un Regard International*. Montreal, Quebec: Remue-Menage.

Tripp, Aili Mari. 2000a. "Rethinking Difference: Comparative Perspectives from Africa." *Signs* 25(3): 649–675.

———. 2000b. *Women and Politics in Uganda*. Madison: University of Wisconsin Press; Oxford: James Currey; and Kampala, Uganda: Fountain Publishers.

———. 2001a. "The New Political Activism in Africa." *Journal of Democracy* 12: 141–155.

———. 2001b. "The Politics of Autonomy and Co-optation in Africa: The Case of the Ugandan Women's Movement." *Journal of Modern African Studies* 39(1): 101–128.

———. 2002. "Women's Mobilization in Uganda (1945–1962): Non-racial Ideologies Within Colonial-African-Asian Encounters." *International Journal of African Historical Studies* 35(1): 1–22.

———. 2004a. "A New Look at Colonial Women: British Teachers and Activists in Uganda (1898–1962)." *Canadian Journal of African Studies* 38(1): 123–156.

———. 2004b. "Women's Movements, Customary Law, and Land Rights in Africa: The Case of Uganda." *African Studies Quarterly* 7(4). http://web.africa.ufl.edu/asq.

Tripp, Aili Mari, and Joy Kwesiga, eds. 2002. *The Women's Movement in Uganda: History, Challenges and Prospects*. Kampala, Uganda: Fountain Publishers.

United Nations Development Fund for Women (UNIFEM). 2004. "Rwanda Gender Profile." New York: UNIFEM.

Urdang, Stephanie. 1985. "The Last Transition: Women and Development." In John Saul, ed. *A Difficult Road: The Transition to Socialism in Mozambique*. New York: Monthly Review Press.

———. 1989. *And Still They Dance: Women, War, and the Struggle for Change in Mozambique*. New York: Monthly Review Press.

US Department of State. 2002. "Country Reports on Human Rights: Senegal." March 4. http://www.state.gov/gov/g/rls/hrrpt/2001/af/8400/htm.

Van Allen, Judith. 2001. "Women's Rights as a Measure of African Democracy." *Journal of Asian and African Studies* 36(1): 39–63.

Vengroff, Richard, Lucy Creevey, and Henry Krisch. 2000. "Electoral System Effects on Gender Representation: the Case of Mixed Systems." *Japanese Journal of Political Science* 1(2): 197–227.

Villalón, Leonardo. 1995. *Islamic Society and State Power in Senegal: Disciples and Citizens in Fatick*. Cambridge: Cambridge University Press.

———. 1999. "Generational Changes, Political Stagnation and the Revolving Dynamics of Religion and Politics in Senegal." *Africa Today* 46(3/4): 129–147.

———. 2004a. "Senegal." *African Studies Review* 47(2): 61–72.

———. 2004b. "Sufi Modernities in Contemporary Senegal: Religious Dynamics Between the Local and the Global." Unpublished manuscript.

Villalón, Leonardo, and Ousmane Kane. 1998. "Senegal: The Crisis of Democracy and the Emergence of an Islamic Opposition." In Leonardo A. Villalón and Phillip A. Huxtable, eds. *The African State at a Critical Juncture: Between Disintegration and Reconfiguration*. Boulder, CO: Lynne Rienner Publishers.

Vines, Alex. 1990. *RENAMO: Terrorism in Mozambique*. London: Christian Geffray.

Waliggo, John Mary. 1996. "Women Reps Should Be Elected by All Voters." *New Vision* (Kampala), January 23, 4.

Walker, Cherryl. 1982. *Women and Resistance in South Africa*. Cape Town, South Africa: David Philip.

Waylen, Georgina. 1994. "Women and Democratization: Conceptualizing Gender Relations in Transition Politics." *World Politics* 46: 327–354.

———. 1996. *Gender in Third World Politics*. Boulder, CO: Lynne Rienner Publishers.

WEDO. n.d. "50/50 Campaign Declaration Statement." www.wedo.org/declaration.htm.

Wells, Julia. 1993. *We Now Demand: The History of Women's Resistance to Pass Laws in South Africa*. Johannesburg, South Africa: Witwatersrand University Press.

West, Lois. 1999. "The United Nations Women's Conferences and Feminist Politics." In Mary Meyer and Elisabeth Pruegl, eds. *Gender Politics in Global Governance*. Lanham, MD: Rowman and Littlefield.

Williams, Stephen. 2001. "Polls Back Wade." *African Business* 266: 39–40.

Women and Law in Southern Africa. 1997. *Families in a Changing Environment*. Maputo, Mozambique: Eduardo Mondlane University, Department of Women and Gender Studies, Center for African Studies.

Women's International Resource Exchange (WIRE). 1980. *Resistance, War and Liberation: Women of Southern Africa*. New York: WIRE.

Women's National Coalition. 1994. *The Origins, History, and Process of the Women's National Coalition*. Cape Town, South Africa: University of the Western Cape.

World Bank. 2003. *World Development Report 2003: Sustainable Development in a Dynamic World*. New York: Oxford University Press.

Yoon, Mi Yung. 2001. "Democratization and Women's Legislative Representation in Sub-Saharan Africa." *Democratization* 8(2): 169–190.

———. 2004. "Explaining Women's Legislative Representation in Sub-Saharan Africa." *Legislative Studies Quarterly* 24(3): 447–468.

Young, Crawford, and Babacar Kanté. 1992. "Governance, Democracy and the 1988 Senegalese Elections." In Goran Hyden and Michael Bratton, eds. *Governance and Politics in Africa*. Boulder, CO: Lynne Rienner Publishers.

The Contributors

Gretchen Bauer is associate professor of political science and international relations and associate dean in the College of Arts and Sciences, University of Delaware.

Hannah E. Britton is assistant professor of women's studies and political science, University of Kansas.

Lucy Creevey is emeritus professor in the Department of Political Science, University of Connecticut.

Jennifer Leigh Disney is assistant professor in the Political Science Department, Winthrop University.

Shireen Hassim is associate professor in the Department of Political Studies, University of the Witwatersrand.

Timothy Longman is associate professor in the Department of Political Science, Vassar College.

Aili Mari Tripp is professor of political science and women's studies and associate dean in the Office of International Studies and Programs, University of Wisconsin–Madison.

Index

About the Book

Working together across religious, ethnic, and class divisions, African women are helping to formulate legislation and foster democracies more inclusive of women's interests. *Women in African Parliaments* explores this phenomenon, examining the impact and experiences of African women as they seek increased representation in national legislatures.

The authors' carefully constructed case studies allow cross-national comparisons of the range of strategies that African women have used to achieve greater involvement in national politics. A unique feature of the work is the voices of African women, who explain how they achieved or continue to fight for electoral success, how they learned to work with lifelong adversaries, and how they have begun to transform their parliaments.

Gretchen Bauer is associate professor of political science and international relations and associate dean for social sciences and history at the University of Delaware. Her publications include *Politics in Southern Africa: State and Society in Transition* and *Labor and Democracy in Namibia, 1971–1996*. **Hannah E. Britton** is assistant professor of political science and women's studies at the University of Kansas. She is author of *Women in the South African Parliament: From Resistance to Governance*.